D0099032

THE HARDER YOU WORK, THE LUCKIER YOU GET

An Entrepreneur's Memoir

Joe Ricketts

FOUNDER OF AMERITRADE

SIMON & SCHUSTER

NEW YORK LONDON TORONTO SYDNEY NEW DELHI

Simon & Schuster
1230 Avenue of the Americas
New York, NY 10020

First Simon & Schuster hardcover edition November 2019

SIMON & SCHUSTER and colophon are
registered trademarks of Simon & Schuster, Inc.

For information about special discounts for bulk purchases,
please contact Simon & Schuster Special Sales
at 1-866-506-1949 or business@simonandschuster.com.

The Simon & Schuster Speakers Bureau can bring authors to your live event.
For more information or to book an event, contact the
Simon & Schuster Speakers Bureau at 1-866-248-3049 or
visit our website at www.simonspeakers.com.

Interior design by Ruth Lee-Mui

Manufactured in the United States of America

1 3 5 7 9 10 8 6 4 2

Library of Congress Cataloging-in-Publication Data is available.

ISBN 978-1-5011-6478-1
ISBN 978-1-5011-6480-4 (ebook)

Insert photos 1 and 2 are courtesy of Nebraska City Historical Society.
Insert photos 3, 4, 6, 7, 8, 10, 15, 16, and 17 are courtesy of the author's
collection. Insert photo 5 is courtesy of Ed Regan. Insert photos 9,
11, and 13 are courtesy of TD Ameritrade. Insert photo 12 is courtesy
of Peter Ricketts. Insert photo 14 is courtesy of Jerry Gress.

Contents

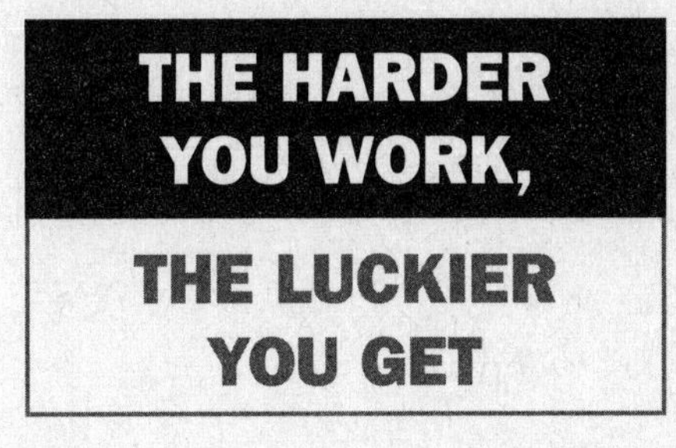
THE HARDER
YOU WORK,
THE LUCKIER
YOU GET

CHAPTER 1

I remember that day vividly, the smell of wood, the sound of hammers banging, the sawdust scattered on the ground. My father had brought me to a construction site where he and his men were building a new home. I was still a boy, and this was in Nebraska City, where I grew up, a town of a little over seven thousand. The decade was the 1940s, but from the way the men were putting up that house—without electrical power, using only their hand tools and the strength of their muscles—it could have been much longer ago.

Each carpenter wore an apron around his waist, with pockets for the different-size nails he used for different tasks. He would pull out a nail with his left hand, hold it in the spot where it needed to go, and bang, bang, bang it in with the hammer in his right. Construction then was altogether different from the way buildings go up now. Nothing was prefabricated and shipped to them, like the trusses of today. The men had to put up every piece of the building one at a time.

My father had brought my younger brothers and me to the job

site and told us to keep out of the way and to pick up trash. When the men finished sawing a board to size and the scrap end fell on the ground, I would pick it up and throw it out. Other than that, I watched. The work was hard and hot. The men got so wet with perspiration that the sawdust stuck to their clothing and their skin. Sometimes they talked with one another about the tasks they were doing, sometimes they joked, but mostly they sawed and hammered without speaking. I remember them as happy—working together, getting something done.

Now here is a mystery. That boy who was brought along to clean up the wood scraps, who grew up in a working-class town with a frontier mentality, would go on to found one of the most disruptive businesses of finance's computer age. That business would utilize the latest communications and digital technologies to revolutionize and democratize the clubby, old, highly regulated, East Coast–based financial industry—and in the process, the founder of that business would become a billionaire.

I was that boy, but if you had asked me then to share my daydreams and talents, they would have revealed no knowledge of computers or special gift for mathematics, and no visions of vast wealth. My idea of financial success back then went no further than the well-off men of our town—the owner of the drugstore or grocery store, our local dentist and doctor. I had no expectation that I would ever work in the finance industry, let alone help remake its services industry. And in fact, if you had asked my wife, Marlene, who met me in school, she would have told you that I seemed like the other young men. Maybe a bit more of a dreamer, imagining myself in charge of the businesses where I cleaned or clerked, but basically like the others, the sort who grows up to work hard all week to support his family, then goes out on Friday night and feels happy to talk with his friends and drink his fill of beer.

But on the day I'm thinking of, there was something new. My father's construction company had been able to buy a new tool called a buzz saw. I watched the men lay a board across the sawhorses they used to hold it still, put a mark on it, and then switch on the new electric circular saw. It really did buzz. And that was it—in a moment, the board was cut to the length they needed.

The men were ecstatic. Dad, though, was calm, quiet. The Rickettses were stoic people. He worked seven days a week, either on the job site or keeping the books. Most days I saw him only at dinner, where it was my mother who would tell us kids if we'd done something well, and my father who would let us know what we had done wrong. He was the disciplinarian. I don't believe he ever hugged me, and I knew better than to hug him. You never expressed your emotion in that way, or by saying "I love you." But on that day, I could tell by his body language that he was happy. His shoulders were relaxed, and his movements were easy, jovial. "This is so wonderful, Joe," he said. "It will allow us to get so much done so fast."

That was what he wanted me to understand: the effect this tool could have on their work and their lives. In that sense, he had an innovator's eye, not because he had invented the buzz saw but because he saw the possible benefit in it. I did not need to know the concept of productivity or the term *early adopter*. I could hear the meaning in my father's voice and see it in the men's smiling, sawdust-covered faces.

When I founded my own business, I would push hard, often against intense resistance, for my company to make advances like that one. Part of our success came from new communications and computer technologies that didn't seem valuable to others back then, and that sound almost like a horse and buggy today—we were innovating with toll-free long-distance phone calls, touch-tone phones, data storage on cardboard punch cards, early personal computers and slow, primitive email. In discount brokerage, as on my father's construction sites, success came down to how fast you could execute without a loss of quality, so we were always looking for a faster, better way.

Yet I did not grow up to become a midwestern Steve Jobs, some tech geek in a barn. It was never my interest to understand how the machines worked. I had no special enthusiasm for technology. In fact, I had very little exposure to new technology at all. We were one of the last families in Nebraska City to own innovations like air-conditioning or television, because my parents did not count those things among life's necessities. But maybe because we didn't have the new machines, I could see better what they could do and what a difference they could make in our lives.

Perhaps it's surprising that a little boy who was tasked only with keeping the job site clean and staying out of trouble would have been so affected by the new tool the men were trying out or would remember its effects so well. I think there are two reasons I paid such close attention, and they both go back to my parents and my upbringing.

First, I had seen how very hard my father worked, the double pressure he was always under, to keep revenue coming in while sustaining his reputation for quality. I remember once we heard that a tornado had hit a farmhouse and destroyed it. The people whose home was destroyed belonged to our church. We kids were excited because building a farmhouse meant that Dad would take us out to the farm where we could do things we thought were special, like riding horses, though the farm kids had horses around every day and seemed to think they were boring.

One day, as the house was going up, my paternal grandfather came out to look over the work. He was old by then, done with physical labor but still healthy and active in the business. He bid the jobs before the men took them on, and he would come out and review their progress. The carpenters had spent all of that day building a stairway, and when they got to the bottom, they discovered that their measurements were off by a quarter of an inch. Now they had a choice: Did they put a shim under the bottom to fill the gap, along the floor where no one was likely to see it, or did they tear it out and rebuild the whole thing?

My grandfather was the boss of the business right up until he died. A tall, broad-shouldered man with a big waist, his authority was almost military. When he came to inspect that day, Dad was visibly nervous. The men worked for wages, so if they had to build the stairs again, that would cost my grandfather an extra day's pay. But at the same time, it was the Ricketts reputation that brought in business. A lot of the houses in town had been built by my father and grandfather, and sometimes when they were up for sale you would see a sign on the property: RICKETTS BUILT. That reputation was their method of marketing—if they built well or badly, the whole community was going to hear about it.

When my grandfather saw that the stairway was off a quarter inch, he knew his reputation was at stake. He didn't want to take that risk. He looked the staircase over, mused for a minute while the men held their breath, and said, "Build it over."

The second reason I was so affected by that buzz saw was the context I brought to it, based on what I saw and heard at home, where my mother's parents lived with us. Even as a child, I could feel they were broken people. My maternal grandfather had suffered what adults called a nervous breakdown, and he lived mostly in his own world, out of touch with reality. I never knew him as a healthy man. My grandmother had diabetes back before doctors knew how to treat it, and both her legs had been amputated clear up to the hips. She needed assistance to get in and out of her wheelchair. Although my cousin

Mary Ann Weidemann remembers my grandmother affectionately, to me she seemed depressed and mentally absent. They lived until I was in my teens, and the explanation for all this waste and sadness came from my mother.

My mother didn't tell their story all at once. There were many different parts and versions, and they would come out while she was cleaning the house or painting, home all day with us kids and thirsty for someone to talk to. I can picture her with her sleeves rolled and her hair tied up in a scarf—she reminded me of the wartime poster of Rosie the Riveter, with the slogan "We Can Do It!" Like my father, she was a person resigned to adversity, but she could not talk about her family history without emotion.

My paternal great-great-grandfather, she said, had been born in Germany, but he wanted to come to the United States. He wanted to leave before he was drafted into the Prussian army. His father had died young, though, so the only way he could leave was with his mother's permission, which she wouldn't give. Before he turned seventeen, that young man decided he had to leave his country and stow away on a ship because he lacked her approval.

His mother fixed him his Sunday meal every week. The following Sunday, when he didn't show up for dinner, she took his meal, a waffle, and put the plate on the mantel to wait for him. It stayed there until she died. She was heartbroken. He made it past the Prussian authorities and ultimately immigrated to the United States. I think he became a blacksmith.

In the next generation, my great-grandmother was ambitious and married a banker. This was before federal regulation of banking, so a local banker was like the owner of any small business: He made his own decisions and lived with the consequences. That meant that our family had access to capital. They had seven children and wanted a farm for each. My grandfather was the oldest child, so they bought the first farm for him, taking on a lot of debt. The crops were good, the farm made money, and as soon as they had some equity in it, they borrowed against that and bought another. In time, they owned farms from South Dakota down through Kansas. You could say that for their time and place, my immigrant forebears were very successful entrepreneurs.

My great-grandfather died knowing he had succeeded. My mother grew up on the first of those seven farms. She lived in Manley, Nebraska, in a family that was not only one of the most successful farm families but also one of the prominent families of the community. They were Catholic, and in those days in their church the people who gave the most money got the first pew, and the second biggest donors got the next pew, and so on. My grandfather's family had the first pew in the church. They bought a new car every few years. Their house was big for its time, with a pillar on each side of the front door, as compared to my father's family home, which was at that time a log cabin. They covered it with siding, so it looked like a regular house. But it was still a log cabin. Growing up in the 1920s, my mother's family was not wealthy, but they lived well as proud and prominent members of the community.

One day my grandfather bought a new bull, a major purchase for a cattle farmer, and the family threw a big party. The kitchen tables were brought out into the yard and laden with all kinds of food. There was a lot of competition among the farmers over who could produce the most from an acre of land, display the best animals, grow their crops in the straightest lines, and other tests of agricultural achievement. People were invited to come to this party to admire the new prize bull. It was like their own private county fair. There were games—my aunt used to tell me how guests would place bets on the number of eggs they could balance on a bull's back before the eggs started falling off—and other kinds of fun that we don't think about anymore.

Sometime after the party, it was discovered that the new bull was diseased. It might have had tuberculosis or hoof-and-mouth, a deadly infection that could spread through a community and ruin all the farmers around. This was before science understood the transmission of the disease, so to make sure it would not pass beyond my grandfather's farm, his entire herd had to be destroyed. Once the vet made his diagnosis, my grandfather had no more say in the matter. The state sent men to dig an enormous hole, drive the animals in, slaughter them all, and fill the hole with dirt.

Because his entire herd had been destroyed, my grandfather did not have enough income to make the payment on his farm loan, and over time, as he missed more payments, the extended family defaulted on all the loans that had supported the family's farms. By now, the Depression had begun. This was before welfare or social security was established, and so my grandparents became paupers. They lost it all.

My grandfather heard that there were jobs at the packinghouse in Nebraska City, so he moved his family there. They left without any assets, and when they arrived, they rented the cheapest home they could find, one with dirt floors. My aunt was so embarrassed to have her boyfriend see where she lived that when he picked her up, she asked him to meet her at the corner.

My grandfather's plan was to get a factory job because that was the work available to a man with no skills except farming. The packinghouse was tough, dirty work. Today those places are as clean as hospitals, but back then there were blood and guts and feces lying all over.

He tried, but he couldn't bring himself to go to work in the packinghouse like a boy. His life's goal had been to become a big cattleman, and before he'd lost his farm, he'd had a big sign on the side of his barn with his name and the phrase "and sons." That cattle herd had been the worldly representation of all his success and his legacy. Losing it destroyed him. He suffered a breakdown and never worked again. When I knew him, he spent the day in his rocker, looking out the window.

His sons went to work in those packinghouses to support the family, and his daughters got jobs in town. My mother was fortunate that she had an aunt who sponsored her to complete high school in Omaha. Her aunt found her a family to live with in exchange for housecleaning and babysitting along the way to earning her diploma. She learned to live as a city girl. After she graduated, she took a job at a five-and-dime store called Hested's, where she would eventually meet my father's sister and, through her, my father.

From then on, my mother was very, very conscious of the social standing her family had lost, and she was bound and determined to get back to where they had been. When she left the house, she was always dressed properly—no one but us kids ever saw her dressed for housecleaning. In church, we all had to be neat and clean, my younger brothers and me in our sport coats and freshly ironed shirts. The Latin Mass lasted an hour and I couldn't understand a word of it, but I knew when to give the proper responses and understood that this was my mother's social show-off time. There was no choice about being there. It was always very important to her that we put on our best show. I remember when I first started going to school, I came home from kindergarten and she received a phone call from a neighbor who had seen me walking across the street kitty-corner. "People are watching you and they know who you are," she told me. "You've got to act right!"

I understood when she told me how her family had lost their farms that she was again teaching me a lesson in how to act right. If you wanted what she called a nice life, you had to make it yourself. You had to work hard every day, and when you got what you were after, you had to keep working hard because you could lose it all. And so, I understood early that I had to succeed on my own.

These lessons were not meant to be tucked away for the future. I think I was in third grade when the janitor who worked in the courthouse called to speak to my parents. His assistant was on vacation, he explained, and he had observed me in town and judged me to be an enterprising young man, mild-mannered, reliable, and obedient. He asked my parents if I would be interested in assisting him in the afternoons for a couple of weeks.

My mother told me, "You ought to be proud of yourself, Joe, because he called and asked specifically for you. He wants you to work for him because you look like a person of worth. Take the job and prove to him that you are."

The janitor was a short, thin, gray-haired man, wiry and a bit stooped, close to retirement. He showed me how to sweep the floor thoroughly by tossing oiled sawdust in front of one of those wide brooms, to help pick up the dust and shine the floors. He taught me to empty the wastebaskets in order, so I didn't work randomly and miss one. He showed me how to clean the bathrooms. After that, we did our work and didn't say much. And I got money for it. I spent it as I wanted to—it wasn't a lot. My parents cautioned me not to waste it.

Then I got interested in getting a new bicycle. I suppose I thought my old bike wasn't good enough. So, I asked my father if I could have a new bike. He said I could have one—I just had to make my own money to pay for it. I asked him how I could go about doing that. He said there were jobs listed in the newspaper, in the section called the want ads. He showed me where they were and promised he would help me understand how to talk when I went for an interview.

I know that plenty of other young people would not have had this reaction, but to me it was like that scene you saw sometimes in adventure movies, where someone opens up the pirate's chest and everyone's face brightens with the light reflecting off the treasure inside. You could open up the paper and it showed you where the money was. With this, a whole new era of my life began.

One of my first jobs came not from the want ads but from a family friend, a man named Mr. Verrett, who had some cleaning work he needed done, moving some trash. He paid me with a check, and he said, "Joe, I'm going to take you to the bank," where he helped me open a savings account. I recognized some of the tellers from church, and one of them gave me a little savings account passbook. Every time I gave them more money, the clerk would write by hand the amount of the deposit and the interest I had earned, so I could see the savings accumulating. I can't express how important I felt when I handed my couple of dollars through the window and the clerk wrote the amount into my passbook. Some kids got that feeling from sports, but my body never functioned in the way that makes a good athlete. I never knew if that was because I didn't have the interest in sports, because I didn't try hard enough, or because I was simply born awkward. Playing sports, I felt like a clumsy kid, but at the bank, I felt like an adult.

I loved seeing the money add up, watching it grow by two, three, four, eight dollars. I kept adding to it. To work, to make money, to watch it grow—that was my secret thrill. None of my friends were doing it. School was not exciting like that. When I was older, in the tenth grade, my algebra teacher took me aside after we had taken an IQ test and she said, "Joe, you can do better. You have an IQ of 120, and that means you can get better grades." But I had no desire to achieve better grades. If I could get a C and get through the class, that was enough for me. I did have the desire to work, though. I always had a job—first a paper route, then a position as a clerk at the grocery store. I was a carryout boy and stocked shelves and swept floors, and I enjoyed it. If a skill is something you have to learn and a talent is a gift you are given, then working, liking to work, was part of my talent.

These jobs became a kind of parallel schooling for me, not in knowledge but in responsibility. I was fortunate to work for people who honored me by taking an interest in the character of a young man. My boss on the paper route was Mrs. Enright. She saw her role as teaching young boys to understand what it meant to do the job well. She gave us reasons: You have to be here by four in the afternoon and here is the reason why. You have to count your papers, and this is the reason why. You have to remember your bicycle or wagon, and these are the reasons why. She was a caring person who was teaching us responsibility with love and with explanations.

Then I became a clerk at a grocery store, working for Norm Stellick, who was not a gregarious man. He did not use a word if he didn't have to. He was a good man, but darn it, he never said a nice thing. The floor wasn't clean enough, the bread wasn't stacked right—he would always call your attention, very sternly, to what was insufficient. His tone made you think to yourself, *Boy, I hope I never get that wrong again*. He'd correct with a reprimand or a frown. He used harsh words. In retrospect, I can see that he wasn't cruel, and that the grocery business was hard work for little money. He hired me when I was in eighth grade, but he expected me to take responsibility like an adult—here's what you have to do, now do it.

Based on my experience at the grocery store, I was then able to get a prime job: clerk at our local Rexall drugstore. With a job like that, you weren't out in the Nebraska weather, you didn't have to get dirty, and you were helping people. It was the crème de la crème for a boy in Nebraska City—none of my friends thought so, of course, but I sure did. My friends Jerry Gress and Jerry Schmitz worked for a while in a grocery store, and they recognized that I had a better job situation than they did, but it wasn't meaningful to them the way it was to me. Jerry Gress remembers my telling them that one day I would like to be a millionaire—a million dollars was, to us, the epitome of rich.

"Why, Joe?" they asked me.

"It would be an achievement," I said.

That didn't seem to mean anything to them.

The owner of the drugstore was a rough, gruff old man named Fred Whit. Big and heavy, he walked around the store passing gas, but he was so old, he didn't care. Mr. Whit had opened the pharmacy back when the town didn't have one, so people had to go there to shop, but he made some customers uncomfortable. My mother was one of them. She was afraid I wouldn't be able to get along with him and also afraid that when she came in, he would embarrass her.

I got along with him fine because he seemed like a step up from Mr. Stellick; when Mr. Whit was disappointed, you could hear the words he was thinking in his head, but at least he didn't actually say them to you. And working for him, I learned that you couldn't crap your pants every time someone chewed you out. You have to do your job, and if you get something wrong you just take the criticism and try to make him happy the next time.

One day old Fred Whit passed away, and his younger partner, Lee Jessup, bought the store. In a lot of ways, they were opposites—Mr. Jessup was short, skinny, and well attuned to the fact that his customers could choose to take their business to the competition. He worked with a smile on his face, always deferential, making customers feel good. At a drugstore, you sell awkward things. Ladies came in to buy big boxes of Kotex, so he taught me to speak discreetly and wrap their packages so they felt comfortable carrying that large box out of the store. Men came in to buy prophylactics, and to hide their embarrassment they used slang terms. It was a time when people didn't talk about such things in public. I had to know what it meant when a fellow asked me in a low voice, "Do you sell raincoats?" Under Mr. Jessup's more customer-focused management style, the once-struggling store prospered. I absorbed all the experience from using the sales techniques I learned and their effects on customers as if they were passing through the cells of my skin.

Mr. Jessup got sick and passed away while I was still a young man. Bill Carroll, the pharmacist, bought the store. He had gone to Creighton University, the Jesuit school in Omaha, and he was a Catholic. He took a special interest in me, and later, when I was applying for jobs as an adult, he wrote me character reference letters and customized each one to suit the job and place of business to which I was applying.

Each of them, I felt, honored me by taking an interest in me. I learned social skills that many other young men, who knew only school and sports, didn't learn, and that gave me an advantage. They helped to shape me and also, I would realize later, to shape my ideas on how a business owner should treat their employees.

Every once in a while, as I worked my jobs and made my deposits into my savings account, I'd want to buy something. I would go talk to my dad about it. "You can buy it, Joe," he would tell me. "It's your money. You earned it. But understand what that's going to do to your savings account, and what it's going to do to you in the future."

I wasn't told no. I was reminded that I could do with my money what I wanted, but I was also given some direction. Sometimes, when I told my mother about a new job and the money I had made, she would say, "That's what you're going to use to go to college. We can't afford to send you. You're going to have to do it yourself." And that was why I didn't buy the bicycle or the gun or whatever I was thinking about.

My friends would ask me why I wasn't playing baseball, why I wasn't playing basketball. I told them, "I got a job. I prefer to work." My parents had never discouraged me from playing sports, but they did encourage me to make money. And my friends didn't understand that I did not have the urge to do what they did. It hurt sometimes that my peers rejected what I cared about. Especially with girls—it seemed the girls all went after athletes, but I was carrying newspapers, clerking in a drugstore. None of the girls seemed to care about boys with jobs.

My best friend would ask me, "Don't you feel bad that you're giving up all this fun? Sports?"

I said, "No, I enjoy what I'm doing."

Senior year, though, they needed a fifth man for the school basketball team, and I had gotten tall. I quit my job and joined the team, but I was never a good athlete. There was only one guy bigger than me, but I was not a good basketball player, and I didn't really care for it. I never seemed to have that physical gift that athletic kids have. One summer, I tried to work for my dad as a carpenter's apprentice, but I was no good at it. He fired me.

I know that some kids imagined I didn't care for fun, but that wasn't true. I liked having a good time as much as the next person, and Nebraska City was really quite wonderful for a kid growing up. I feel now like I grew up in heaven and didn't know it. In the summertime, when I was still little, my mother would pack me a lunch in a sack and I'd tell her I was going to the park or what we called the camp, a place in the woods that was good for playing and fishing, and then she wouldn't see me until suppertime. For a boy growing up, you couldn't ask for anything better. You had your fun and you went home, and you didn't tell your parents what you did. Maybe you had a scratch, and your mother would ask, "What happened?" And you'd say, "I got in a fight with Bob." And that was the end of it.

She never worried about me all day long because everyone in town knew who I was, and there were eyes everywhere, watching me. Every once in a while, somebody in town would call her because they saw me doing something I shouldn't, like tipping over somebody's garbage cans. We always had that awareness: *Gee, no matter what I do wrong, I might get in trouble here*. It was nice from a parent's point of view, and it was nice from a kid's point of view because it allowed for a lot of exercise in judgment and character development.

When I was in the Boy Scouts, for example, we had to cross a bridge to get to the meetings. We used to bring eggs with us, hide under the bridge, and throw the eggs at passing cars. We thought we were smart and that no one knew who was doing it. Then one day we went into the police station to get a drink of water, and the police officer called out to us, "Quit throwing the eggs at the cars! It ruins the paint!" And that was the end of that.

Most of all, I loved the Boy Scouts. We had a wonderful scout leader who didn't worry about merit badges, he just let us run free and have fun. Generally, that meant fighting with the other camp. We'd have a sort of war. We'd see who could collapse the most tents by pulling up the stakes, who could pour water in the other camp's sleeping bags, who could beat up the most guys—just wasting time and playing tricks like that. I can remember sneaking up on their campsite at night, with all the guys standing and singing in front of their bonfire, and tossing a cherry bomb into the flames. That stopped the singing right away. After the explosion, the whole group came after us, and we ran away through the forest, laughing.

At Boy Scout camp, it felt like we were a thousand miles away from home and church and all the rules, with nobody to oversee us. There was still somebody keeping an eye out though, so if a kid broke a leg, somebody was going to take care of it. I still remember our troop leader. He lived in the neighborhood and everybody knew and respected him. He was a bachelor, and later some people got upset because he was rumored to be a homosexual. He was made to leave the organization. We kids never had any idea about that, and he never did anything he shouldn't have. He was a great scout leader—I can't imagine anyone better as an ideal for young men—and I thought his being asked to leave was a tragedy. It made me sad.

As I got older, of course, I had to give up that kind of freedom. And by the time I was a senior in high school, I knew that what I wanted was to go away to college, not stay in town and get a job. As one of my friends from Nebraska City liked to say, it was a great place to grow up and then a great place to get away from. I'd had enough of a place where everybody knew everybody else, where there were eyes and expectations everywhere.

I had saved a few thousand dollars, but Creighton University was expensive, and after my first year all the money I had saved up back home was gone. One of the first things I did when I got to Creighton was look for work. I became the dormitory janitor, cleaning the bathrooms so I could have a free room, and the busboy in the Jesuit dining room so I could have free meals. Then my friend Clark Smith told me about a job opening at a bread factory that paid more than two dollars an hour, and I thought that sounded great. I worked twenty or thirty hours a week, off and on, mostly evenings and weekends, and those were the dollars I used to pay my tuition and buy my beer.

Sometimes they would get big orders at the factory before a holiday weekend. Once, I worked twenty-four hours straight. The first eight hours I got the regular wage, two dollars and twenty-five cents an hour, and I thought that was high. The second eight hours, I got time and a half, which was great. But the third eight hours, I got double time, four dollars and fifty cents an hour, and I couldn't pass that up. The unionized employees wouldn't work three shifts in a row, but to me it was an opportunity.

For meals, they only had vending machines with candy bars. To get energy, we'd take a bottle of honey, steal a loaf of bread, break off a piece, dip it in the honey, and eat it. I got sick to my stomach eating so much bread. Sometimes I worked while I was close to throwing up. And it was hard—really hard, exhausting work in very hot spaces. The older people there were very tough. Once, there was an accident and a worker lost a finger in one of the machines. Only after they'd gotten him to the hospital did someone think to ask: Where'd the finger go? It wasn't on the ground outside. It wasn't on the factory floor. It wasn't in the machine. We went out to the docks, where there were three semitrucks full of packaged bread, and we realized the finger was in there somewhere on one of those trucks. Then the manager said, "Hey, ship it." So, the bread was shipped, and some customer found a finger in her loaf. To this day, the smell of a bread factory reminds me of working those long hours with an upset stomach. It makes me feel sick.

Thrilled as I was to have that factory income, I learned that I was going to have to find another way to be thrilled, because the work was not the kind I wanted. That was further motivation to get through college, even though the classes were difficult for me and my progress was slowing. I kept shifting time away from earning credit hours so I could earn more money to pay for them, which meant I fell behind the other students.

One Sunday morning, after I'd been working all night on the production line, the sun was coming up, ushering in a bright, beautiful day. We didn't have any windows we could see out of, but there were windows near the ceiling. Later, I climbed up on some of the huge pans to look out, and I could see young people in convertibles going on picnics or to the beach. They were having a nice, leisurely day. I thought, *Boy, you know, that looks fun. I want to make enough money so I don't have to work on Sunday and I can go to the beach too*. I felt what it would be like to get out of that factory and make sure I could have a good job, a house in a nice neighborhood, a car, and some leisure time.

I could claim that at that moment it all became clear. "That's what

I want someday! And I want my kids to have that too." I could say that this vision inspired me for all I achieved later. It would make a great story, but the truth is that with all the money I earned later on, I never bought myself a convertible. My son Todd eventually gave me one, a Mercedes 280 SL, a beautiful classic car. He said, "You're never going to buy it for yourself, so I bought it for you." I enjoyed that he bought it for me, and I enjoyed driving it, but did I drive it to the beach like I imagined that morning in the factory? Never. I've been to the beach once or twice, but the truth is that to me, things like cars and seaside vacations are pleasant, fun now and then, but not deeply satisfying.

For me, it's the getting there. It's the competition, the problem-solving. It's being right when no one thought you were right and winning when the stakes are high. Even after I had more money than I could spend, I went on working forty to sixty hours a week. I still wanted to succeed at business, not for the increased buying power that success would earn me, but for the pleasure of making a business succeed.

To me, looking out that factory window at the beautiful convertible, the open road, the day that could take me anywhere, was a vision of freedom. To know that I have earned the freedom to do something, that feels glorious. But actually doing it? That's not the point. Rewards, for me, were the wrong motivation. I wanted to work hard, make money, give it everything I had, and build something that would last for myself, my children, and the people who worked for me. I just didn't know, yet, what to build.

CHAPTER 2

In college, I got serious about dating Marlene Volkmer, a girl I knew from my high school class back in Nebraska City. Our entire class had numbered only twenty-two kids, and because Marlene had a very large relation, including ninety-eight first cousins, the joke had been that she would have to marry me because everyone else was a relative.

Back in high school, she had dressed in the style of the boppers, in full skirts—what they called poodle skirts—with bobby socks and black-and-white saddle shoes. All the girls dressed like that, but Marlene stuck out to me as more attractive than other girls. From my point of view, she was beautiful, lovely, but we never considered each other as someone to date. Our class had eleven girls and eleven boys, so already we knew each other a little too well for dating. We all went around in a big group as friends. On top of that, I was afraid to date a Catholic girl because of the rules they grew up with. If I took a girl's hand, I was afraid she might call out "Mortal sin!" So, I never thought of finding a girlfriend at my little high school. I was more comfortable with the girls from the public school, and Marlene preferred to go to the town of Syracuse, where there was a dance hall on Friday nights. You paid to get in and you could buy some beer and meet other young people.

Marlene says that when we were kids, she was aware of me as a clean-cut boy, neat and groomed all the time, with good manners, a gift for debating, and a bit of a swollen head. I had two friends both named Jerry, and the three of us went around together calling ourselves the Three Js and, according to Marlene, bragging about how great we were.

While we were still in high school, Marlene's older sister Lynne decided to join the convent. This came as a shock to a lot of people. Lynne was a vivacious girl, twenty-two years old, with blond hair. She drove a white-and-baby-blue Chevy. To a lot of young guys, I think she probably looked like everything you might hope for in a girlfriend. Before she decided to become a nun, Lynne had even gotten engaged. When she told her fiancé her decision, he was heartsick.

Her ex-fiancé asked to take her out on one last big date, dinner at the Lincoln Country Club. She said yes, but she wasn't comfortable going alone with him. Marlene wanted to come along, but Lynne did not approve of the boy her younger sister was currently dating. There was nothing wrong with him, Marlene felt, but Lynne said, "You can only come to the country club if you find a decent boy, someone with some class."

Marlene says she thought to herself, *I'll ask that John Joseph Ricketts*—my full name—*because there is no one more stuck-up than Joe. He thinks a lot of himself.* She knew that my mother was very aristocratic and prim, so she expected that Lynne would like my good manners.

I had never been to the country club, so I was excited to see what it was like and how the waiters acted. The double date was awkward, though, because Lynne's date was still madly in love with her. I remember he tried to put his arm around her, and she pushed it away. You could see the anguish on his face.

After that night, Marlene and I went out a few more times, and she found she didn't think I was so stuck-up after all. We got to know each other better. Marlene was the third of seven children and her family lived on a farm about ten miles outside town. They raised and grew a little bit of everything: corn, wheat, hay, cattle, pigs, and chickens. As a girl, she milked cows, gathered eggs, and generally helped with everything on the farm except tending the crops. Her father didn't believe in women working in the fields. She and her sisters gardened, cooked, and helped their mom do the laundry and the ironing. Marlene told me that they had an electric washing machine, but that after they ran the washer they had to put the wet clothes through the ringer to squeeze out the soapy water. Once they had put them through the ringer, they moved them to the rinse tub, then a second trip through the ringer, and then they carried them out to hang on the clothesline to dry. Her mother wanted an electric clothes dryer so it wouldn't be so much work, but her father said he didn't see the need for it. He liked to see the clothes drying on the line. Later, when her mother got sick and her father had to handle the clothes, he bought an electric dryer.

Marlene was an A student who seemed to have a natural gift for learning. Graduating first in our class, she was offered scholarships to the University of Nebraska, Creighton University, and a small women's school in Omaha—the College of Saint Mary. She chose Saint Mary's because one of her many cousins went there and loved it. Located on the west side of Omaha, the college was operated by the Sisters of Mercy. The girls didn't have cars so they couldn't go anywhere, and the nuns kept a pretty good eye on them. Later she would say that I had more fun than she did in college, because I didn't have the nuns watching me, and because I was a boy.

In college, we started dating more often. Some other girls were more glamorous, but I didn't want glamor. Marlene was nice, and she was kind. We went to dances with the swing music of the era, the Glenn Miller Orchestra and that sort of thing, or the new style of music, typified by Elvis Presley. There were movie theaters, and in the warm weather you could go to the drive-in. We would walk through Fontenelle Forest, which was bordered by the river, one of my favorite places. Once, on a nice day when I really wanted to see her and I had no transportation, I walked all the way from Creighton to St. Mary's, more than five miles.

I had always wished for a big, warm family, but my house growing up was quiet and somber. I had two brothers to tell what to do and beat up if they didn't listen, but we didn't have a warm give-and-take. I wished we were more like my cousins' families with eight or twelve kids. As I started to get to know Marlene's family, it seemed big and happy, like visiting my cousins. There was a lot going on in that house, a lot of enjoyable chaos, and the fighting and teasing was never malicious. They had a lot of fun. Marlene's brother, I remember, could not take the teasing, and she'd irritate him all the time and he'd get all upset, but mainly her family was easy with one another. They joked and laughed and enjoyed one another's company.

Marlene's dad was a jolly old fellow known for singing in the fields while he worked. He'd go to social gatherings, have a drink or two, and have a pleasant time. I came to love him. Sometimes I'd sit on the porch and visit with him and smoke cigarettes, and he would tell me stories and jokes. I can remember my own dad having a drink or two and having a good time, but I don't remember my mother ever enjoying herself that way. It was as though she was too serious about life.

Marlene wanted to be a social worker, but once we got together, she decided she was unlikely to make it through the required six years of higher education before we got married. She switched to a two-year teaching-certification program with continued coursework over the summers, and found she loved teaching in the Omaha public schools.

We married in 1963 and moved into an old carriage house behind the nurses' dorm at Duchesne College, a Catholic institution operated by the Society of the Sacred Heart. In exchange for lower rent, I worked occasionally as a janitor in the dorm. I could walk to classes at Creighton. Marlene was a good teacher for her students and, I found, a good influence on my studies. She liked to tell people, "Joe was not an A student until I married him and made him do his homework." I was also fortunate that my friend Tom Guilfoyle suggested I take a course in economics. I didn't generally love my studies, but economics fascinated me.

Those were great times—we had this nice little apartment above the garage, which had been the stables until automobiles came along. There was a family in the main house, and the neighbor kids, who must have been nine or ten, would come over to watch our black-and-white television. Marlene loved to have those kids around. When we talked about having children of our own, we thought we'd like to have twelve.

In those early days of the marriage, we had the time to go to the movies. I especially liked the ones based on Edna Ferber's stories, where she traces the fortunes of families over three generations or more. Whenever there was a movie based on one of her stories, I made sure we saw it. One of the most popular was *Giant*, which starred Elizabeth Taylor, Rock Hudson, and James Dean. You meet these cattle ranchers and then oil is discovered, and the oil business turns everything in that part of cattle country topsy-turvy. Ms. Ferber wrote one story on the Oklahoma Land Rush and another on prospecting for gold in Alaska. In those movies, you could see how new opportunities change everything in life. I was cutting my teeth on those movies, learning to think in longer stretches of time—how decisions today would make a difference not just in a month or a few years, but decades ahead, when the world would look very different. The friends and family we knew who saw those movies enjoyed them, too, but they didn't seem to share my interest in learning to think with a longer view in mind.

My dreaming about long-term opportunities and change got interrupted when we realized that Marlene was pregnant. Now we had to make some difficult choices. She was teaching fourth grade to the children of workers in the big meatpacking plants and she loved her work. She wanted to continue, and I had planned to finish my bachelor's degree as the starting point for my career, but as she said, "When you've got a baby to support, you've got a baby to support."

I was unhappy with myself. I should have been out of college with a degree before I started a family. And I could have been, if I hadn't slowed my progress repeatedly so I could work more hours to earn my tuition. Now I considered trying to borrow in order to finish college, but I had borrowed money in the past and found it very, very difficult to repay. I was not inclined to support a wife and child with borrowed funds. This was a discouraging time.

I concluded that I had no choice but to leave school and find a full-time job so Marlene could focus on the baby that was coming. Our plan was that once the child was a little older, she would go back to teaching, supporting us while I finished my degree. Many young couples had arrangements like that, though they didn't usually have babies so early on.

I began to read the want ads in the Omaha newspaper. I applied for whatever sales or business jobs were open to a young man without a college degree. In the end, I was offered three positions. The first and highest paying was as a salesman with a wholesaler of frozen vegetables. That sounded easy—I would just have to hurry, hurry, hurry from store to store, making sure my company's vegetables were well displayed in the frozen-food department and trying to get the buyers to increase their orders.

The second job, which paid a little less, was in the camera business. A chain of stores that sold camera equipment and developed film was looking to expand, and they wanted someone they could train to be a manager of one of their new stores. I had helped customers with cameras and film back when I worked at the drugstore, and I enjoyed taking pictures. I thought it would be exciting to get to use all the new products as they came out and to try to position them in the store to improve sales. This was the job with the most personal appeal.

The last job, which paid a little less than the others, was to work as a credit reporter for the credit information bureau Dun & Bradstreet. It would involve some travel, but beyond that, I really had no idea what it would entail.

In choosing among potential jobs up to that point, I had always taken the highest pay. Now, I wasn't sure. There wasn't a big degree of difference among the three salaries and I knew the position wouldn't be permanent. I decided to bring the choice of work up with my dad.

In those days, after we were first married, Marlene and I would often drive to her family's farm on Saturday, stay overnight, and go to church with them out in the country. Then, late Sunday morning, we would drive to Nebraska City to have dinner—that is, the big midday meal—with my parents. Mother made fried chicken, mashed potatoes and gravy, creamed corn, and salad. Those sorts of things.

That Sunday afternoon, I sat with my dad out on the patio in the backyard and reviewed the opportunities before me. He was able to teach me about the Dun & Bradstreet job because he had received their credit reporters and answered their questions. He used their service, he explained, because when he ordered supplies, especially if it was something new that was coming from another part of the country—like that buzz saw years before—he would put his order in and the seller would have no idea who he was. If they shipped him the equipment and a bill, would he be able to pay it? At those moments, he depended on his credit rating. He could give the supplier the name of his business and they would look him up via Dun & Bradstreet.

Dad thought I should take the credit reporter position, even though it meant a little less money. He said, "If you go with them, you're going to learn a lot because you're going to travel around, calling on different businesses and seeing how they run. That's probably more valuable for you in your long-term career than the difference in the salaries."

I accepted the job with Dun & Bradstreet and finished up my semester at Creighton. Marlene and I moved to Syracuse, Nebraska, where her brother owned a restaurant. That way she would be near family when the baby came, and I could help her brother keep his books. It didn't matter so much to me where we lived because on Monday mornings I got in our car, a new, dark-blue Chevy four-door, and paid calls on Nebraska businesses until the end of the day on Friday. Weeknights, I'd stay in a motel and write my credit reports.

Marlene's pregnancy went well. Hospital policy required the father to wait outside during the labor. Even after the baby came, only the mother could be in the room. They put all the new babies in cribs behind glass, and the fathers had to look through the window. Peter's birth had been hard, I learned, and the doctor needed to use forceps, which left the baby's head bruised and misshapen. But I couldn't see it. I thought he was the most beautiful baby in the world. Then the guy standing next to me said, "What's wrong with yours?" I wanted to kill him. Soon, though, the doctors explained to us that the injuries were temporary.

Besides joy, fatherhood meant greater responsibility. Now, I felt, I had to work harder so I didn't fail as a father. I went back on the road, and it was rough on Marlene with me gone so much and the new baby to care for. "But if you get hungry enough," she sometimes said, "you can learn to live with anything." We had both worked hard all our lives, and our expectation was that we would keep on working hard.

At first, my work felt a little awkward. I showed up at a stranger's business with my briefcase containing the previous year's credit reports for the company and the blank questionnaires to fill out. Even wearing a jacket and tie, a credit reporter did not command a lot of respect. The role did not require any special intelligence or talent, and people did not regard it as having any social benefit. It wasn't as if they thought you were the scum of the earth, but they let you know that you and your job were nothing special. Also, the information I needed was private, revealing the merchant's wealth, and so I had to put them at ease to help them trust me. Often, I interrupted merchants in the middle of their day, and I suppose they regarded me as a minor, necessary evil. They needed the credit report, so they couldn't tell me to go away, but they had no special enthusiasm either. It helped that I had worked sales jobs before and was used to people telling me no.

Another awkward aspect was interviewing the owners of businesses I knew nothing about, such as lumber or shoes. But it didn't feel odd for long. To me, these owners were important people, small businessmen like my dad, and I felt glad for the chance to talk to them. My grandfather had enjoyed the independence of his own business, and I admired and respected that. I had grown up around the men my father associated with—plumbers, electricians, plasterers—self-made men, confident and comfortable, pleased with themselves. That's what I thought a man should be, and here I was getting to meet these successful men in person. I say "men" because in those days I never saw a woman entrepreneur. Most women I knew stayed home and took care of the house. If they were in the workforce, they were in a health profession, such as nursing, or they were schoolteachers or secretaries.

One day I paid a call on a man in, I think, the clothing business. The address I had been given turned out to be his home. When he came to the door, he explained that he was Jewish and was about to observe a Jewish holy day with his family. Could I come back some other time? I said I was sorry, but I couldn't do that because I only stopped in his town for one afternoon. He grudgingly invited me in.

The man's home was beautiful. He called his two sons to join us and told them to listen, to consider it training in business. I felt guilty encroaching on their special time, but it was important for him to have a current rating, and we both knew that. When the interview was finished, I left thinking: *That's how I want it to be. A nice house, a nice family, and the chance to show my kids how to conduct themselves in business.*

I liked to imagine myself enjoying the independence and joy of these men who had done their own thing and made a success of it. For me, privately, there was a current of excitement beneath every interview—a feeling that any day I might discover how I could achieve as they had achieved. They had the knowledge I needed, and through them, I hoped, I might discover what I wanted.

I paid calls on merchants during the day and ate my meals alone at the cafés, diners, and hamburger stands you found in small midwestern towns. Places that served sandwiches for lunch, roast beef or meat loaf for dinner. You could have a slice of pie. At night, I'd go back to my motel room and write my credit reports. I didn't mind, as I didn't have anything else to do. The truth was that I preferred to be out on the road rather than back in the main office in Omaha. In December, because of the holidays, we couldn't call on businesses, and so we were all called back in from the field. I felt like an outsider in the main office. I never worked with those people long enough to get to know them, and I've always felt more comfortable by myself than in a group. Only rarely have I felt lonely, but in those years, I was lonely for Marlene. I was deeply in love—just to see her made me happy. It was hard to spend all that time away from her and Peter.

In retrospect, I could have written a lot of my credit reports faster than I did. The data didn't change that much from year to year, and I could have touched up the prior year's report and submitted it with the relevant changes. But I wrote each report as if it were brand-new, noting distinctive facts about each merchant. This annoyed the ladies back at the main office, who typed up the final drafts, because their job was easier if I stuck to the standard template. But I didn't want to cheat the businessperson who had confided in me, returning his trust with some half-assed rewrite. I wanted each report to be as accurate as it possibly could be.

My dedication was partly for my own benefit. I wanted to learn all about these businesses, to get all the details right, because I found them fascinating; it was exactly the education I'd been looking for. In college, my social science teacher had said that America was wealthy because of its natural resources, such as minerals in the ground and rich soil for farming. But on the road, I saw something different. I met entrepreneurs creating wealth out of their own ideas, energy, and commitment, some of them making a great deal of money. It wasn't all a matter of natural resources. It was thanks to free enterprise.

Another thing that captivated me: the people who were successful were not necessarily the ones you would expect. One day I went to call on a retailer of Caterpillar construction and farm equipment. Boy, did his operation look impressive. Inside a big fence, he had all these big, clean yellow machines—tractors, loaders, backhoes, dozers, graders—gleaming in the sun and looking expensive. Inside the office, the owner wore a beautiful suit and tie. I asked him my questions and as he answered from behind his big office desk, I thought about his cash position, his accounts receivable, and his inventory. As I worked out his cash flow, I realized he was almost broke. This impressive-looking man was getting ready to declare bankruptcy.

My next interview was supposed to be right across the highway, so close I didn't even move my car. The office was located in a railroad yard, or at least I thought it was, but there were no numbers on the buildings. I couldn't locate the address. Then I saw a man walking across the yard in bib overalls and an engineer's cap, so I called out to him asking where to find the owner of the business. He kept walking. Didn't say a word. I thought: *You son of a bitch!*

He walked to one of the buildings and put his hand on the doorknob. Then he said, "That's me," and went inside. I suppose he didn't know who I was or what I was doing on his property—I was just some intruder in a jacket and tie.

I followed him inside. There was a foundry, and the equipment was dirty, covered in metal dust. Even his office was dusty. The owner was gruff, but he let me interview him, and I learned that he'd built his business during World War II, manufacturing artillery shells for cannons. Now he was a multimillionaire.

The contrast was stark: the man in the fine suit with the beautiful display in his yard, going broke; the man in coveralls with the dirty machinery who wasn't looking for any attention, a multimillionaire. It was intriguing. How had the foundry owner done it? I wanted to know. What motivated him? How did he get started? What did he own and how did he invest the money he made? Out poured my questions about becoming one of the independent businessmen I admired. And this rough, brusque, standoffish man was kind enough to talk with me well beyond what I needed for the credit report.

Another time, over in Iowa, I called on a sort of garage where the floors were dirt, not even pavement or wood. The owners were two brothers who repaired farm implements. They bought the Dun & Bradstreet service to know the credit quality of customers who wanted to buy expensive machinery. When I walked in, the brother I had to speak with was lying underneath a truck with his hands up in the grease. He was too busy to take time to talk to me, he said.

"Don't you want to renew?" I asked.

"You have to come back."

"I can't come back," I told him. "You're way out in the country. This is the only time I'm going to be out here."

We argued some more, then he finally slid out from under the truck on his mechanic's creeper. He reached out his grease-blackened hand and said, "Okay, give me the goddamn contract." Then he took his thumb and pressed it on the signature line. It left a grease thumbprint.

"That's not going to work!" I said.

"Well, I'm not going to sign it. If my fingerprint isn't good enough, I'm not buying."

There didn't seem to be much point in arguing further. I took the contract into the office in the back, where his brother was sitting at a rolltop desk. He asked me, "Do you know what these cards are for?"

He handed me a pile of computer punch cards. At the time, IBM kept records of wealth on cards like those. He had a whole stack of them.

"My God," I said. "Do you know what each of these cards represents?"

"No."

"This is thousands of acres! Did you know you've got that much land?"

"Yeah," he said. "I did. But I didn't think anyone else knew."

Then I understood. These people with the dirt floors and the grease under their fingernails had quietly figured out how to accumulate a huge amount of money. They just worked and bought more land, worked and bought more land until they were incredibly wealthy. I thought about that as I drove back to my motel. At the end of the week, I turned in their contract with the thumbprint for a signature. The company accepted it.

My father had been right. Here was the education I wanted, an education in thinking bigger than owning a grocery store or becoming a local dentist or doctor. An education in the difference between looking successful and building true wealth. So much of the business acumen I would depend on later came from this time.

And it was exciting! This was another thing they hadn't taught me in school. Business was an act of creativity and courage. Other people didn't seem to see it this way, but to me, business was where life came alive. Some people were alive but dead in spirit—merely functioning. To be *alive* alive, there had to be a creative challenge. Running a business made you work creatively to achieve, and then feel the joy of achievement. At some point, I had come across the following quotation from David Kelley of the Institute for Objectivist Studies, and I often returned to it: "Business is a creative activity, just like writing a novel or sculpting a statue. And it requires the same traits as other creative activities: imagination, self-discipline, and, often, courage."

Being a credit reporter was a nothing job in society's eyes. But to me it was wonderful. The only thing I disliked was the volume of work. At home on weekends, I'd still be at my desk. If we were invited to a big dinner with Marlene's family and they rented out a hall to fit all her relation, I'd go out to my car after the meal and keep filling out reports. I was probably working sixty hours a week. Often, I wouldn't finish until Sunday evening, which meant I had to drive from Nebraska City to Omaha to drop the finished work into the mailbox before I went to bed. If I got my envelope into the box for local mail on Sunday night, the post office would deliver it to the main office in town the next day.

Marlene thought it was kind of crazy to work such long hours. She had known from the start that I was a hard worker, but she also knew that I didn't make any additional money for putting all that time and energy into those reports, so what was the point? I'd hear her talking to family members, explaining why they saw so little of me: "He's gone all week. He writes those things all weekend. I think the word *workaholic* might come into it . . ."

Still, my supervisors were impressed. They promoted me and moved me to the Omaha office. By then, Marlene's brother had closed his restaurant, so we moved to Nebraska City to be near to our families. She was able to do some substitute teaching and we stayed long enough for our second son, Tom, to be born in September 1965. Marlene gave birth during the day, and I was called from Dun & Bradstreet to join her. This time, the nurse thought I'd like to see the baby right away, so she brought him out to me. He was all bloody. I thought, *Clean that baby up! I'm not used to all this!* Nobody had ever explained to me the details of how a baby was born. I was shocked. They had wrapped him up in a sheet, so he didn't get blood on my suit, but I would rather have seen him neat and clean. Later, I told Marlene, "Don't do that to me again. They had to call me away from work! Next time, have the baby in the evening." Boy, was she angry. That's how insensitive I was in those days about such things.

Dun & Bradstreet offered to put me in charge of the Sioux Falls office, making me the youngest manager the company ever had, and I moved the growing family to South Dakota. I was managing the other credit reporter while at the same time selling the service to new clients, meaning that I now received a commission as part of my income. That was very exciting, to be paid on the basis of my own performance. I began to think that I could make my way in life without ever finishing that bachelor's degree. I would simply find a good corporation and work my way up.

In Sioux Falls, I called on a furniture wholesaler. He needed our service for his furniture business, but he talked to me about another of his ventures, a hamburger franchise called McDonald's. Sioux Falls was a much smaller town than Omaha, around seventy thousand people, but this guy owned four or five locations and it seemed they were always busy. I remember how the simplicity of it impressed me: they had a fifteen-cent hamburger and ten-cent french fries, and it all came out hot as soon as you ordered it. This was a relatively new idea then, that a restaurant would cook your hamburger before you even arrived. To make that work, they had to have customers coming in all day long to buy those waiting burgers, and their surprising idea was to take the law of supply and demand that I'd learned in college and work it in reverse. Instead of raising the price of a burger to discover what the market would bear, they lowered it enough to drive up demand and get people to come in all day. With the lowered price, they didn't make much per burger, but with so many customers, they still made a healthy profit. I admired how they went against the normal way of thinking, then found the courage to take a risk on their idea and follow through. That was an interesting conversation.

I began to have my own ideas about what could be done, beyond hamburgers, with a low price point and a high volume. I suppose I could say that thinking about McDonald's gave me an aha moment, that now I knew the kind of innovative approach I would later take with Ameritrade, but that's not exactly true. When we look backward, knowing how our stories are going to turn out, we tend to make our creative processes sound neat. But actually getting there is messy. Even the McDonald's story is messy. Richard and Maurice McDonald developed a revolutionary restaurant kitchen, as efficient as a factory, but although they were the pioneers who invented it, they didn't fully grasp the opportunity that their factory-kitchen represented. Someone else, Ray Kroc, went on to do that. For me, observing McDonald's helped develop my eye for ingenuity and entrepreneurship, but did I know what difference it would make? Did I have a plan for what was to come? Not at all.

What I did have, as I made connections between the economics I had studied and the merchants I visited in my work for Dun & Bradstreet, was a newly clear idea of what I wanted from life: to found my own business. I felt as if I'd wanted it all along but hadn't known the word for it. Now that I knew, I was surprised to realize that there were other people who didn't share this goal. To be honest, I was stunned. When I was young, I assumed I was like everybody else. I can see now that it is a good thing that we do not have a world of people who all want to do the same thing—it would be a chaotic world if we all wanted to be entrepreneurs and take risks or to be painters and make art or to be accountants and keep the pennies straight. Back then, though, I thought everyone must look at the world as I did and see a place where free enterprise brought prosperity and took away misery, where starting a business was the thing to make you feel alive.

Unfortunately for me, this vision of innovation and prosperity was completely out of my reach. I didn't have any money to start a business. I had no access to capital I could borrow, and I didn't know what kind of business it would be, anyway. But I enjoyed thinking about it. I thought about it a great deal.

One day I was on the road in southeast Nebraska. I went to interview a young married couple that had opened up a successful shoe store. They were hardly older than me, just a snot-nosed couple that had taken a risk and found a way to make a living for themselves. They had plans to open another store in another town nearby, and to their surprise they had discovered, as had I, that few people cared about it the way they did. No one seemed to grasp the excitement or to savor all the details of their plans and their attempts and the lessons learned. The three of us were weird. They seemed so pleased with themselves, working so hard and getting such a reward for their effort. I would not say I ever set a conscious goal of seeking out other people to partner with who wanted to make a business succeed as much as I did. But I remember that after I said goodbye to that couple, I thought: *Man. I'd like to be that happy.*

In Sioux Falls one day, I recall picking up the current issue of *Time* magazine. I can still see in my mind what I remember as the image on the cover—a tall man wearing a beautiful suit and shiny wingtip shoes, stepping into a taxicab at the end of the workday. The article described his career as a stockbroker, selling stocks and bonds on commission, and how very, very well his industry was doing.

I wanted those shiny shoes, the beautiful shirt and tie, and the fine tailored suit—not because I was suddenly excited about high fashion, but because those were the markers of someone who had achieved success in business. The picture showed a man who had won at being a stockbroker, and I wanted to be that man. I wanted to work on commission in a booming industry where the possibility for success was limitless, which was probably as close as someone like me with no access to capital could ever get to owning my own business. Boy, did that thrill me.

It seemed the moment was ripe to become a broker. I learned

that since 1960, the stock market had experienced explosive growth. Except for brief but steep drops in 1962 and 1966, the Dow Jones Industrial Average had risen at an unprecedented pace, led by electronics, computers, and space technology, as well as a wave of horizontal mergers that created a new form of company, the conglomerate, which combined disparate holdings under a single corporate structure. Gulf and Western, for example, owned sugar-production facilities, auto-parts manufacturers, and moviemakers like Paramount Pictures. Ling-Temco-Vought pieced together slaughterhouses, steel production, and aerospace. These acquisitions had created a buying frenzy on Wall Street and the Dow nearly broke the one thousand mark in February 1966.

For the first time since the stock market crash of 1929, large numbers of individual investors had jumped into the market. Many bought individual stocks, but others invested in the growing field of mutual funds, which accounted for 25 percent of trading activity on the New York Stock Exchange by 1965. As trading volumes rose to record levels, many stockbrokers, paid based on the number of shares sold, were earning well over a hundred thousand dollars a year, an enormous figure for the era—twenty or more times the average American family's income, which was about seven thousand dollars.

The brokerage business sounded like my best chance to get paid relative to my own talents, skills, effort, and energy. In my mind, from that day on, I have carried that picture from the magazine cover of that prosperous stockbroker. I could see him, the image of success, stepping into that cab and heading to the railroad station. Only later did I discover that there had been no iconic *Time* issue on The Stockbroker. The press did write about the phenomenon of the changing brokerage industry, but apparently they did not rate the news highly enough to feature it so dramatically. It was I, in the newsstand of my imagination, who made it the cover story. To me it was the story of the decade.

Taking a day off from Dun & Bradstreet, I put on a pressed shirt, my best suit, and freshly shined shoes. I drove from Sioux Falls to Omaha, hoping to find a brokerage firm that was hiring. At that time, if you wanted an office job, you walked in the front door of the establishment and walked up to the receptionist, who would ask who you were and what you were there for.

"I'm here to apply for a job," I said. "I'd like to see a manager."

If you walked in with dirty jeans, you wouldn't get past the reception area. If you wore a suit and tie but you couldn't speak well, they wouldn't give you a second thought. But I had on a suit and had a salesman's way with words, and I got through. I told that manager my goal, and he answered me right away.

"I'm sorry," he said. "We don't even look at applicants who lack a college degree."

For the rest of the day I went around to the other brokerage firms in Omaha. They wouldn't even let me fill out an application. Finally, I drove back home and explained the situation to Marlene. We began to brainstorm on how to change the family budget so I could go back to college. I needed one more year of coursework to get my bachelor's degree.

At that time my brother Dick worked at Boys Town, a nonprofit organization founded by Father Edward Joseph Flanagan and dedicated to caring for orphans and families. They were known for their logo, showing one boy carrying another boy on his back, with the caption "He ain't heavy, Father, he's my brother." I thought I could work nights at Boys Town and go to school during the day. It meant a cut in pay, and now Marlene had two children to look after and a third on the way, but we worked out a budget, itemizing what we would spend for food, clothing, and other necessities. We looked at it together and thought we could manage.

I spent most of my time that year either working or going to school. At night, I supervised the boys in their dormitories, checking to make sure each one was safe in his bed. One boy I remember was what we called an Indian. I had never spoken to a real Native American before. He would be in bed at lights-out and again at the first bed check, but then he would disappear. I couldn't understand how he was sneaking out or where he could be going in the middle of the night. When I confronted him about it, he said he'd never slept in a bed before and couldn't get comfortable. He snuck out at night to sleep in the fields.

My college courses came no easier than before, but my motivation was strong. Marlene would explain to people, "It's a pretty normal life, except Joe works *and* goes to school." Although she disliked that I was home a very small percentage of the time, she did enjoy where we were living: a big, old, two-story brick house close to many of our relations, so there was some help and company for her. It was not a comfortable life, and there were times we wished we had more money, but our friends weren't rich, either. As my mother used to say about the Depression, "It was tough, but everybody was in the same boat." You learned to get along.

The following spring, with graduation on the horizon, I started applying for brokerage jobs again. My first choice was Dean Witter & Company, one of the largest investment houses on the West Coast. I liked the manager, I liked their systems, and their training program was regarded as the best in the industry. This time, with my college degree expected in May, they took me. I was invited to join a six-month training program at their headquarters in San Francisco. At the end of the training, there would be an exam; those who passed would become brokers. It meant more school, but then I would be only one exam away from the life on that imaginary magazine cover.

Peter was now four years old, Tom three, and my daughter, Laura, was one. After my year of working nights and studying days, Marlene was pretty well adapted to not having me around. She probably would have been content to stay home with our little children in Omaha while I completed the training, but the company required married participants to bring their wives. It was 1969, only two years after the Summer of Love, and San Francisco was filled with hippies and others drawn to the promise of free love and psychedelic experimentation. Apparently, there had been trouble in the past, with the Dean Witter management getting calls about husbands taking up with other women. So that was their policy, and it was probably a wise one. San Francisco was a heck of a lot of fun, and I probably would have had more fun than I deserved if my wife and kids hadn't been there with me.

One other Nebraskan was joining the training program when I started, and the company introduced us in the Omaha office. Bob Perelman was a tough, fatherly-seeming man about twenty years my senior who had recently sold his family's grocery stores. He helped me find an apartment to rent in San Francisco and chose one for his family down the hall in the same building.

By the time I took my last exam at Creighton, we were all packed up and I was more than ready to be done. The past ten years had been such intense work and I felt so happy to be finished with it all. I walked out of that test and dumped my textbooks in a wastebasket. I never wanted to see them again. Then my youngest brother, Jim, and I got into my car and he helped me drive it out west. Marlene and the kids flew out to join us.

• • •

San Francisco then was still a small city, beautiful and charming. We lived in the Richmond District, just a few blocks from the ocean, between Golden Gate Park and the Presidio. Although we were in the capital of the hippies, the seventy members of our Dean Witter training class showed up every morning in jackets and ties, short hair neatly combed, ready to learn. Most of my classmates were older than me, well into their thirties, with some professional success already behind them. Scientists, attorneys, vacuum salesmen, pharmacists, car salesmen—they were talented men who expected big things, with strong egos to match. That was probably the most fun part of it. I enjoyed their company.

As we listened to our lecturers, we could hear the bang of pile drivers and construction equipment working on the construction of the Montgomery Street BART station. The smell of cigarettes and coffee filled the room. We learned sales techniques and the rules and regulations of the business. Some of the rules had been crafted by the industry—through the New York Stock Exchange and the National Association of Securities Dealers (NASD)—and some had been imposed by the government through the Securities and Exchange Commission (SEC). We learned aspects of how to analyze a company financially, but not thoroughly. The instructor's attitude was, "We don't want to spend a lot of time on this because we're going to hire analysts to do that for you. We will tell you what is good and bad. Your job is to sell."

There was a lot of information to assimilate. We worked hard. My new neighbor, Bob Perelman, and I found we were good study partners. Forty-seven years old with curly salt-and-pepper hair, he was no longer used to book learning. He appreciated working with a recent graduate. For my part, I learned from his two decades of practical experience in every facet of the grocery business and from his personal knowledge of investing.

On the surface, Bob Perelman and I seemed very different. He was Jewish, an A student who had taken a leave from the University of Nebraska to serve in World War II. With the 232nd Infantry Regiment, he helped liberate the Dachau concentration camp. He returned to civilian life believing that his grades were good enough to get him into Harvard Business School, despite the quota at Harvard limiting the admission of Jews, but he came home to discover that his father, who owned a grocery store, had bought a second store for him to run. Bob didn't want it. He hated the grocery business with its long hours, small profits, and lack of opportunity to use all he had learned in college. But his father had bought it for him as a gift, and Bob didn't criticize him. "God bless him," Bob would say, "he was looking out for me." He took the store on out of respect and ran it for twenty years. In time, first father and then son served as president of the Omaha Retail Grocers' Association. Only after his father died did Bob sell the business and turn his sights on a career more to his liking.

Bob was a natural salesman. Ambitious and competitive, with a strong work ethic, he called things as he saw them. I remember hearing a man push him to explain why he had chosen to become a stockbroker. What did he like about it? "I just like it," Bob said. "Because I do. Why does anybody like what they do? I like it because I like it. There's no reason. That's all." I came to love this gruff, fatherly man, to trust him as my mentor. In time, we would become business partners.

At the end of the day, when I was home from work, Marlene and I might take the kids over to Golden Gate Park or walk the hilly streets of the city with them, which offered a lot that was new for the children. They learned about riding the bus. For the first time in their young lives, they experienced people with different skin colors, different languages, different smells, and different clothes. They just took it all in. I remember I took my kids out on Halloween, and at one house a black man answered the door. My oldest son, Peter, still very short and very small, called out, "Trick or treat!"

"Just a minute!" the man said. "I'll be right back with some candy."

While he was gone, Peter turned to his little brother, Tom, and said, "Hey, he speaks English!" They had expected a man with a different skin color to speak a foreign language. So, San Francisco was not just a beautiful town but also a necessary education for my kids.

Overall, we men in the training program—they had hired only men—enjoyed ourselves. We knew that as brokers we would soon be competing with one another for clients, but for now we shared the camaraderie of students. We went out drinking after work and Dean Witter threw us some parties. Bob liked to go out with some of us younger guys, to drink and joke and flirt harmlessly with the waitresses. It was a fun time.

Marlene's experience was different. From the day we arrived, our life in San Francisco was hard on her. Back in Omaha, the only place you would find a home without a yard was in the poorest areas. When we first arrived at our apartment in the Richmond District and she saw that we had only two bedrooms in a building with no garage for our car, no lawn, no fenced-in yard where you could hang your laundry while the kids played in safety, she said, "This is a slum. Joe, we're living in a slum." Richmond was a middle-class neighborhood, but not to her. There was no baby bed for Laura, so Marlene piled some bedding in an open dresser drawer in our room until the landlady brought a bed for her.

Then there were the earth tremors. Marlene had grown up with tornadoes, and said she would take a tornado over an earthquake any day. When the dresser started to bang against the wall, all she knew to do in an apartment was to gather the children in the bathtub and pray. She had no love for San Francisco.

Most of the Dean Witter trainees had already found success in other careers. They had a cushion of money to ease them through six months of lowered income. I did not. Down the hall, Bob's wife, Betty, would get their little boy off to school and then go shopping and enjoy the city. Marlene took our little ones to the zoo or Golden Gate Park, the inexpensive things you do when you have to get out of a cramped apartment and don't have much spending cash. In the park, they met other children, many of them from hippie families, but Marlene found the hippies strange—dirty and sickly, she said. Back at the apartment, the smell from the hallway that she at first thought was incense turned out to be marijuana. She had never lived near drug users before, and I suppose that added to her feeling of living in a slum. Even when we drove through Haight-Ashbury, the now-legendary center of the counterculture, she said it gave her only a vague impression of sadness.

In the evenings, we could not afford to go out on the town, and Marlene did not believe in leaving children with a babysitter who was a stranger, anyway. The way she looked at it, all the men in the training program had taken a cut in salary, and all the wives had to make do, and so once again we were all in the same boat. But down the hall, Betty Perelman was living differently. She was free to go out and explore the city during school hours. The two women did not become close like Bob and I did.

Back in our apartment, Marlene would launder the children's soiled diapers and carry them up to the roof to hang on the clothes-line, watching the San Francisco fog roll in. She knew that if the fog reached the clothesline before the laundry was dry, it would get damp all over again. She watched that fog and wished we could move across the bay, where it was warmer.

And so, San Francisco was another of those experiences that we just had to get through, a necessary step toward better times. Marlene knew it would be temporary and she did not complain. We talked sometimes about the advantages of having our children so young—one day, we dreamed, when I was successful and the kids were grown, we would still be young and could do the things together that we couldn't do then.

In retrospect, there was one thing that changed for Marlene and me in San Francisco. When we had first gotten together, we dreamed of having twelve children. After Pete was born, we were a little more realistic and scaled it back to eight. With Tom, we changed our goal to six. But after living in San Francisco, we would have only one more child.

At the end of the training program, I took the exam to become a broker. Then, over a couple of days, we drove back home to Omaha. I felt confident coming out of the test that I had scored well—the company had paid my salary for six months in this training program, and they had made sure we were prepared to pass. Back in Nebraska, they told me my grades, but I wasn't interested. The point was that I got the job.

A friend took a photograph of me from around the time we got back to Omaha. Marlene and I had gone to see a production of *Fiddler on the Roof* with our friends the Regans. Afterward, we had a few drinks, and someone snapped a picture of me performing for our friends in the style of the show. I'm wearing purple pants, which you can blame on the era, and a red baseball cap turned backward to serve as my orthodox head covering, like Tevye in the show. I'm dancing with lighted candles in both hands and singing "If I Were a Rich Man." I look happy, confident, a little drunk—ready for the song to come true.

Unfortunately, in the months of studying leading up to the exam, the market had taken a downturn. We didn't realize it, but it had topped in November of 1968. Still, my classmates and I were not concerned. We believed the bear market would turn around within six months, as it had in '62 and '66, and we counted ourselves lucky that we had missed the down months while we were hitting the books. We were wrong. The go-go sixties were over. Two bear markets in a row would last five years.

CHAPTER 3

It was an evening sometime in 1974, and when I came home from the office, I saw what was on the dinner table: frozen chicken pot-pies, again.

"Oh, Marlene," I said. "I can't take this anymore. I mean, I don't want them."

I'd been working long days at Dean Witter and going back in again at night. I felt I would really like a steak.

"I'd prefer to have something else," I said.

Marlene was independent by nature—not one who answered *Yes, sir*.

"Well, Joe," she said. "You've got to give me more grocery money for the budget. If I can't have any more money to buy groceries, I can't buy anything outside of those pies."

With that, she took my argument away. We had agreed to keep our family operating expenses in line with our budget and she was doing her part. Friday was the end of the week and she was nearly out of money. Potpies were what we could afford. Was I really going to tick her off by complaining about it?

I had become a stockbroker at exactly the wrong time. In the sixties, the Dow had reached highs of nearly one thousand, but by May 1970, it had fallen to 631, and the total value of the New York Stock Exchange was half what it had been the year before. While I had been training to become a stockbroker, individual investors began leaving the market in droves. We couldn't know it then, but by the end of the seventies, the number of Americans who owned stock would fall by seven million, and the share of households with assets in the market would fall from about one in four to less than one in ten. I felt those headwinds every day at Dean Witter as we struggled to sign up clients.

Some of the decline was due to larger economic trends. The productivity of American manufacturing had slowed as the United States struggled to compete with the growing economic might of Japan and Europe in basic industries such as steel, textiles, automobiles, electronics, rubber, and petrochemicals. The stock market had also suffered from the excesses of the go-go years. When David Babson, an old-guard investment counselor on Wall Street, was asked in 1971 what had gone wrong, he pointed to a general loss of responsibility. His list of faults included investment advisors who "massacred clients' portfolios" while trying to "make good on the over-promises that they had made to attract the business in the first place," and too many "security analysts who forgot about their professional ethics to become 'story peddlers.' " Unethical practices had made the problem that began with weak economic fundamentals even worse.

With demand for stocks down so far, many brokers could no longer support themselves on their commissions. The industry was shedding jobs. Bob and I were keeping our heads above water, but to do it we worked all the time. The Dean Witter office in Omaha was at Nineteenth and Douglas, and during the week I'd leave about seven thirty in the morning and work until I came home for supper. As soon as I finished eating, I drove back downtown and got on the phone again, coming home about ten o'clock. I worked on Saturdays, too. Saturday nights, I kept my habits from college, drinking my fill of beer with our friends. That was the extent of our leisure time. I didn't take the kids fishing or anything like that, and we certainly couldn't afford vacations.

Sundays, we went to Mass at Christ the King, and then I'd go home to rest from the previous week. I would not say I ever lost interest in the work of being a broker, but I did get worn down, deeply exhausted. Sometimes when I was home, Marlene would ask me to take care of the kids while she went out. When she came back, she might find me with a pillow, asleep on the living-room floor.

"You were supposed to be watching the kids!" she'd say.

"I told them to behave" was my answer.

Some weeks, I worked on Sundays as well. Meanwhile, Marlene was busy all week with four young children and part-time teaching when she could fit it in. These habits, though stressful, didn't seem strange to us. Many of the people who became our close friends worked similar hours, but plenty of them were making more than I was. They asked me, "Joe, why don't you just stop? Why not work for IBM or some other company that can pay you a comfortable salary?"

I wasn't interested. It felt like when I was in grade school and my friends wanted me to play sports, but I wanted to work and to earn. I told them, "I enjoy this kind of work more, and I have a feeling there will be an opportunity that is huge, somewhere, sometime."

That's when they would laugh and shake their heads. They didn't see any huge opportunities waiting around the corner. Even Marlene sometimes asked me, "Joe, wouldn't you like to try something a little easier?"

"Those things," I told her, "are never going to make me a millionaire."

But my motivation was never simply money. Working in the brokerage industry energized me. There was opportunity and risk. There was the need to compete and better myself, which for me has always been incredibly exciting. When there was no risk, no excitement, I became a zombie. My biggest fear was that I would have to get some job I hated in order to support my family, and it would feel like a living death. My long hours at Dean Witter could be exhausting, but when I was there it didn't feel like a *job*. I felt alive, and that was hard to explain. With most people, I didn't even try.

At times, naturally, I doubted myself. Maybe, I thought, I was just an idiot. What did I have, really, besides this idea—an idea that no one else seemed to share—that a great opportunity was waiting out there for me? I took solace in the words of George Roche III, president of Hillsdale College, who wrote, "Ideas rule the world—not armies, not economics, not politics, not any of the things to which we usually give our allegiance, but ideas."

My day-to-day work was mainly cold-calling. That meant dialing phone numbers to try to get potential customers on the line, then persuading those who answered to become clients. When I had first become a broker, I expected to have an advantage because my travel for Dun & Bradstreet had introduced me to a lot of successful business owners who would want to become my clients. I soon found out that all the brokers in Omaha knew the same people, and we were in competition with one another to get the same accounts. Most people you cold-called said no, and I had to develop a kind of callous inside to accept that. A small percentage agreed to become clients, and then I would ask them, "When I have an idea for you, may I call you again?"

Statistically, we all knew the percentage of attempts that yielded clients and sales, so I had to maintain the discipline to make so many calls every day, with the pressure of knowing that if I didn't make the calls and my commissions fell, I couldn't support my family. Dialing a certain amount of numbers per day did not feel like the excitement of competition. That was unhappy drudgery. When you finally got someone on the line who was willing to talk, you had to dig deep inside yourself to find the enthusiasm to make those pitches, and frankly, most people don't like that work. When our friends asked Marlene about the cold-calling at my office, she would say, "They all hate it."

To me, though, making the pitch when I finally got the chance could be fun. I liked the challenge of calling up a guy who owned a business, someone successful and sophisticated, the kind of man I had enjoyed interviewing for Dun & Bradstreet, and telling him, "I want to do something for you. I'm going to help you out. Are you interested in talking to me?"

To help us advise clients and increase sales, the company maintained a research team. That was part of what made us "full-service brokers." The research department was a big expense that the company passed on to clients, but I discovered in a very short period of time that the research didn't put any more money in a broker's pocket. The recommendations were for blue-chip stocks, suited to the clients who wanted a good stock that they could hold on to forever. But a lot of the clients I spoke with were interested not in patient, long-term investing but in short-term growth: stocks that would go up soon.

I went looking for better research, to find my own stocks to peddle with greater potential for growth. The company discouraged independent recommendations, but we were paid on commission, so I didn't care. Bob Perelman, who had been successful at investing his own money, had taught me charting, which includes various methods for calculating the supply and demand for a stock. There was a great deal of disagreement between analysts who called themselves chartists and those who called themselves fundamentalists, but I found that if you put the two methods together you could sometimes predict the psychology of when a stock would move.

I learned about the Natomas Company, which was developing profitable offshore oil concessions in Java and Sumatra. Over a year or so, the stock price quadrupled. Many of my customers bought it and made money, and that was when my reputation as a broker started to take off. Because I had recommended one stock that went way up, people were willing to sign up as my clients. They seemed to feel that made me a serious professional.

In retrospect, what lifted the stock was mostly rumor, and we brokers were helping it along. All of us at Dean Witter were living through the same challenging bear market; when somebody got an idea that seemed to work, they would tell the rest of us about it. We were naïve enough not to realize that we brokers were probably helping to push the price up, or, if somebody did understand, they had greater insight than I. In any case, it worked to raise the stock price. It worked well. And a crazy story like Natomas was fun to talk about, which fired up my enthusiasm. That enthusiasm traveled through the phone line to my potential clients, and when they felt it, more of them would agree to buy.

Later, we started pushing a company that made Wankel engines for cars and other vehicles. The pistons in this engine rotated in a kind of figure eight instead of pumping up and down, though there was some concern about pressure building up and bursting the engine's seals. It seemed like the future, like the Tesla of the 1970s. We really had no idea how those engines would ultimately affect a car or airplane maker's bottom line, but the stock price soared. We started buying that stock in the twenties, and I believe it went over a hundred.

Those big successes were rare. We didn't know it yet, but between 1968 and 1982, the Dow would lose three-quarters of its total value, adjusted for inflation. In that environment, there were few stocks that I could in good conscience tell my clients to buy. After all, I expected the market to go down or at least sideways. I began to recommend shorting: borrowing shares of a stock that you think is priced too high, selling it as soon as you borrow it, and then, when the price goes down, buying it again at the lower price and paying back the borrowed shares. Shorting lets you reverse the usual order of stock investing—you sell high and buy low. We were able to help our customers make money by shorting, but I got a lot of pushback from Dean Witter, which said you couldn't build a long-term clientele by going short. And whenever I had my customers buy stock that was not in a Dean Witter–researched company, the branch manager would come with questions: "Where are you getting your information? How valid is it?" They would make sure that I wasn't doing something improper, harmful to clients, or most of all, illegal.

Slowly I observed that in this down market, some brokers at other companies were finding unethical ways to pad their commissions. Some guys I had trained with were selling warrants, which are options attached to another kind of security. If you bought a company's bonds, for example, they might come with an option, or warrant, to buy the company stock at a set price. You could then sell that option to someone else. The guys I knew priced the warrants at two dollars, which sounded like a simple, inexpensive way to speculate in options, but they kept twenty-five cents as commission. There was nothing wrong with the warrants and nothing illegal about adding a commission, but with customers paying 12.5 percent commission for the warrant, it was very unlikely that they would ever earn a big enough return to make it worthwhile—and many customers didn't realize their two-dollar purchase included that big commission. In the long bear market, there was a lot of pressure to find questionable maneuvers like that.

By the midseventies, our youngest, Todd, had started school, and our family was outgrowing its home. My colleagues advised me to buy the most expensive place I could afford and live in it forever, so we bought a three-bedroom house, figuring the boys would share a room and Laura could have her own. The price was forty-one thousand dollars, more money than I could ever imagine making. I remember thinking, *I'll never get this debt paid*. It was a huge commitment, but by pinching here and there we thought we could afford it. Marlene was happy because it was a pleasant house located in the best public school district in Omaha.

There was also a new source of stress at the office. A manager was allowing some of the older brokers to hire secretaries based on their looks and their willingness to go on dates with brokers. "It's basically a whorehouse," Bob would say. What upset him, besides his objection to that sort of thing in the workplace, was that those secretaries gave priority to the work they received from brokers who showed an extracurricular interest, and delayed Bob's and my work because we did not.

At the same time, I realized that since I had passed my test to become a broker five years before, I had gathered a good number of clients, but my income just barely covered our expenses. Marlene shopped for discount brands and served potpie on Friday nights. My kids saw me mainly at dinner. My present employment situation was barely sustainable, and when we looked ahead, Bob and I both recognized that a change was coming to the industry. Our situation as stockbrokers was about to get worse.

From the time of the creation of the stock exchange, for over 180 years, the commissions received by stockbrokers had been fixed by the predecessor of the New York Stock Exchange. The buyer and seller were not allowed to negotiate the fee. That may have made sense when there were few trades that happened slowly and the industry was small, but with the rise of mutual funds and other changes, these fixed commissions came to the attention of regulators, the Justice Department, and Congress, as a violation of antitrust laws and harmful to consumers. Prominent economists suggested that reduced commissions would increase trading and stimulate the economy. The government made the decision to phase out the fixed commissions, starting with the highest-dollar trades and gradually including trades of any size, including those of the individual investors who were our clients. That change was scheduled for May 1975.

Other than Bob, my colleagues seemed unconcerned. Commissions wouldn't change, they said. We'll be fine, they said. But in the *Wall Street Journal*, if you knew where to look, you started to see little advertisements for brokerages in New York City that offered "third market" trades, meaning that instead of buying your stock from the issuer of that stock (the "first market") or from one of the traditional stock exchanges (the "second market"), you could trade stocks "over the counter" from a third-party securities trader not bound by the old rules on commissions that applied to the stock exchanges. It was a crack in the dam of the traditional broker rules.

My colleagues did not seem to pay much attention to the coming changes. Throughout my life, I have observed that most people tend to believe that life will continue on in the way it has gone before. There is some expectation that tomorrow's weather will be more or less like today's. To me, though, the world never seemed that way. I was still thinking about the Edna Ferber stories I knew about people facing times of enormous change. In *Giant*, when Jett Rink (played by James Dean) is offered money by cattle ranchers for a small acreage he has inherited, he refuses to sell. He says he'd rather keep the land. He digs and discovers oil, a new and greater source of revenue that the cattle ranchers don't understand. I didn't want to be like those cattle ranchers. I wanted to be like Jett Rink, recognizing that changing times were creating big new opportunities.

I also loved Jack London's stories about the Klondike Gold Rush in the Yukon. London describes people who saw a new opportunity and leapt at the chance to get rich without first learning to understand Alaska's hostile climate. With no idea how to survive an Alaskan winter, many prospectors died on the trail. I carried those two ideas with me, tucked in the back of my mind—that most people will miss a new opportunity when it comes, and that those who do see it need to prepare as thoroughly as they can for its dangers.

Most of the brokers that Bob and I knew believed that the rule changes wouldn't hurt us as long as brokers kept charging the same commissions they had always charged. That didn't make sense to me. I had observed small businesses throughout the region, and it seemed there was always someone willing to lower prices as a way to win customers. The traditional price that had seemed like an impenetrable dam would crack, and a tiny leak could become a flood.

"Somebody will break ranks," Bob agreed, based on his years in the grocery business. "Somebody will see an opportunity to make a profit, and they'll take a risk."

One day I walked across the Dean Witter office, past the ticker-tape machine, to Bob's desk. An advantage of being paid on commission was that we could stop and talk when we felt like it—when you're paid only for what you earn, no one tells you to get back to work.

"Everybody says this new rule on commissions won't affect us," I said.

"But it will," Bob said.

"When it does, we're going to have to work even harder just to do as well as we're doing now."

Bob had seen in his grocery store what happened when he

introduced lower-cost products, what we called "plain label" canned goods: the name brands lost customers to the generics. I had seen the same result from the customer side, when Marlene switched from Green Giant vegetables to a generic brand in order to keep within our food budget. Now, Bob and I were coming to the same thought: Why should we stay at a full-service broker and lose the customers who want a lower price? Why not become the new brokers who get to welcome those customers?

In my lifetime, the national brokerages like Merrill Lynch and Dean Witter had bought out the local firms of the previous generation. The big national firms benefited from economies of scale that small firms couldn't compete with, and it was almost impossible for a new player to break in. This new rule change, though, had the potential to disrupt the entire industry, as we would say today. With less regulation came new opportunity—a small local brokerage might be able to offer a lower price to the customers who would appreciate it.

How exactly would we do it? What steps would it take? We had no idea. We were so unprepared, so inexperienced, so just plain stupid that it is hard for me, looking back, to believe it. All we had was the intuition that if it could be done in the grocery business, it could be done in the stock business. We could not fully explain what "it" was, but we could feel that there was an opportunity to be pioneers, setting out to explore and map and make our fortune in this uncharted territory of negotiated commissions.

I had always loved to read about the early Americans of the colonial period. For years, they stayed near the coast, not daring to enter the thick forests of the Appalachian Mountains. It was hard for me as a reader to believe that the colonists wouldn't go into the forest, but to them, it was terrifying. There were bears and cougars. There were hostile Native Americans. It took a pioneer like Daniel Boone with the courage and curiosity to learn how to live off that unknown land. And that, at the start, was what Bob and I had in place of a business plan—curiosity and courage.

Saturday nights, when I talked over beers about starting my own brokerage, my friends called me crazy. Where was I going to get the money to back a new firm? And even if I did, the brokerage business was famously cutthroat. If a lack of capital didn't stop me, the competition would kill me. What was there really to talk about?

But with Bob Perelman, for the first time, I had a partner to dream with. We traded ideas back and forth. We feasted on each other's enthusiasm. Because I had someone to share my ideas with, the thoughts came even faster. My youngest son, Todd, remembers me working in the basement office I'd created, barely speaking to anyone. Todd would be playing with his cowboys and Indians, and I might come up from the basement now and then to mow the lawn or do some other chore, and then down I would go again, never saying a word. I was studying, planning, dreaming.

One day Bob and I took a research trip to Chicago, where a couple of our former classmates from the Dean Witter training program worked on the new options exchange. Stock options are now a common part of corporate compensation packages, but at the time most people didn't even know that a stock option was a contract that gave you the option to buy or sell a stock at a certain price or by a certain date. Buying and selling options was not an investment but a kind of speculation, and as a young man, that sort of risk appealed to me. Our classmates painted a rosy picture of how trading in stock options would grow once commissions came down, and as it would turn out, they were exactly right—profits on the options exchange were so high, for a while, that exchange memberships that would have cost us $12,500 in 1974 would be valued a few years later in the millions.

At the time, options trading was a new operation, very small. The traders had been given a large room in the Chicago Board of Trade Building, but there were only enough of them at their standing desks to fill about a quarter of the floor. Our colleagues gave us the chance to see how it all worked up close, and it looked attractive, though Bob and I both felt we would be more comfortable starting a business back in Omaha rather than coming to Chicago.

Walking out of that big room, we happened to bump into another classmate from our Dean Witter training days. Bob told him that we were looking to make a change, and the fellow said, "Come with me." Bob had that essential quality for a good salesman: people just liked him. There were people Bob didn't like, but everyone liked Bob.

We followed him into an elevator that opened onto a dark, dingy hall. I saw a door with a sign in red cursive: ROSE AND COMPANY. Inside, we stepped down into a small room where three people sat at metal desks. At the first, a lady was answering calls as fast as she could. At the next two, men were taking orders for stock trades. There was a ticker tape running at the far end of the room. That was the whole operation, but they seemed to be doing a tremendous volume of business. I could hear them on the phone, and they weren't offering stock research or making any kind of sales pitch. The callers, I realized, must already know what they wanted to buy or sell.

Did that ever get my attention: Clients could call you! You didn't have to call them. What fun! No more long days dialing for dollars. No more asking strangers for permission to call them again later with stock recommendations. It was as if I'd spent five years crossing a desert and now I discovered the oasis. The phone orders just kept coming in! The thing that excited me most was that they weren't trying to make customers feel happy with the enthusiasm in their sales pitch. They were satisfying a practical need by executing orders quickly and accurately. Wow. That, to me, was what the brokerage business was supposed to be.

The trades we observed at Rose and Company were occurring on what was called the third market. This was early 1975, and the major stock exchanges had not yet gone to negotiated commissions on all trades, but it was possible to trade a listed stock on the third market, the over-the-counter market, which is now called Nasdaq. And because you could do that, you could avoid the high minimum commissions of the New York Stock Exchange or the traditional brokers.

Let's say you bought General Electric at fifty dollars on the NYSE. Their required commission might be two hundred dollars or so. In a third-market trade, however, the customer paid a little more than the listed stock price, maybe fifty dollars and an eighth, meaning an additional twelve and a half cents per share, plus a twenty-five-dollar commission. The extra eighth they paid went to compensate a market maker to perform the trade, but the overall cost including the commission was still far less than it would have been with the required minimum commission. By going through the over-the-counter market, the customer effectively got a negotiated commission before the law required it, but only an experienced investor would understand that or know where to find it. So, the kinds of customers who found and patronized third-market brokers were sophisticated. That was compelling. Customers who could understand the third market would also be customers who didn't need research and advice.

Our colleagues at Rose and Company were generous in sharing what they knew with us, in part, I think, because they operated only in Chicago. The whole brokerage business back then was based on local branch offices and local calls—at that time, long-distance calling was still a significant expense. Our colleagues didn't see Bob and me, living far away in Nebraska, as competition, nor did we worry about them. No one imagined that technology would soon put every broker in the country in a head-to-head struggle for market share.

With their example in mind, Bob and I began to estimate the practical ways we might cut costs compared to full-service brokers. If our orders were coming from experienced investors who did their own research, we wouldn't need to fund a research department. If clients were going to call us instead of the other way around, we wouldn't need to rent branch offices and pay commissions to brokers making cold calls. And if we could pay an exchange broker for each trade as it was made, we would not need to hire our own clerks on the exchange floor, like Dean Witter did, and pay their salaries. *Disintermediation* was not yet a common business term, but we could see that by providing our customers with lower-cost trades, without offering any of the additional services and functions that brokerages had traditionally provided, we could cut our costs by 75 percent or more while giving the sophisticated clients exactly what they wanted.

Bob and I came back to Omaha eager to start our own third-market operation. Could we pull it off? There was no way to predict, but I felt we made a good team. He was of course far more experienced as a businessman, and often described me to his colleagues as "green," "inexperienced," and "just along for the ride." He also said that I was one of the hardest workers he had ever come across. He seemed to enjoy training me, telling me when to heel and to sit, while at the same time I was helping the older dog learn new tricks. Every time Bob pointed out a problem with our plans, I had an answer. Every time I pointed out a problem, he had an answer. If he didn't see our contributions as equally balanced, I didn't mind. I felt grateful to have a mentor.

To be honest, it was more than mentorship. My father had died of a heart attack around the time I became a broker. There were no more trips home to sit on the back patio and ask his opinion about my career decisions. I didn't think about it a lot, but Bob slowly took my father's place as my gruff but caring guide through the business world. I loved him for it. Most of the emotion went one way, me to him. I don't think I was a son figure to him, but he trusted me. He knew I would be loyal to him and not bring him heartache.

Unlike me, Bob had money to invest in a new business, which meant his money would be at risk. He had more reason to be scared. Part of what I contributed was my lack of fear. For one thing, I didn't have money to lose. For another, I felt motivated: I was thirty-three by then and felt my life was passing by. It could take twenty years to build a business the way I had dreamed—I would be fifty-three! This might be my last chance.

More than all that, though, I had the gift of enjoying risk-taking. To me, the most exciting things in life are the dangers you can control. I have never enjoyed gambling because there is too much luck involved. It's risk without control, which to me is just a discomfort to be endured. But starting our own business meant the freedom to make our own decisions in the face of serious risk. I had hungered for that all my life. Bob, though a successful businessman and a good salesman, was not a natural entrepreneur. He would never have attempted a third-market operation by himself. He was daunted by too many uncertainties. I had to help him think through ways to reduce his concerns to a level he could accept.

It's hard to convey today how new all of this felt at the time—and just how much we didn't know. What had to happen after a customer called us and requested a trade? Somehow, the buyer's money got to the seller, and the seller's stock certificate (a physical piece of paper with monetary value) got to the buyer, and records of this trade were provided to the buyer, the seller, the stock exchange, and the government in legally specified ways. This is called clearing. We didn't know the first thing about it. Our experience was in sales; up until this point all we had done was get people to agree to trade, then step aside. "We knew bubkes," Bob would say later. "We knew bull. I knew nothing, and Joe knew less."

Looking for more information, we went to visit the NASD at their office in Chicago. They were kind enough to talk to us. We told them we had questions about starting a brokerage and their response was, essentially: *Why even try? People are going broke in the brokerage business. The market is down; no one is making any money. What kind of masochists are you?* These were guys who knew how the entire investment system worked, and even they couldn't see the opportunity we thought we saw. It was that new.

I felt that we were like the fur trappers Lewis and Clark encountered when they were exploring the Missouri River, coming into the country to trap beaver for their extremely valuable pelts. The trappers knew that the opportunity was immense and the unexplored country hostile, but they had no practical idea what to expect. Faced with that kind of uncertainty, you either give up or say to yourself: *Okay, I'll figure out how to do this, and when I do, I'll show them how it's done.*

We didn't know what clearing meant, but it sounded like it must be a banking function, so we paid a visit to the trusts department of the Omaha National Bank.

"We'd like to start a brokerage operation," Bob told the head of the department, "and we'd like you to clear our trades for us."

"No," he said. "We can't do that."

We were kind of floored.

"Why not?" I asked.

"We don't do that," he said. "I don't actually know what that means."

"Well, gee," I said. "We don't know what it means either."

That banker had no practical information for us at all, but he did leave us with a suggestion.

"You know," he said, "you might go across the street and talk to this fellow, Cliff Rahel, who has a firm on the first floor. He's thinking about closing his doors, but I bet he can talk to you about clearing."

I did not know Cliff, but Bob was familiar with his family. Bob knew a lot of the history of the successful Omaha families. The story Bob told me began with this man's father, J. Cliff Rahel, who was the CEO of a local brokerage firm in the forties and fifties. The firm did the underwriting for municipalities and large corporations around them that needed to finance large projects such as highways, swimming pools, factories, and especially schools. They were successful with the elder Rahel in charge, growing many branch offices, until company policy required him to retire at sixty-five.

Rahel felt he was still too young to stop working, so he started his own firm, J. Cliff Rahel and Company. He had the brains to run the business, but he discovered he no longer had the energy for all the legwork. He decided to put his son in charge, and so the son, Cliff Rue Rahel, would drive out to small towns that needed bonds underwritten and visit with city councils and the other players involved. The father, back at the office, would do the complex analyses to determine the correct interest rates to offer on the bonds, which were issued in numbers too small to be rated by Moody's or Standard & Poor's. The company was still called J. Cliff Rahel, and a lot of new customers never realized that Cliff Rue Rahel, whom they dealt with day to day, was not J. Cliff Rahel, who made the big deals and did the underwriting. The father never told them otherwise.

The son had another advantage, besides his father's brains. He had married a woman who inherited a large amount of money. His wife's money provided a funding source for the firm to take on new projects. The new firm prospered, issuing bonds for school districts, municipalities, and corporations on a local basis, and they gradually grew into several offices.

Then, in 1969, two changes befell Cliff Rue Rahel. First, his father died, and the company lost its brains. Second, he did something to anger his wife and she divorced him. He lost his brains and he lost his money, and he had to sell the business.

Cliff kicked around for about a year, to the best of my knowledge, and didn't or couldn't find a job. Then he and his former branch manager in Lincoln, Nebraska, decided to start another brokerage firm to do the same thing that J. Cliff Rahel had done: be a primary issuer of bonds. The manager's name was George Knack, and they called the firm Rahel, Knack, and Company. This was the firm located across the street from the Omaha National Bank, that the head of the trusts department suggested we visit.

The operation was very small, and it had not grown as hoped. The two men bought a propane gas business that was for sale near their summer homes in Iowa, and Knack left to run that. Cliff hired a registered representative named Ernie Field to assist him in the office. By the time I knocked on Cliff and Ernie's door in 1975, they had five years' experience running a brokerage firm, with all the licenses it would have taken Bob and me a couple of years to collect. But interest rates had gone up, and municipalities were not issuing bonds as they had in the sixties. The firm was struggling.

"This was a hand-to-mouth little business," explained David Kellogg, the CPA who used to do their yearly audits and later came to work for Bob and me. "As long as they were both there trying to make a living at it, I suspect they were going to be okay. But they certainly weren't getting rich, and they weren't getting any bigger. It had to be a heck of a comedown for Cliff."

The office was in an old retail store with big plate-glass windows.

Cliff turned out to be middle-aged and balding, the sort of man always seen in a suit and tie. He drove a Thunderbird, the famous luxury car, and he let you know right away that he came from the upper crust of Omaha, the country-club set. When he spoke to me, I felt he was looking down his nose. I figured him right away for a stupid rich kid.

We had heard he might be ready to sell his business outright, but after Cliff heard me describe our plans, he said he wanted to see what would happen with negotiated commissions. He wasn't interested in selling his business, he said, but he might be willing to be partners.

That was a dilemma. Cliff hardly seemed a natural match for Bob and me. He was not enthusiastic about lowering commissions and trying our low-cost approach, and more than that, Bob felt he wasn't a straight shooter. Marlene, when she met him, said she couldn't quite trust him. But what choice did we have? He had the registrations and licenses we needed. He had a worker in the office named Ruth who knew how to keep proper records of stock trades and submit them to an investment banking firm called A. G. Becker, which handled their clearing. He was our only chance to launch a brokerage in Omaha anytime soon.

Cliff didn't seem especially keen on working with us, either, but he liked that we would bring new energy and new money into his business. At first he suggested that he would put in twenty-five thousand dollars to recapitalize, and that Bob and I together could put in another twenty-five thousand, making him the senior partner and Bob and me the junior ones. He knew how to run a brokerage firm, he argued, so he should be more important.

We said no. We appreciated that he had knowledge, licenses, and connections that we needed, but he couldn't be above us. "We're going to be equal partners," we told him. "If you can't do an equal partner arrangement, we're not interested."

When Cliff realized we were serious, he proposed that Ernie Field become the fourth partner. Ernie was a sweet, likable guy, but though I could be wrong, I don't think he had $12,500 to his name, and I'm sure he never had an idea about how to innovate in the brokerage business. I had the sense that Cliff brought him in as a front for his own money, knowing that Ernie would always vote as Cliff said. So now we were looking at an equal partnership arrangement in which, if we ever came to a serious disagreement, that disagreement would also be equal: Cliff and Ernie against Bob and me. Bob and I were not afraid of that because we were good friends and because he knew that between us he was the leader, the older man. He knew I respected him, and that I would pay him deference and not oppose him.

We agreed to launch the business with four partners. For a name, we took Omaha, because we assumed we would be a local business, and we put "First" in front of it, like banks do. I don't remember who proposed it, but we all agreed. We would be First Omaha Securities.

This, finally, was my chance. Everything I had done in business up to this point paled in comparison. I was excited as hell, but my share was a lot of money to me. I had to borrow several thousand from Bob, several thousand more from my brother Dick, and even a little from friends. I knew that if I lost that $12,500, my life would change dramatically. As it was, I was only getting by week to week. How would I pay back that kind of money if I lost it? And yet, at the same time, I remember feeling comfortable. There I was in the middle of all that risk, and it felt normal. It was as if I'd been waiting for it all my life.

Once we came to terms with Cliff and Ernie and the papers were signed, our new company took over their old lease in that narrow, little first-floor office on Farnam Street. You came in through a short hall with a desk pushed up against the wall, and then the room opened up a bit with four more desks for Cliff, Bob, Ernie, and me. Because the room was so narrow, we couldn't fit the desks facing forward, so we lined them up facing the wall. Customers who came in had to walk in front of all four of us. The office was dingy-looking, with linoleum floors, metal desks, and dull lighting. There was a ticker-tape machine and a bookshelf. The room widened a bit in the back, where Ruth kept the account books. She also answered the phones and swept the floors.

Downstairs was supply storage and a bathroom. The building had been constructed before running water, so the plumbing was an afterthought. The bathroom was terrible. In this small, unremarkable office, there was nothing physically distinctive or appealing anywhere, but my spirit was soaring.

I will never forget that first day. The pride. This was our own office, the office of the business we ourselves had started, and our business was to be honest brokers. We weren't padding our commissions or taking our customers' money in ways I didn't think was right. We were not going to cut corners. We could establish the type of operation and the destiny we believed in.

Of course, I knew it would be work, work, work, but this work would be an adventure. There was no class you could take to explain how to succeed as a broker in the new age of negotiated commissions. No one to tell us what to do. We had to get out there with our brains and our strength and make it succeed. We were the first beaver trappers in an unknown river valley. In my heart I believed, *This is me. This is what I was meant to be*. We didn't say it out loud, but I believed that Bob and I both felt it. *This is heaven*.

From the way the brokerage business was conducted back then, we might really have been on the frontier. When a client called to make a trade, we wrote the order out by hand on a preprinted paper ticket, circling the word *buy* or *sell* and filling in the number of shares requested. You gave a copy of that ticket to Ruth, who called in the request to make the trade, then waited for the exchange to call back with the final price. That price had to be noted by hand on the paper ticket, and then the information had to be copied into a big, dark, hardcover general-ledger book. Another copy had to get put in an envelope and mailed to the customer, who wrote out a check (if it was a buy order) and mailed it to our office. The tickets had carbon paper under them, so that writing on the top sheet made a couple of copies underneath. You had to press hard with your pen.

Our customer account records were kept in a bin of paper cards, one card per customer, and we wrote on the cards which stocks they had bought and sold, and whether we had received or paid out any money. Pen, paper, bad lighting—the year could have been 1840. Even having lived it, I can't quite believe that was how investing was done. On our first day, among the five of us, the firm made only a handful of trades. We were ecstatic.

It was also like the frontier in another way: Not every town had a sheriff, and when the law arrived, you couldn't be sure what to expect. Cliff entertained us with a story from before we became partners, when the government first introduced a new customer protection rule. Known as the net capital rule, it was a liquidity requirement, meaning that each week a brokerage firm had to calculate the amount they were holding in customer funds and keep a fixed percentage of that on hand to compensate their customers if the firm went out of business.

To explain the new rule, the Securities and Exchange Commission, the national regulatory body, sent a representative. So did the Midwest Stock Exchange, the regional regulatory body, on the same day. The two representatives sat down at a conference table with Carol Jeppeson, who had worked for Cliff before Bob and I arrived.

But the two regulators couldn't agree on how the new rule was to be followed. Instead of making the procedure clear, they began to argue. Finally, Carol said, "Okay, why don't you two go somewhere and fight this out? When you decide what you want us to do, you let me know."

After they left, Carol had to decide on her own what she thought the rule required. The firm never heard anything more about it, which seemed to be fine with Cliff. He liked to do things the easy way. But all this had happened before Bob and I arrived, and we didn't yet know that Cliff had a tendency to cut corners when it came to regulations.

Once we opened our doors, some of our established customers grasped the advantage of what we were offering and started placing orders. In March 1975, completing ten or fifteen trades a day, the firm made seven hundred dollars. It was a relief to see that we could at least make enough to break even, buying us time to develop the business. To earn any real money, though, given our low commissions, we knew we would have to build up our client base and the number of trades. Like plain-label canned goods, like McDonald's keeping burgers cooked and ready around the clock, we were cutting our profit margin and hoping to make up the difference by serving a whole lot of customers. We had to let investors who had never heard of us know that they had a new choice on price, and to do that, we had to advertise.

We placed our first ad in the *Omaha World-Herald*, offering third-market trades for a twenty-five-dollar flat fee, with a phone number to call. We spent hundreds on that ad, an enormous expense, but we trusted that the ad would bring in new customers whose commissions would pay for more ads, which would bring in more customers in a cycle of increasing growth.

We placed that newspaper ad and then we waited for the phone to ring. We didn't get a single response. For the first time, my sunny excitement felt some rain. What were we going to do now?

Bob and I got on the phones, night and day. We called all our former customers and all our business connections to explain the benefit of choosing a negotiated commission. Many did not fully understand how the third market worked, but on the strength of personal relationships with Bob or me, some gave us their business. I drew clients from a group of employees of Kresge's, the big-box retailer, for whom I had set up retirement accounts. Most of our business, though, in those early days, came thanks to Bob.

As we began to have a little success, we learned that our competitors at the full-service brokerages were bad-mouthing us, saying that our trades were done "under the table," that there was something dark or sleazy about them. In fact, our trades were the same as anyone else's except lower in price, but from the way they talked about us, you would have thought we had leprosy.

Our competitors similarly refused to use the official term for what we provided, which was *negotiated commissions*. That would have sounded too respectful of the customer, for whom we had negotiated a better deal. They called us "discount brokers," as if we were the bargain basement, cut-rate, something less-than. The press picked up the term and the label stuck. We couldn't overcome it, so we had to adopt the term ourselves and try to prove we could offer something good behind that label.

Meanwhile, it became clear that our new partners, Cliff and Ernie, were not hard workers. When they arrived in the morning, it seemed to me, they just sat and waited for the phone to ring. Cliff seemed to feel it was demeaning to pursue individual customers when he had been used to meeting with city council members and corporate executives. Ernie was too mild-mannered for aggressive sales. Bob and

I provided most of the production and most of the revenue, but we didn't mind at first because we were so busy and so relieved that the business was breaking even, and because Cliff arranged the back-office operations.

On Saturday mornings, we had a weekly meeting to discuss the firm's progress. Cliff's attitude was that he had the greatest knowledge and experience with securities, so we should defer to his judgment. Bob disagreed with Cliff's patrician attitude and many of his specific decisions, and when Bob differed with you, he would fight you all day long. He quickly lost patience with normal conversation. Even when he wasn't yelling or cursing, he was adamant and angry. Bob seemed to think he could yell until he got his way, and that was all there was to it.

To me, trying to influence your partners by being emotional and losing your temper seemed counterproductive, a waste of time and effort. But I was still too busy learning from Bob to get too upset about his temper. In those arguments, he questioned Cliff about our operating statement, our balance sheet, our strategy and tactics. Listening to him, I got a tutorial on evaluating a company from the inside. If Bob needed to yell to make his point, I figured, that was the way he communicated. Whether I liked it or not, it was better for the company.

I came to understand that Bob's combative style had two sources. First, he had been raised in an immigrant family's grocery business. Grocery customers can almost always find another store to shop at, which means a constant struggle to keep them coming back. Added to that was the extra pressure of selling products that quickly spoil and lose their value. A bottle in a liquor store that doesn't sell this week can be sold next week. A piece of meat or a head of lettuce that doesn't sell this week is garbage. And because the store had been the sole means by which the Perelmans fed and provided for their family, they had no choice but to succeed. Raised in that environment, Bob became extremely competitive, focused at all times on winning—winning customers, winning market share, winning whatever fight there was to be fought.

Beyond that, his family weren't just any immigrants, they were Jewish immigrants. The family had left Russia because they were treated as second-class citizens. In the United States, they had a chance to overcome bias, but equal treatment didn't come automatically. As a young Jewish boy in the Midwest, Bob was taunted with Jewish slurs in school, and each time, he had to be ready to use his fists to preserve his dignity. Even when he volunteered for the army, fighting the Nazis, some of his fellow soldiers voiced the opinion that when it came to Jews, maybe Hitler was right. Bob felt a constant need to come out swinging, and it influenced his character. "I'm a sorehead sort of a guy," he would say. "I have principles, and either you keep them or you don't." If he felt you disrespected him, or if he saw a chance to compete and win, he was going to fight. His dignity depended on it.

Six months after we launched the business, we were still afloat, but we faced a serious challenge. We didn't offer trades on the New York Stock Exchange because we weren't members. We were members of our regional exchange, the Midwest Stock Exchange, the most prominent one after New York. Our full-service competitors were making it sound as if NYSE trades were the best, and what we discount brokers offered was an inferior substitute. That angered all of us, probably Bob the most. Then we learned that we could in fact trade on the NYSE as nonmembers, if we paid a higher price, somewhere in the range of eight to twelve dollars more per trade. But if we gave up twelve dollars on a twenty-five-dollar trade, that was effectively cutting our already-low commission in half.

Bob proposed that we do it anyway. Twenty-five dollars for all trades. That scared the crap out of Cliff and Ernie. They felt uncomfortable enough already with negotiated commissions. Ernie deferred to Cliff, as usual. Cliff hemmed and hawed. But Bob was adamant.

"We have to do it!" he yelled. "It's the only way. We would be idiots to do anything else."

I wasn't sure. Could we make a profit at that price? Bob didn't seem concerned. For him, I realized, it was no longer a matter of projecting potential income and expenses. It was dignity. The other guy put apples on sale? He would sell his apples cheaper. They cut the price again? He'd cut his even more! If Bob weren't actually broke, he'd keep competing on price. Making money was secondary.

For me, risk like this went beyond welcome excitement. If we lowered commissions too far and it didn't work, we would be in a very awkward position when we told our customers we were raising them again. That could be the end of us.

In frontier days, I knew, plenty of beaver trappers had died unremembered. I wanted to be sure we had a chance of surviving and seeing a profit, but there was simply no way to run some numbers and make an educated analysis. This was hiking into the unexplored forest. This was ignorance, unpreparedness, raw courage, and wild-assed guesses.

One advantage we had, because we were in Omaha, was at nearby Offutt Air Force Base, headquarters of the Strategic Air Command, where AT&T had installed an elaborate and extensive national and international communications network. They had built it for state-of-the-art wartime communication by telephone, but with no hot war in the seventies, most of the capacity of this infrastructure went unused. AT&T began to promote Omaha as a center for toll-free numbers. Catalogue companies and travel businesses, including airlines and hotel chains, responded to the opportunity and opened call centers in and around Omaha. That meant that the price of long-distance calls would not prevent customers from other parts of the country from switching to our brokerage. We could advertise across a wider region, find those customers who appreciated what we had to offer, and give them the opportunity to call us toll-free. It seemed possible that if we could advertise more widely, we might find enough customers to make ultra-low commissions pay.

Bob said we had to go to twenty-five-dollar commissions on all trades. He kept on saying it. Slowly he convinced Cliff. Cliff saw that he couldn't make money the way his father had, and he had no appetite for making cold calls all day just to break even, so why not give this a try? If we continued as before, we were going out of business anyway.

I didn't know what to think, but it helped that I trusted Bob. I believed he would never do anything to hurt me or the business. I said, "Okay, I'm in." Bob had pushed us all forward by sheer competitive force of will, and though it scared me, that was something I admired. I tucked away the lesson: Sometimes you have to be adamant.

Once we had made the decision, I didn't think about what could go wrong. I focused on working harder to get the results that I wanted. We wrote a little advertisement that said "$25.00 for a New York Stock Exchange trade," with a toll-free number to call, and gave the ad to the Midwest edition of the *Wall Street Journal*. Then I went back to cold-calling established customers and waited for the ad to run.

The day it appeared, the phone started ringing off the hook. Suddenly, the orders were coming in as fast as our little band could keep up—in fact, faster. We had found the sophisticated customers we were looking for, the ones who didn't want advice, just a better deal.

CHAPTER 4

I felt great. Our ads were bringing in new clients. The company was growing, and our concept was proving itself. We started getting some good local press that helped us tell the sophisticated, independent, knowledgeable investors that we offered a money-saving alternative to the full-service brokers. And our volume kept growing—twenty trades, fifty trades, eighty trades a day. Each night at dinner I would tell my family how many tickets we had written that day. We hired new brokers and new back-office staff. With each new high, we would all celebrate at the Rookery, a bar down the street from the Douglas Building on Nineteenth and Farnham. I am sure that not one of us laughing at the bar imagined that in just a few months, attorneys from the Securities and Exchange Commission would shut us down and threaten to put us out of business permanently.

People talk so much about the stresses of setbacks and failure, and how those stresses test you. But growth, no matter how much you may have wished for it, is its own kind of stress test. Even as the advertising helped us add telephone customers who used the toll-free number, we still relied on local customers who walked in our front door, got a cup of coffee, and sat around talking to us while we were taking orders. Our entire business model was based on the idea that customers did not come to us for research or advice, only to give them stock quotes and execute their trades, but some people still liked to have a personal relationship, so they would come in and visit. It could be distracting, irritating—I wanted to answer the phone and do work, but we needed their business. We had to continue both approaches at once, answering long-distance calls while making in-person customers feel welcome, which was a strain.

With one office flourishing, we began to test a strategy of expansion by opening branch offices. Some former Dean Witter colleagues started an office for us in Chicago. Cliff knew someone in Lincoln who wanted to test out an office for us there. But the greater the volume of trades we did, the more we discovered the limits and flaws of our methods, which were still the old manual, paper-and-pen systems of a fading era. With just a few of us in that narrow office, handling even ten or fifteen trades a day, plus keeping the books correctly by hand and answering the phones, was a hell of a lot of work. As we hurried to keep up with incoming orders, we made errors recording trades. On top of those, the company that did our clearing made an increasing number of errors in the records they kept for us. We had to issue corrections and cancellations on trades. Customers' monthly statements would be off. Even when it was simply that customers' names were misspelled, or the name was where the address should be, these little errors undermined trust and played into the idea, still dangerous to our reputation, that discount brokers offered an inferior service.

We began taking work away from the clearing broker and doing it ourselves, but that only added to our responsibilities. We needed more hands. One of the most important hires early on was Carol Jeppeson, who had worked for Cliff in the back office at Rahel, Knack, and Company a couple of years before. She started off doing trade confirmations as well as answering the phone and greeting customers when they came in. Many must have taken her for an ordinary receptionist, a pleasant, personable Minnesota farm gal, blond and quick to laugh, who made them feel at home. But Cliff had recognized early on that she had both the mind and personality for brokerage work.

Back before I ever met Cliff, he had pushed Carol to get her brokerage license. He started her on underwriting stocks. Then a couple of things went wrong. To begin, the first stock she sold was in a magazine publisher called Pyramid Communications. She handled the underwriting well, but it turned out that the Mafia was scamming Pyramid. In those days, when an issue of a magazine first hit the newsstands, the newsstand owners were allowed to return the unsold copies of the previous issue for credit. To save on shipping costs, instead of returning the entire magazine, they would send back only the cover of each issue. But the Mafia began printing their own fake magazine covers, submitting requests for more refunds than the company had printed issues. Pyramid soon went out of business, and Carol lost her enthusiasm for underwriting.

At the same time, Carol's marriage was on the rocks. Her husband blamed her job for keeping her away from him, so she quit to try to save her marriage. When that didn't work, she came back to Cliff for a job, and he started her on recordkeeping and receptionist work for us at First Omaha.

Soon she was doing the figuring for commissions on trades, as well as on extensions—different classes of stock shares—and margins, which are stocks bought on credit. Federal rules allowed investors to borrow money from their broker and use that money to buy stocks in what was called a margin account. Such accounts benefited the broker, because we charged interest on the loan and that interest was a significant revenue stream for us. They were also an advantage for customers, because the loan gave them the means to take a larger position in a stock that was going up, so their wins were bigger. In those early days, Carol was the only one at the company who could figure the margins and other calculations that the regulations required. She quickly became essential to the back office.

I also approached David Kellogg, who was our auditor at our accounting firm, Haskins & Sells. Dave was a quiet man, very smart and very funny. Everyone said that his father, for whom he had worked for many years, looked like Santa Claus, and though Dave's hair wasn't yet white, he had the same fair, red-cheeked look. I explained to him that we were having growing pains and needed a higher degree of professionalism in taking care of our books and records. Over lunch, I described the changes from the last time he had come to audit the firm, and he was surprised to hear how fast things were moving—he said he hadn't even heard that we had opened a Chicago office.

Dave had an entrepreneurial streak. An accounting major at the University of Nebraska, Omaha, he had dropped out to help his father with his furniture and architectural/woodworking company, bringing an aptitude for numbers and systems. Over time, while completing his accounting degree part-time, he became his dad's all-purpose problem-solver, pricing and negotiating the company's insurance, handling leases for facilities, developing accounting systems, and even breaking the bad news when an employee needed to be fired.

With Dave on board, we set out to solve the problem of our strained and error-prone recordkeeping, which was far inferior to what Dean Witter had provided when Bob and I worked for them.

We settled on a new company out of Pennsylvania called Computer Research. This was cutting-edge technology at the time—they had put "computer" in their name to show that having computers set them apart from the competition.

Here's how it worked: This service bureau gave us something like a teletype or typewriter, but instead of printing words in ink on a piece of paper, it poked holes in a narrow piece of paper tape. After a customer had placed an order and we had written up a ticket with their account number and the details about the trade, including confirmation by phone that the trade had gone through as ordered and at what final price, we'd give the ticket with all that information to the teletype person. She would then type in all the activities related to the trade—monies received, monies disbursed, all the details. The machine sounded pretty much like a typewriter. Now, all that information was represented by perforations in that tape. At the end of the day, we had to put that tape onto another machine that was a primitive kind of modem: it read the data from the pattern of those holes and sent it over the telephone line. The main office of Computer Research in Pennsylvania then created our daily sales blotter, our general ledger, and all the records we were required to keep. Then that office would transmit those records to their remote office in Chicago, where they were printed with a dot-matrix printer onto wide, green-and-white computer paper. They also printed trade confirmations that had to be sent out to the customers, which our back-office staff would stuff into envelopes and put in the mail.

We were supposed to receive a complete and accurate set of each day's records by ten the following morning, but there were opportunities for errors at every step. Our clerks, rushing to keep up with the increasing pace of our orders, made some mistakes in data entry. Static on the phone line caused additional errors. The reports were often late, and when we got them, the back-office staff was often too busy with the current day's concerns to go back and reconcile older records against the original handwritten tickets. When we did find mistakes, the corrections had to be entered through the same system, then checked again in the next day's delivery of records—if our back-office staff had the time. All of us spent at least an hour a day checking for errors, and still many got past us.

Carol knew that the volume of business was getting ahead of the firm's ability to accurately process orders. As the daily volume of trades rose as high as 150, she suspected the company was failing to properly oversee customers buying on margin. In the back office, they were too busy even to keep track of how far they were falling behind. "We were all just running around like chickens with their heads cut off," she would say later, and as the child and grandchild of farmers, she had seen birds do that. Normally congenial and funny, Carol's mood darkened. She developed migraines. One day she had to be carried out on a stretcher. Dave Kellogg, for his part, was almost always calm, but when frustrated to the point of anger his face turned beet-red.

One thing that especially frustrated him was the lack of back-office staff. Dave warned Cliff, our president, that we didn't have enough staff to keep up with the volume of business. In Dave's estimation, we needed a one-to-one ratio of back-office staff to brokers. Apparently, Cliff promised to discuss this request with us other principals, but nothing was ever said. That may seem like an obvious mistake, but we were all discovering what would be the biggest challenge to our success as a low-price brokerage: our advertisements, promising lowered commissions, reliably won us more customers, but because we charged lower commissions, it took a long time for us to see much income from them. Meanwhile, net capital regulations required us to set aside more money each time we held more in customer funds. To meet those requirements, fund our advertisements, and manage our cash flow, we felt constant pressure to keep all other costs down. Our entire operation was an experiment in keeping costs low so we could reinvest our earnings back into the company. I personally was still cleaning the bathroom on Saturdays so we didn't have to hire a janitor.

It would have been challenging enough to meet the net capital requirements if we had known exactly how much we were holding in customer funds each day, but our recordkeeping kept falling behind our growth. Carol began to fear we were flying blind. Adding to the challenge were regulations that kept changing along with the industry. Before Dave had come to work for us, when he was completing our last audit in his position at Haskins & Sells, he had discovered that we had fallen behind the net capital rules. He brought this concern to Cliff, who pointed out that the SEC had recently loosened the capital requirements. Under the new standard, Cliff reassured him, First Omaha was okay. Dave checked with the experts at his firm, and they agreed. Unfortunately, no one noticed that the new regulations came into effect one day after the close of First Omaha's fiscal year. The audit should have shown us in violation. That was an error waiting to be caught by the regulators.

We were also in bad shape in our handling of stock options. Cliff's old firm had not dealt in options, and though Bob and I had training in trading them, Cliff had no experience in clearing them. He had the back office keep the options records in the same way they handled stock trades, which was improper, but again, no one knew it.

Under increasing time pressure, Dave Kellogg missed the required deadline for filing a quarterly report with the NASD and the SEC. When he did submit the report, it was in poor shape. In May, the NASD sent an auditor to review the books and determine how far out of compliance we were, both in the accuracy of our recordkeeping and in our adherence to the rules. The examiner was a nice-enough guy who conducted his research for a couple of days and reported back to his supervisors. Soon, we learned they had fined us a thousand dollars for mishandling stock options. It felt like a huge amount of money, more like twenty thousand dollars today. It was enough to make us cut back on advertising, and we all knew that if we fell behind in signing up customers, our competitors might overtake us.

At the Saturday morning meeting of the principals, tempers flared. Dave had attracted the attention of the NASD by filing a report late, but Bob and I viewed the fault as lying with Cliff, because he was the president, the financial principal, and the one with experience in clearing. Why hadn't he taken more interest in the regulations? Why had he signed Dave's report if we were not reporting stock options correctly? Why wasn't he, as president, acting more responsibly? Voices rose. Bob threw a chair, denting the plaster wall.

To my mind, Bob was right to be angry, and his temper, which came and went quickly, could even be funny. Marlene, though, saw him differently. She spent her days mainly with children, and she said that when she heard about the way Bob cussed and yelled, practically jumping up and down, he seemed less like a man expressing his views than a child throwing a tantrum. It made me uncomfortable to hear Marlene speaking that way about my mentor.

When we all calmed down, we agreed to pay the fine and get back to getting along so we could develop the business. But as it turned out, even after the fine, Cliff did not require the staff in the back office to update their procedures for stock options. A few months later, we would get charged again with the same infractions.

On September 9, 1976, three attorneys from the Securities and Exchange Commission entered the office. Stiff and straitlaced, they flashed their identification and told us to lock the door. One showed us a temporary restraining order issued by the US District Court, prohibiting First Omaha Securities from acting as a broker or dealer until a complaint filed by the SEC had been resolved. The order cited provisions of the Securities Exchange Act of 1934, including the net capital reserve requirement.

The phone was still ringing with calls from customers wanting to place trades. No one was answering it. Carol sat in a chair, staring straight ahead, stunned. Later, Dave would say the attorneys' arrival reminded him of the time he was pitching a softball game and a line drive smacked him in the forehead. Everything seemed to turn red.

The attorneys told us to tell any customers who called that we were closed for the day. We also had to close our satellite offices in Lincoln and Chicago. Then we four partners met with the attorneys in the back room. They were not East Coast, but they were big city, Denver, and they seemed very different from us. They wouldn't make polite conversation, wouldn't respond to a friendly remark. To me they seemed sterile, stiff. We brokers wore black or blue suits with white shirts and ties. They wore sport coats and colored shirts—yellow or blue. I had the feeling they wanted to let us know with their dress that they were set apart from us, that they had a power we didn't have, and that we were required to wait and find out how they would use it. As it turned out, the head attorney, Joe Cris, a very fine man, had been in military intelligence in World War II, and he had that kind of quiet, intimidating severity.

In the back room, away from the rest of the staff, we principals argued with the attorneys. There was more yelling and cursing. Bob was furious about the interference with his clients. He took it all very personally. Cliff and Ernie seemed overwhelmed, out of their depth. The attorneys told us we should expect to be closed for at least a week, until we got everything to their satisfaction, and then they would allow us to reopen. However, this was only an information-gathering mission. Once they learned what they needed to know, they would start preparing their case against us.

The only transaction we were permitted to conduct that week was to sell stock for customers who wanted to sell. Without cash flowing in to pay our employees, we had to lay everyone off except Carol, because she knew the accounts better than anyone and the attorneys required her to stay. We were so short of hands that Bob and I asked our wives, Betty and Marlene, to come in and assist Carol. We also had help from my little sister, Mary Sue, who was recently out of college.

We were required to reconstruct our records all the way back to the beginning. For days, Carol, Marlene, Betty, and Mary Sue went through the files. They retrieved the stock certificates the company held for customers in a safety-deposit box at a local bank, and Betty compared the paper certificates with our records of trades. Carol worked with the Midwest Clearing Corporation to verify what securities we were holding for First Omaha's customers. Marlene handled the new accounts. Then the women reported to us on what they found. In the end, Dave estimated that there was something on the order of forty thousand dollars in trades that we never accounted for correctly. Bob, though, disagreed. He would always maintain that there were no trades misrecorded and no missing securities certificates.

Because Dave was an accountant who had audited businesses, he knew the little tricks and irritations people used to nudge auditors to finish up and leave: desks with poor lighting, tables that rocked back and forth, chairs with one short leg. But there were limits, and one of those was the expectation that the employees of the business having an audit, or, in this case, an SEC exam, would treat the examiners with respect. Bob mainly ignored the attorneys. When they talked to him, though, he was nasty. On the last day of their work, Joe Cris walked up to Bob and stuck his hand over Bob's desk to shake and say goodbye. Bob slammed his book closed and called Cris a son of a bitch.

As the attorneys filed out, I ran to the door to catch them.

"Please forgive Bob," I said. "He's short on temper, but he's a good person. He's honest."

Cris said, "It's okay," but you couldn't tell with these people what they were thinking, or what they intended for you.

After the SEC attorneys left, we were free to reopen, but every day we were aware that the crisis wasn't over. The attorneys had done their fact-finding, but there was still the court hearing to come, and they had made it clear that our multiple violations of the net capital rule were potential cause for a shutdown. The feeling they left behind was that we were too stupid to handle other people's money correctly and that they wanted us closed for good. I think that was what provoked Bob to be so distant and rude.

Of course, we were not stupid, but I felt they treated us that way and I suspected it was because we made them uncomfortable. As discount brokers, we were something new and unpredictable, a challenge to the establishment, and I was afraid that made us dangerous and unattractive. We had limited staff, which meant we couldn't afford to have employees dedicated to regulatory compliance. My sense was that in the industry overall, there was a tendency to believe that we were doing something wrong.

There was also the problem of simple bias. The NASD, which had called in the SEC to take legal action, was governed by a board made up of representatives from the full-service brokerages. The full-service guys didn't like our business model, which was taking customers away from them, and it seemed they were pushing the regulators to look especially hard at the new players. At the same time, there was evidence that some full-service brokers were colluding to keep business away from discount brokers. The Department of Justice convened a federal grand jury in 1976 to look into whether New York

Stock Exchange firms had conspired to divert business from Kingsley, Boye & Southwood after that market-making firm slashed prices in half for individual investors. But after eighteen months on the case, the grand jury disbanded without returning any criminal charges.

I suspect as well that the New York Stock Exchange, where we were not members, was fighting to preserve its status as the rule maker and primary stock exchange. Within the business, we had an idea that they were putting pressure on the regulators to make sure everyone, especially the discount brokers, played by the full-service brokerage rules.

Of course, the attorneys never presented it that way. In their communications with us, their only stated concern was technical compliance with regulations designed to protect the consumer. It was as if they spoke another language. They had found irregularities in our books and records resulting from a period of rapid growth. We were failing to reconcile customer security positions with the records of the outside third-party firm we had contracted, and it was their obligation to protect consumers by guaranteeing that we would bring our recordkeeping into conformity with the applicable rules, including the net capital rule. And so on. Nevertheless, it felt as though they were out to make an example of us.

Lou Lipp, our lawyer, agreed. He was a short, slender man of about seventy who dressed in fine suits and drove a Jaguar. His firm, White, Lipp, Simon & Powers, was highly respected in Omaha. They had represented both Cliff's company and Bob's in the past, so we were all inclined to take Lipp's counsel seriously. In his office, he sat in a great big chair behind a great big desk. He told us that because we were accused of so many different errors and violations, ours would be a very difficult case to win. In addition, the lead SEC attorney, Joe Cris, was considered to be as inflexible as he was smart; Lipp didn't think Cris would negotiate a settlement.

Lipp gazed at the four of us from across that great big desk with a grim look on his face. "You must know that if you want to fight, the United States government has unlimited funds to prosecute you," he said. "This fight would be a challenge for a wealthy company, and your company isn't wealthy. So, what do you think? Do you believe you have a viable business here? Are you willing to put up your own personal money to defend it?"

He looked first at Cliff, because he was president.

"I don't think it's a viable business," Cliff answered. "You can't charge twenty-five dollars per trade and make a profit. We're never going to make enough money to support all our costs."

I wanted to argue with him. I wanted to tell him that he'd always been used to spending a lot of money, that he just had to learn to keep costs down. But I could see that the whole venture had become unattractive to him. He didn't like working night and day. He resented the pressure to keep costs low. He hated being investigated and blamed. By this point, he was finished with it.

Ernie spoke next, and of course, Ernie was with Cliff. Then came Bob.

"Well, you know," he said, "I have to agree with Cliff and Ernie."

It all happened so fast. I was used to thinking of Bob and me as standing together, united in our understanding and our commitments, but now I looked at Bob and Cliff and I saw two of a kind, a couple of men of means, graying, established and comfortable in their financial success. Why should they risk the nice net worth they'd worked all their lives to earn?

I thought: *Oh my God*. I was going to lose my investment. I was going to lose all the money I had in the world—and I couldn't afford to lose it, because most of it was borrowed. Bob and others had lent it to me, and they had trusted that they would get it back even if it took the rest of my life to pay them off. Now that might just be my fate.

"All right, then," said the attorney, serious as an undertaker. He was playing with a pencil between his fingers. "We'll make the arrangements to shut the business down."

"Hey," I said. "Wait a minute! I own one-fourth of this business. You cannot do that. I'm sure you can't do that without my permission. I'm not giving you permission."

Lipp got a disgusted look on his face. In his view, our odds were worse than David's versus Goliath. There I was, the youngest, most inexperienced of the principals, the corporate secretary, going against the older men in the room. He threw his pencil down on his big wooden desk and walked out of the room.

Lipp returned with someone I recognized, a classmate from Creighton University. I had not known Tim McReynolds well when we were students, but he was hard to miss—tall and lanky, with big bushy eyebrows and a long, curving nose, like Ichabod Crane from "The Legend of Sleepy Hollow." Tim was a brand-new associate at the firm—Lipp was offering me the firm's most inexperienced attorney. Maybe he thought someone my own age would be better able to talk sense into me. Maybe he thought that this way I could lose this hopeless case as quickly as possible and learn my lesson—if, that is, Tim consented to take it to court.

After a brief introduction, the two attorneys left, leaving me with Bob, Cliff, and Ernie. They had no interest in talking to Tim, but I went looking for his office. He proudly showed me his leather desk chair, delivered just that day. I told him that my brokerage had a 15c-3-3 violation, and that I believed the SEC was doing the bidding of the big, traditional brokerage firms and trying to shut us down. I told him that Lou had just recommended we liquidate my company.

"Oh," Tim said, "I wouldn't do that."

It was a foolish thing to say. He was thirty years old and he'd been at the law firm all of two weeks, but he was saying what I wanted to hear. Once we got started talking business, it went on and on. I took him out to dinner. Over a couple of bottles of wine, he told me he had followed an unusual career path, working for labor unions, practicing with an accounting firm, advising businesses on strategy, and doing programming in, he said, twelve or thirteen computer languages. It was clear he was highly intelligent and that he liked having a puzzle to solve. He had also met the SEC attorneys who had come to shut us down. Tim agreed with Lou Lipp that we probably wouldn't win in court, and that Joe Cris was unlikely to negotiate with us. But Tim also said that the youngest of the three, Harold Golz, was fairly idealistic, a true believer in the mission of the SEC to protect ordinary investors. Tim thought we might be able to appeal to him by arguing that it was in the public's interest to have a lower-cost option for trades, especially with a broker who did not have the usual conflicts of interest that come from recommending stocks and then profiting off those recommendations. Tim said we should try to show Golz that shutting us down would be hurting rather than protecting the public, who, after all, were the ones meant to benefit from the government action that ended fixed commissions. That, he said, might make the SEC more open to negotiating a settlement.

The next day, Tim would tell me later, he was sitting in his new leather office chair when Lou walked in and said, "I understand you've been giving out advice that's contrary to mine."

"You talked to Joe Ricketts?" Tim asked.

"I did. And we are having a meeting of our board of directors in the conference room, starting right now. I'd like you to make a presentation of your advice."

Tim thought this might be the end of his very short tenure as a law associate. Empty-handed, with no time to prepare, he followed Lipp into the meeting and tried his best to explain his approach. Then he went back to his office.

A few hours later, Lipp returned to say that the board had voted, and Tim would be handling the case. Tim was amazed. I felt that, financially at least, it was a smart choice. Tim, as a first-year associate, billed at a much lower rate than a name partner like Lipp. We would have a better chance of paying our bill if the case was handled by the firm's least-experienced member. Assuming, of course, that we won.

In March 1977, the government announced that it would hold a public hearing on First Omaha's violations of the Securities Exchange Act. The announcement, noted in the *Wall Street Journal*, alleged that the four of us principals had "willfully aided and abetted violations of certain provisions of [the Act]" related to recordkeeping and reserves. This was not the way I had dreamed of making our debut in the *Wall Street Journal*. We told their reporter that the SEC's allegations stemmed from "an incident that occurred last summer" and that the partners were confident that the dispute "will be resolved favorably."

In fact, I was not confident. I was even worried whether we would be able to compensate those who were helping us fight these allegations. I knew that even if we failed in court and First Omaha couldn't pay its legal bills, Tim would receive his regular salary. But in addition to a lawyer, we needed a well-recognized accountant to go over our records and vouch for them to the SEC.

I got in touch with Mike Naughton, a partner at Haskins & Sells. He was also a Creighton graduate. I had to tell him that I had no money to offer up front. If we were successful in our fight with the SEC, I explained, I was confident that First Omaha would make money again and be able to pay its bills. If the company was liquidated, though, I couldn't make any guarantees. Mike took a big risk in agreeing to help, and that meant a lot to me.

Mike came from a large Catholic family that lived on a farm in

South Dakota. I knew that farmland—hardscrabble, marginally productive, and lacking the irrigation and fertilizing methods that would be used later. But Mike was one of those amazing men who came from almost nothing, men who worked hard and sometimes benefited from government programs that helped send them to college, and he became a CPA. He was as honest and hardworking a man as you could ask for. Drank a lot, laughed a lot, took no shortcuts, and always made me feel he had my best interests at heart. When the young man he put in charge of our audit fell behind schedule, Mike was out of town, but he came back on the day it was due and lost his temper and made sure we got that audit to the SEC in time for our court date.

The hearing was scheduled to take place in Denver in early 1977. The three of us, Tim, Mike, and I, held meetings in preparation. The other principals had not agreed with me about fighting the charges, and while they went into the office every day to work, they did not help fight the SEC.

The night before we left for Denver, Mike stood up from the table at about nine and said he had to call his wife in the hospital.

"Why?" I asked. "Is she all right?"

Mike explained that she had just given birth. I was astonished that he was working with us that night instead of being by her side, but he said that it was their eighth child, so she had been through it all many times before.

The next day, Tim and I arrived for the hearing. It was like in the movies—their legal team sat at one table, we sat at another. The SEC's attorney, Harold Golz, seemed friendly. "We're hired guns, Joe," he said. "We're marshals. You broke the law and the government sent us in. Nothing personal. Don't have any anxiety about our personal feelings." It seemed that Tim had successfully raised the issue of whether we had been singled out or misunderstood because we were discount brokers, but there was no way to tell if that would make a difference.

Besides us, the hearing room itself was empty. I asked, "Where is everybody? Where's the jury? Like the movies, where are the reporters? Where are the people watching?"

"This is an administrative law hearing," Tim explained. "A judge will come in, and he'll listen to them and he'll listen to me, and he'll decide."

I asked him to tell me about the judge. He said the judge we had been assigned was a retired SEC examiner. My heart fell through the floor. I felt sure the odds were against us.

Golz and Joe Cris presented the government's case. Tim offered First Omaha's perspective. He didn't argue that the SEC was wrong or that we were blameless. He conceded that we had made some mistakes but said that we understood the importance of keeping the firm in compliance with regulations. He suggested that exactly because our recordkeeping had fallen behind, we couldn't know for sure if we had failed to reserve the required percentage of capital. Possibly we had been in compliance all along and we just couldn't prove it. In any case, Tim concluded, those responsible would accept any required sanctions so that the company could go on, for the benefit of our customers.

The judge left the room to consider the facts. When he came back, he said that First Omaha had to be penalized, but not necessarily shut down. The first penalty was for Cliff. Since he had been the officer in charge, and responsible for the back office, his registration would be taken away.

I said that would be fine, because Cliff and Ernie wanted out of the business anyway.

The judge also said that Bob and I would have to take a suspension and agree to the entry of a permanent injunction against the company. We would have to give up the satellite offices and pause our advertising and opening of new accounts until existing accounts were in order. Bob and I would be suspended for a few weeks. If we would agree to all that, our doors could stay open.

I asked for a break and ran to the anteroom to call Bob from a pay phone. I was excited to explain the judge's proposal, but Bob hated it.

"I didn't do anything wrong," he told me.

I explained that if we didn't agree, we might lose both the business and our licenses.

Bob said, "Joe, I won't accept it. I didn't do anything wrong, and I'm not going to take any punishment. I have my reputation to think of! Screw them." Then he went through a whole litany of bad words. He lost his temper—what Marlene would have called one of his tantrums.

I thought maybe if I waited until he calmed down that I could get through to him, but there was no time. Bob was going to keep fighting, keep cursing, keep defending his dignity, and insisting he could win. His entire life had shaped him to be tough and to not back down, and now he couldn't stop, even when it made no practical sense. Even when it endangered our business.

My God, I thought. *You're a fool.*

I walked heavily back to Tim and gave him the bad news. Bob was not going to change his mind. I had tried. But Tim was wonderful in a fight. His spirit and inventiveness never died. He loved the chance to place another bet, to find another way to solve the puzzle. Tim went back over to Golz and said, "Harold, you need to understand the situation. Bob Perelman simply is not going to take any penalties. He doesn't think he's done anything wrong. But Joe wants to stay in business."

Harold considered that.

Then Tim asked the judge, "Do the penalties have to be split between the two of them? If Joe took them all, would it make any difference?"

And I think at that point the judge was a little lenient with us. He said, "The only thing that we care about is that somebody takes these penalties. Would Joe take them all?"

"Oh, yes," I said.

Without admitting or denying the allegations, I agreed to a suspension. It meant negative press for the company, but even that we would try to turn into a marketing opportunity. The *Wall Street Journal* would quote us as saying: "We would like to fight these very old charges. However, that would take a great deal of time and money and keep us from introducing our new commission plan. We feel our customers would prefer being able to trade five hundred shares for a twenty-five-dollar commission rather than seeing us win a moral victory in a long court battle."

After the hearing, I was very happy with Tim. I felt he had saved the business because he had gotten through to Harold Golz and shown him that we were not the bad guys. And in fact, when we said goodbye, Golz said, "Why don't you fellows open an office in Denver? We could use a good, honest broker in this town."

That was a surprise, but I certainly did appreciate it.

Officially, we were suspended for six months from associating with any broker, dealer, investment advisor, or investment company. But for Bob, that suspension was held in abeyance for all but one week, which meant he was banned from the office for only seven days. He called that week off a vacation. I had to stay out of the office for a month. I told people I was using the time to catch up on my reading, but my thoughts were always with the company. I remember one day I was downtown, and without meaning to, I walked down our street and stared at the First Omaha sign. I felt so full of emotion, but I knew I couldn't go in.

What weighed on me was that Bob had allowed me to take on his suffering. That was not what you do to the people you love. I had believed we shared a commitment to the business we founded, almost like parents to a child. When your child is threatened, you step forward. But the crisis had come, and Bob hadn't stepped forward. He had failed me, and he had failed this venture we were trying to create to be our legacy. He never even said to me afterward, "Congratulations, Joe. You were right. You saved the company."

I had never thought of myself as having the skills to become a leader. I was content to let others do that. But now it seemed the only one left to do what was necessary was me.

CHAPTER 5

I was never sure if that administrative law judge in Denver believed we had a chance of surviving his penalties. Was he letting us down gradually, sending us back to Omaha to discover that he had given us a slow poison?

My goal for the company was always to achieve a 30 percent annualized compound return on equity, meaning that the company would be worth 30 percent more each year than the year before. If we could maintain that rate, then thanks to the magic of compounding, we would double the company's value every two and a half years.

Of course, no one expects a new business to achieve a 30 percent return on investment, minimum, year after year. Had I told anyone that this was my plan, they would have told me it was stupid to think anyone could achieve that. But I was committed to the idea and so I focused on trying to raise our income while keeping costs low. All our effort and all our thrift were in the service of that goal, and in our very first year, 1975, we succeeded, achieving a 30.3 percent return on equity. But the company's financial performance had dropped in the next year to 17 percent and in the next to only 5 percent. I knew that if we couldn't turn it around, at that rate of decline we would not only miss our targets, we would soon be out of business.

One Saturday, not long after I had finished serving my penalties for the SEC, I went to lunch with Bob and Dave. I felt down. First Omaha Securities owed a substantial sum to Haskins & Sells, about forty thousand dollars, which we had agreed to pay off over time. We owed seventy-five thousand in legal bills. We had given the guys in the Chicago office their freedom, and they were going to continue on their own as an independent brokerage. Cliff and Ernie were waiting to sell their shares back to the corporation, but we didn't have the cash to buy them out. I was feeling the weight of all our financial obligations, plus the many restraints the settlement still put on us. I felt especially concerned because the SEC had required us to temporarily stop advertising, which was tantamount to starving the business. We were a hand-to-mouth operation. I couldn't help but worry we might never regain the momentum we had enjoyed with our first regional ads.

In a time of serious transition, your mood shifts up and down; or at least, mine did. As we waited for our sandwiches, I think both Bob and I were uncertain there was a way forward. Dave leveled with us. "From my point of view," he said, "there is nothing wrong with this business. The concept is right. The timing is right. All the problems have been in the implementation. If you take exactly what you have been doing on a small scale and do it on a large scale—advertise, compete on price, keep your costs down—it could be extraordinarily profitable."

We were all in agreement on that. I don't remember if it was Bob or I who challenged Dave to back up his brave words with his own money, but once the topic was raised, he agreed to put up twenty-five thousand to recapitalize the business, assuming Bob and I did the same. This was a significant commitment for Dave, not least because the money we invested would be held to protect our customers. None of us could get it out again unless the NASD said it was all right.

We needed one hundred thousand in total capital, so we were still looking for the last twenty-five thousand. Bob had a couple of prospects, and we had some talks with them, but nothing came of it. I canvassed my family and friends in search of investors. (My brother Dick likes to tell the story that I'd call him up sometimes and ask, "Can you lend me a hundred bucks? I need to feed my four kids.") Marlene's brother, Lee Michael Volkmer, was an attorney, so I thought he might have the means to invest something in First Omaha Securities. I was sure he said to himself, *I'm going to give some money to my stupid brother-in-law, and he'll lose it, but he's family. I owe that to my sister*. So, he invested.

Another of Marlene's brothers, Keith Volkmer, wound up a shareholder indirectly. We had put money together into a corncob grinding business in Shenandoah, Iowa, that was called Agri-Firm, but it had not done well. As part of closing down that failing company and making its investors whole, I gave Keith stock in First Omaha.

I still hadn't put together the full twenty-five thousand, though, and I was running out of people to ask. I had gone to our relatives. I had gone to our friends. I was afraid I had tapped them all. Then I thought to ask my childhood friend Jerry Gress. His dad, who was a bricklayer, had been a co-leader of our Cub Scouts den along with my dad, and then we had wound up at the same high school, St. Bernard's. We used to read travel books—we made a vow that we were going to buy 1956 MG Roadsters when we got out of high school and see Australia.

I knew that Jerry and his wife, Patty, didn't have a lot of money, so it seemed like a long shot. Even so, I told Marlene, "I'm going to invite them for dinner. Let's have a couple bottles of wine." Marlene served a nice meal, and after, as we sat around our dining room table, I explained what a fantastic opportunity the company represented. "But if I don't get this money," I told them, "I'm not going to be able to stay in business."

Jerry volunteered to loan me about four thousand dollars. What I didn't understand at the time was that he did not have it. He and Patty were like a lot of people we knew then, just getting started with no savings to speak of. He got about half the money by cashing in his life insurance. My guess is that Patty encouraged Jerry—she was more of a risk taker than he was. In any case, he didn't tell me he was cashing in his life insurance for me. Had he done so, I wouldn't have accepted his money, which I think he knew.

I was glad to have the loan, and I hoped to pay him back soon, but I was not able to do that. A few years later, I sent him a letter explaining that I still couldn't repay him, so I was going to give him a share in the company for every dollar he gave me, four thousand shares. After that, every three months, I sent him a letter with a quarterly statement. I don't think he ever looked at them. Most of our early investors just stuck their statements in a drawer somewhere until years later, when we got ready to go public. I tried to make the statements readable, and to someone like me they were exciting as hell, but remember, I was weird. I knew that most of our investors found those statements too boring to read.

At last, after calling in all the favors I could, sitting down with friends and family and selling the potential upside of the business while twisting their arms a bit, I gathered the full twenty-five thousand. Under the new arrangement, we three principals, Bob Perelman, Dave Kellogg, and I, each owned 25 percent of the company's stock. The others collectively owned a 25 percent share under the business name of Agri-Firm, Inc.

At the first meeting under the new corporate structure, we had to choose officers. With Cliff gone, we had lost both our president and our financial principal. Dave Kellogg became the company's new controller, taking the required exams and getting the necessary registrations so he could supervise the accounting, the back-office processing, and regulatory compliance. That was an easy call, and crucial to the future of the company. I took the tests as well.

Who should be president? Bob said he wasn't interested. Since the hearing in Denver, my mentor had begun to withdraw. He still raised his voice in meetings—that was his style—but he had less to say. Part of his silence was due to Cliff's absence. Their big Saturday morning fights were over. Another part of his silence, I thought, was an awkwardness between us because I had taken his penalties. I was quiet with him too. But as disappointed as I was in him for leaving me to defend the business alone, I could not express any rancor. If the company was going to develop, I needed his capital and his hard work.

I told Bob and Dave I wanted to be president. Their attitude seemed to be, "Well, we're not really excited about being president ourselves, so we'll let you." Nothing changed very much at first. There was no shiny new sign on my desk saying PRESIDENT. Big decisions were still made by taking a vote, and two still prevailed over one.

Inside, though, I thought a great deal about what was necessary for our success. During the thirty days when I had not been permitted to go to the office, and ever since, I had tried to understand the mistakes we had made. What would we need to set them right? How could we avoid them in the future? Some of those mistakes, I felt, had been mine. At the hearing, Tim had argued that because Cliff was the financial principal of the company, only he should be held responsible for our errors. The rest of us should not be blamed. But the judge had rejected that view, saying that all officers of the company had a duty to make sure the records were accurate, the rules obeyed. I felt the judge was telling me: *Grow up, Joe. You can't give an excuse and get out of it. It's your company and you're responsible for the whole thing.*

That meant expanding my focus. Up to that point, I had seen my function as making the company grow. I had focused on getting better at advertising, marketing, and developing customers, and doing it all in a cost-effective way. Now, for the first time, I admitted that the company could not succeed unless I understood the regulations and how they were evolving along with the industry. I realized we had not one but three areas where I had to take responsibility for making sure the company would survive and succeed: growth, yes, but also regulatory compliance and recordkeeping.

Once the SEC let us start running newspaper ads again, we began to serve more out-of-state customers with our toll-free number. This was very exciting. We were signing up customers who had been to college and studied enough about business that they felt qualified to make their own investment decisions, and because of the toll-free number, we could harvest those customers even if they were dispersed over a wide area of the country. In doing so, however, we came to the attention of state regulators. Their rules said that if you "solicited customers" with stock offerings in their state, then you needed to be registered as a broker in that state. This was separate from our registration with federal organizations like the SEC and the NASD, or with the Midwest Stock Exchange.

When some states first asked me to complete their registration process, I tried to make the argument to the regulators that discount brokers were not like the brokers the rules were written to cover. We didn't tell anybody which stocks to buy, so we were not "soliciting."

In fact, I explained, people wanted to do business with us exactly because we did not solicit or recommend or whatever they wanted to call it. I invited them to come visit our office and see that what we were doing was different.

At first, this caught the regulators off guard. For a while, I got no response except "We will get back to you." I believe it was some months later that they came back with a new argument: Advertising is soliciting, they said, so you have to register with each of us after all. I don't remember which state said so first, but once you had one state doing it, then they all had to do it, like buffalo charging over a cliff. And I couldn't talk them out of it, because, I suspected, once they saw that they could regulate an entire new business, discount brokers, they realized this would broaden their responsibilities and entitle them to ask for budget increases.

Now, when I came home at night, I worked on our state registrations: filling out the forms, signing the papers, mailing them in. Roughly half the states required that I take a test relative to their state law, and each state's laws and tests were different. Some let me do it at a testing center in Lincoln at the university. Two states would not, one of them being Washington. I had to fly halfway across the country, get off the plane, get in a cab, take their test, get in another cab back to the airport, and fly home. I hated the expense, and all the time, effort, and energy spent in having to do so. It did nothing to make the business grow, but I took it on, registering in all fifty states. That turned out to benefit us because some of our competitors did not get registered properly, preventing them from advertising nationally. Later, the states got together and established one standardized test for all of them, but it was too late for me.

I also decided to take the financial principal test, so we could never be shut down for failing to have an officer who was approved to sell all the financial products we sold. I took the stock options principal test, the bonds principal test, all of them. But while I could pass the tests, the truth was that I didn't have the proper background to understand all the rules and regulations, and to implement them in all their complexity. Accounting had never seemed important to me, and I didn't understand a lot of the terms. If you said "credit," then sure, I had an idea what you were talking about. But if you said "debit," I didn't know exactly what that meant. What's a debit? Is that the same as a debt?

Of course, I knew from my work for Dun & Bradstreet how to read a balance sheet, and what a profit and loss statement could tell you, but SEC regulations were something different. Those rule books were composed of long paragraphs full of colons and semicolons—by the time I got to the end of one paragraph, I'd forgotten how it started. I had to admit to myself that even though I could study well enough and pass the tests, I would never have the understanding or, frankly, the patience to fulfill the requirements. It would be critically important that I rely on Dave and others with a deeper understanding, not just for our accounting needs but to bring that regulatory perspective to everything we did. Carol was good at the clearing part—very, very good, and as the industry grew and changed, she just kept learning. But now I realized we needed a broader understanding of what the regulators expected from us.

Over the next few years, this became the first glimmer of our hiring philosophy. To find forthright people, honest, up-front people with accounting backgrounds who could communicate with an accounting dummy like me, explaining our changing regulatory obligations in layman's terms.

The decision to hire people with backgrounds in accounting had a more immediate benefit. Accountants were the people most likely to appreciate our seriousness about keeping costs down, which Cliff and Ernie had not. At First Omaha, we counted our pennies. We reused our paper clips. If a piece of paper had writing on one side, we'd turn it over and write on the other. Once, when my son Todd was six years old, he visited the office and made a photocopy of his hand. I explained to him that he had just wasted five cents that could have gone back into the business.

Although I wore a suit every day, I owned only three or four of them, and I kept wearing them until the pants were shiny from use. We controlled our costs and put the savings toward achieving that yearly growth of 30 percent. Bob Slezak, who began performing our audits for Haskins & Sells after Dave came to us, called my commitment to cost control "messianic," as if watching our pennies carefully enough could bring on the Second Coming. He said it with admiration.

We still faced the second problem that had gotten us into trouble: recordkeeping. Our service bureau, Computer Research, would deliver those big boxes of green-and-white computer printouts pretty much every day, and everyone in the office would spend an hour a day or more looking through those reports for errors. We knew we couldn't continue spending so much of our time cleaning up after a flawed computer system, but we couldn't go back to paper and pen, either. There were other service bureaus and information-system providers, but they charged by the trade, which meant that our costs would keep rising the more trades they recorded for us—not a winning strategy for a business built on the goal of continuously growing our trading volumes. To keep our per-trade costs as low as possible, it seemed wiser to have our own in-house system. Should we rent a computer? Buy? With what software? And what, exactly, was software? This was 1977, and small businesses were just starting to own computers. We hardly knew where to begin.

Bob Perelman and I invited Dave Kellogg into that conversation. Dave had a remarkable mind. He was so quiet, you might have called him an introvert, and for sure, there was nothing social about him.

He never came to the Rookery for a drink. But he was very funny and very likable—I think rather than any distaste for social situations, his difficulty was that he was so smart, and thought about things so intensely, that he had a hard time finding common ground with other people. What he did enjoy was challenging his mind.

At the University of Nebraska, Omaha, Dave had studied computers a little—just one three-hour course in programming in BASIC, the first widely available computer language for users who were not mathematicians or scientists. He found that he liked computers because, as he said, "Computers yield to perseverance. You can do most anything if you've got some basic knowledge and you ask enough questions and you work hard enough." Dave had a lot of basic knowledge—math, statistics—and he liked to learn.

When he got to Haskins & Sells, he volunteered to become the point person for understanding and deploying a new nationwide corporate computer system. The system used regression analysis to detect suspicious transactions in customer accounts, alerting auditors to possible fraud or management problems. Haskins & Sells sent him to a week-long training in New York City, where most of the attendees were local and went home for the night. Introverted Dave, though, had nowhere to go but his hotel room, and no interest in going out. Instead, he volunteered to help the instructor, who was running more advanced computer programs at night. The big, slow computers of that decade could take hours to run a complex calculation, so there was always competition for "computer time." Dave kept raising his hand to do more computer work, and his knowledge grew. He liked to say that he became the Omaha expert on computers with absolutely no prior qualifications.

Following his lead, and with the help of a consultant, we explored buying our first machine, taking trips all the way to California and St. Louis to observe stockbrokers using computers in their offices. Dave found software he liked, called BOSS, for Back Office System

Software, meant to run on the IBM 360, a mainframe computer as big as two refrigerators. The basic model came with only one-quarter of a megabyte of memory. It ran so hot that you needed to keep it in a special room to air-condition it properly, which was a substantial extra cost.

The IBM machines looked as if they would do the job for us, but the problem was price. The 360 had been introduced in 1964 and was becoming obsolete. We couldn't afford the new model, the 370. We were all nervous about making such a significant purchase, though honestly, we weren't as nervous as we should have been. Investing in our own computer was a risk that could have bankrupted us.

In the end, Dave proposed that we buy the BOSS program and a less expensive Honeywell computer. The disks it used for storage were platters about two feet in diameter and weighed about eight pounds each. Dave volunteered to rewrite the software to run on the more affordable machine. Personally, I didn't understand the workings of the Honeywell and had no interest. I couldn't program a computer any more than I could build a buzz saw. But I could see what the technology could do for us, so I was willing to place a big bet on someone like Dave Kellogg, who was as smart as he was fascinated by the challenge.

We hoped to have the system ready by April 1977, but we kept running into problems. Dave and his staff had to invent as they went along, and there were setbacks. In hindsight, I see that we were at a fortunate stage of growth when we addressed the computer problem. Smaller firms couldn't afford one, and bigger ones had more to lose if the system failed. We were small enough that if the software didn't work, we could still get by with paper and pen. It was like knowing you could always go back to your horse and buggy if your new Model T broke down.

By the end of 1977, the system was up and running. Looking back, it seems very unsophisticated—at first, it could only keep records of our cash accounts. We still used a fully disclosed broker to handle our margin accounts, which meant that some customers received two entirely different sets of statements from us each month. They put up with it because they appreciated the low cost and the freedom we secured for them. Nevertheless, this limited system allowed us to automate the daily trade settlements with the exchanges, and it proved much more reliable than our old system. It worked so well, in fact, that we could stop using our service bureau, a real cost savings. Just like the buzz saw at my father's job site, our Honeywell-BOSS hybrid was faster, cheaper per hour, and more reliable than working by hand. Thanks to Dave, we could operate and maintain it ourselves. I think that, all told, we would spend about $700,000 on that system, an amount almost impossible for us to comprehend. It had never crossed my mind that I would ever spend that much money on anything. By contrast, a couple of years later, in 1979, Charles Schwab & Company, which would become our main competitor, was said to have bought a used IBM 360 with readymade software and spent $2 million, equal to the firm's entire net worth.

As we officers settled into our new roles, our new three-way partnership worked remarkably well. Dave Kellogg ran the back office and took responsibility for the accounting. Carol Jeppeson reported to him and handled the clearing, and the two of them got along wonderfully keeping our records. Bob Perelman and I were in charge of new accounts, advertising, and taking orders from customers. Every Saturday morning, the three of us got together at eight in the office. There was still some yelling and screaming because Bob communicated that way, but he wasn't actually losing his temper. It all went more smoothly than when Cliff Rahel had butted heads with Bob. We were making money and we all agreed on the importance of keeping the money in the business, rather than increasing our salaries.

After the morning meeting of the officers, we'd go to our desks and open up new accounts and answer correspondence—catching up on the things we couldn't get to when the markets were open. That was how we spent our Saturdays. It was really quite a pleasant time.

The more print advertisements we ran, the more customers called. We couldn't afford to pay for more staff to answer the phones, so Bob asked Betty, his wife, whose kids were grown, if she would come in and take calls. She was a good worker and smart. She took a motherly approach to the other women in the office and played cribbage with them at lunch. I was grateful she was willing to give us her time without pay. As those new calls led to new client accounts, though, and those new clients began placing orders, we had the usual problem—our revenue grew slowly because our commissions were low, so although we had more work, we didn't yet have much more income. We realized we needed even more help taking orders, but we couldn't afford to hire another broker, so Betty studied evenings and weekends to get her license. Meanwhile, the phone kept ringing. I asked Marlene if she could come help out.

Marlene had always been my champion. She had the 1950s attitude that her job was to be a mother and take care of her husband. Whatever I asked her to do as far as supporting me at home and making it possible for me to work effectively was all right with her. But except for that one terrible week after the SEC shut us down, I had never asked her to step out of her life as mother and teacher and step into mine. She loved the life she had made for herself. She had started teaching at a preschool where the head of the program was so impressed with her teaching that she asked Marlene to rewrite their entire curriculum. I knew that Marlene loved her work and loved being home in time for our youngest, Todd, to return from elementary school. Every day, the first thing he said when he came in the back door was "Mom!" If she wasn't there, he would come home to an empty house.

When I told Marlene that I needed her at the office, she said, "Joe, I don't want to do this."

"I need it," I said.

"But I like teaching," she would say. "If I liked the business world, I would have gone into that in the first place."

"The company is showing a lot of promise," I would explain. "We just have to open up the accounts to get the revenue. I need you."

"I don't want to do this," she said, again. "But I will."

She had grown up in a family where the wife was the leader. But she was devoted to me and she wanted to do whatever would make it possible for me to succeed. If I told her my success depended on her coming to work at the office, then she would resolve to do it. And then, because the business kept growing, she stayed.

Our oldest son, Peter, was given the role of babysitter, with the responsibility of enforcing the rules. Marlene taught Tom, our next oldest, how to start a roast cooking, so the major part of dinner was ready when we came home. Sometimes she'd call him at three from the office and say, "Put the meat in the oven," and give instructions for the side dishes. At the end of the day, Marlene and I would drive home after work. The kids met us at the door.

We ate dinner as a family, then often all four kids came back to the office with us, so Marlene and I could open up new accounts. The kids had to go along with that. They would run in the hallway and play with the Quotron machines that gave us stock market quotes for our customers. There was a big old safe in the basement that the kids played with so much they learned to pick the combination lock. Marlene would joke that it was good they had learned a valuable skill.

In summers, when school was out, the children were more or less on their own. Todd recalls it as a free-for-all, with the kids fighting physically and making up games that they would never have been allowed to play if an adult was home. Apparently, they would climb up on the roof with hoses and race objects down the gutters with the force of the water. They had bottle-rocket fights, one team on the roof and one in the yard, each launching the little fireworks at the other. When they had water-gun wars, to settle arguments about who had been hit, they filled old spray bottles with water and food coloring then chased each other through our home spraying colored water that faintly stained the walls.

All of this unsupervised running around led to a fair amount of breakage. One of my aunts used to make little ceramic holiday decorations that hung around the house, and the kids broke a lot of them throwing balls and other toys. Marlene used to keep all the pieces in a bag and threaten the kids that she was going to make them glue all the figures back together someday.

Pete and Tom, so close in age they were often taken for twins, could play with each other, and being the older kids, they had more freedom to come and go around the neighborhood. They remember those unsupervised times as fun. Todd remembers spending a lot of time in the house alone. Later, he would joke that he raised himself.

Laura would say that she didn't remember a lot of specifics about the company from that time, other than her mom and dad being gone a lot, but that she felt the company as an enormous presence, a presence that required each of us to sacrifice. Marlene's sacrifice was giving up the teaching career and the traditional role of stay-at-home mother that she so loved. Years later, when she told the story of agreeing to work for the company full-time, she would say, "It broke my heart. But do you ever listen to country and western songs? There's always somebody whose heart is breaking." She meant that heartbreak was common, something you just learned to accept.

• • •

Marlene started out doing filing, answering the phones, and opening the new accounts. I thought of the arrangement as a necessary evil, but as time passed, the job became important to her. She got licensed as a broker, too, and I saw her learn the ropes. In those days, with fewer than ten employees, it wasn't as if we thought of any one person as the boss. Marlene wasn't assigned a supervisor or manager, but it was assumed that Bob and I would each manage our own wives. If Betty made a mistake and needed a reprimanding, it wouldn't be me who had to tell her, it would be Bob. The same went for me and Marlene. In the office, even if I upset her, she'd keep her mouth closed. When we got home, though, it was a different story. "You might be president at work," she would tell me, "but I'm the president at home!"

Marlene came to find that she enjoyed the phone calls, the contribution to the business, the feeling of independence. She recognized that our filing was badly organized, so she designed and implemented a new system that helped us make a more complete transition to computerized recordkeeping. I saw her begin to catch the bug for helping to build a business.

She also enjoyed the status. Being a broker at that time meant you were an esteemed member of the working community, and I could see it meant a lot to both Betty and Marlene. They were proud to get their broker's registrations and to speak on the phone with authority.

That's not to say working in the same office with your spouse didn't have its share of tensions. Carol Jeppeson remembers being in the back office one day when Marlene and I had some kind of argument. Marlene stormed into the back to get a little break from me, I suppose, and the staff were all afraid to say a word. Finally, Marlene told Carol, "You know, I'm mad at him. But he said he was going to be a millionaire. I'm going to hold him to it."

• • •

Our volume of trades kept growing, and we expanded by offering jobs to brokers we had known at Dean Witter. Instead of the stress of pressure selling for commissions, we offered a reliable salary. "You'll enjoy yourself more when you don't have to hustle for commissions," I told them. With a few of our former colleagues, including Bob Carley and Elton Semke, this argument worked. We also hired a young man named Duffy, a very nice guy who had worked for a full-service broker where, of course, he had been expected to push stock recommendations at customers. It was a revelation and a relief to him just to take orders and not try to influence which stocks the customer chose. I remember once, when he first joined us, he hung up the phone with a client and started laughing and laughing. He almost fell out of his chair.

We said, "What's wrong with you, Duffy?"

"That guy just lost his ass," he said, "and for once it wasn't my fault!"

Despite all of our new accounts, our bottom line was still not growing. We increased our revenue, but we couldn't increase our profits because our costs kept rising. It concerned me very much that although the advertising was a great success, we had not yet proved that we had a successful business model.

We thought the answer might be to open more branches, as some of our many competitors were doing. A salesman for a full-service broker in St. Louis who saw himself losing business to discount brokerage applied for a job with us. We found him office space in St. Louis, put in the communications system, and started advertising, and very quickly customers started walking in off the streets. He hired a young lady to help him, and then they needed another registered rep to keep up. Our main office provided support—if one of the St. Louis staff went on vacation, we'd have to send somebody down to help them out. In Century City, Los Angeles, we started an office in the same way.

After a couple of years, however, with a lot of energy spent reproducing the success we'd had in Omaha, Bob took a close look at the accounting for the branch offices and made the case that the main office was really carrying the branches. They were not profitable on their own. The solution was either to increase our commissions to pay for the branch offices, as some of our competitors were doing, or close them down. All three principals agreed on closing the branch offices. We all recognized that the only reason a broker-dealer in Omaha could compete with New York or Los Angeles was that we offered a lower commission.

We had no choice but to concentrate on telephone customers, but they were still not bringing a bigger percentage of profits. I went looking for economies of scale, so that when my revenue went up, we would keep a bigger share of it. One day I was having lunch with Tim McReynolds, my attorney, and I explained the problem.

"When we put an office in another location, people like it. Even if they never come to the office, they seem to like knowing it's there, and it's a reason they open up accounts with us. But we don't make enough revenue out of it to offset the cost, so branch locations are basically a wash."

Everyone I had spoken with saw it as a simple choice: Either raise prices to pay for the cost of branch offices or close the branches and keep commissions low. But when I told Tim, he took it as a puzzle to be solved. How could we keep our low prices and still open branches?

"What if you didn't have to open your own office?" he asked me. "What if you could partner with someone who already maintained an office in a community, so you didn't have to pay the expenses?"

"That's what I want!" I said. "That would be perfect."

"Why don't you make an association with a bank?"

"Well," I said, "it's against the rules."

That was putting it mildly. In the 1930s, during the Depression, Congress had separated commercial banking from investment banking. The mixing of the two forms of banking was believed to have started the Depression, and although that wasn't true, the idea was anathema. Only someone like Tim would have persisted in thinking there was a way to make it work.

"Is it really against the rules, though?" he asked. "Let's take a look."

Tim believed that it was a regulatory gray area. What we wanted to do wasn't exactly within the rules, but it wasn't exactly against them, either. To his way of thinking, the real question was whether the SEC would choose to come after us if we did something that was borderline incorrect. I was intrigued enough to engage him to start studying the matter.

To me, Tim's efforts were a highly worthwhile investment. To my partners, however, hiring Tim to research a hunch that went against more than forty years of settled regulations seemed like stealing resources from our core business. Their objections were warning signs that although Dave and Bob and I worked so well together, we did not see the future of the business the same way.

My partners and I also disagreed about where to get more capital, which would have allowed us to grow faster. Bob was financially independent, so he had his own capital and access to credit, and although he wasn't rich, he didn't need his salary to live on. He would have grown the company by investing his personal money, but he wanted us all to go in equally, and I depended on my salary. Bob wanted to bring in outside investors, but Dave and I didn't want to give up stock and control to outsiders. Bob set up some meetings, but Dave and I voted those plans down. Up to now, many of the partners' decisions had been unanimous, but if they weren't, Dave and I had sided against Bob. He put in his two cents, but mostly he sat and listened.

Now, though, there was a new pattern in our meetings. I kept seeing what looked to me like opportunities, but to my partners they seemed like dangerous or at least wasteful distractions. Now that we could clear our own retail trades, for example, I saw the opportunity to pick up additional income by clearing the trades for other retail brokers. Getting into clearing, though, in which our name would appear on the trades we cleared for other brokers, would mean that we would take on a higher level of financial responsibility. In those years, regulations gave buyers five days to pay for the trades they agreed to make. After ordering the trade, buyers would wait to receive a written confirmation of their trade, then they would mail us a check. We would deposit the check and wait for their funds. Meanwhile, we were already sending funds to the seller and moving the stock to the buyer's account. As the clearing broker, we were the ones who would have to guarantee that each side got what they had agreed to—payment or stock—and if the buyer didn't pay or the check didn't clear, we were left responsible. To Dave Kellogg especially, that seemed too risky.

Another initiative I wanted to explore was offering our customers trading not just for stocks but for commodity futures—bets on the changing prices of agricultural commodities such as corn, wheat, pork bellies, and so on. Bob and I had looked into handling futures when we first were starting the business, and he had felt comfortable taking the risk of doing that himself. Bob was not risk-averse like Dave, but he was comfortable only with risks that he could keep under his own control. Like a lot of small-scale entrepreneurs, he would not let anyone but himself take the gamble. I wanted to have the company try trading in commodities futures, but I knew it would not be cost-effective for me, personally, to take the time to learn a whole new market. Commodities trading attracted speculators who put up only 5 or 10 percent of the purchase price of the commodity, then sold it again quickly. I saw that I would have to hire someone to do it for me, just as I relied on Carol Jeppeson to take responsibility for the details of clearing our stock trades. I felt ready for the company to take risks that went far beyond my personal abilities, but my partners refused.

My partners objected not only to the risk but also to what they saw as my loss of focus. They believed that to be successful in a given business, you had to pick a focus and not get distracted. I agreed with that principle, but I disagreed that we had found our true focus. Advertising for low-commission trades was not going to be sufficient to increase trades enough to make profits grow the way I wanted. I still remembered the stories about my grandfather, whose impressive cattle farm, the biggest in his town, had allowed him to throw parties and enjoy life—until it collapsed to nothing. I wanted a company so big and well established that I could pass it on to my grandchildren. From my point of view, we were still launching the business, just getting started. With that goal in mind, I grew increasingly comfortable with experimenting and making mistakes.

This was a change for me. Like most people, I had started off trying to avoid mistakes as much as possible, but the more I considered the first few years of First Omaha Securities, the more I saw that we had made plenty of errors. We had thought we would find our customers by advertising locally, in Omaha, and we were wrong. We had thought it would be most efficient to have our records kept for us by an outside service bureau, but we were wrong. We had thought to hire an outside firm with computing power, but then we realized, hey, we need our own computer, our own software, and our own in-house programmer. We had made mistake after mistake, and from each of these failures we had learned valuable lessons. These experiences were changing my attitude about mistakes. Failure, I realized, was better than school. Failure showed you how the world actually worked.

Mistakes were fine—as long as you identified them quickly. You had to be willing, even eager, to learn where you were wrong. Instead of trying to avoid mistakes and hiding the ones you couldn't avoid, it was more valuable to get a lot wrong, then think and talk about your errors immediately.

The person in the office who understood this best was Carol. I would tell her, "People don't understand. To succeed, you only have to be right fifty-one percent of the time. That means you can be wrong forty-nine percent of the time, as long as you admit it quickly." Carol saw the wisdom in that more entrepreneurial approach, but it made Dave uncomfortable. It scared him to death. As an accountant, he'd been trained to catch all the mistakes, 100 percent. Bob, meanwhile, wanted to sell stocks and bonds and options the way we already did. He seemed happy just to answer the next call, talk to the next customer, write the next ticket. He wasn't looking for another home run. We had a business that was succeeding, and he was content.

That is not a criticism of Bob Perelman. Most people, including most entrepreneurs who found businesses, are content with a small, reliable success. The Gallup organization conducted a study of high school students in 2013, looking for the "builder" quality. They concluded that only half of 1 percent of those high school students had the talent and the drive to build a business greater than $100 million. I didn't know those findings back then, but I had felt for years that I couldn't pay too much attention to business advice from other people. Other people were wrong. You had to listen, but then you had to focus on discovering what your specific business needed and not worry about who agreed or disagreed with you.

Slowly, among the three principals, it became clear there was a conflict of vision. In disagreements about overall strategy, increasingly, the vote would be Bob and Dave for maintaining the status quo, against me, for experimenting and making mistakes. It might sound as if I now chose to side with the risk-takers like Tim McReynolds and against the accountants like Dave Kellogg, who strive to be 100 percent right, but that was not how I felt. Risk and control now seemed to me like two gears. The power came from forcing them to turn together. I could see that if I had both, the results could be extraordinary. But I didn't appreciate how hard it might be on those caught in the turning of the gears.

As president, I would send official quarterly reports to our shareholders. Our return on equity in 1979 was 61.8 percent. The next two years it was 48.4 percent and 55.4 percent, respectively. To my friends and relatives who had invested a few thousand dollars here or there, these numbers seemed huge. My brother-in-law Keith, the biggest of the shareholders that we called collectively Agri-Firm, approached me one day to suggest that it was time for the company to pay shareholders a dividend. That was unacceptable to me, but I couldn't tell him so. He did not understand that the more our business grew, the more money we needed to devote to meeting the net capital requirements and to paying for new advertising to increase our growth. I couldn't show him my true reaction, though, or he might ask for his money back.

Each time Keith brought up paying a dividend, I would explain why we needed to keep the money in the business, but he wasn't satisfied. He was supporting his family, but in those years a little extra money would have made a big difference to him. Finally, he asked me to propose the dividend at a meeting with Bob and Dave. I felt that was a waste of time, but at the same time I felt a responsibility to the shareholders. I would not have had a company without them. I put the question of issuing a dividend on the agenda for an upcoming officers' meeting, assuming it was a dead letter. That way I could tell Keith I had done it.

Around the same time, another issue divided me from my partners. Back before we had founded First Omaha, I had set up some retirement accounts for employees of Kresge Corporation, a growing chain of big-box department stores headquartered in Illinois. I had offered some of these customers the opportunity to generate income on their Kresge stock by selling "covered calls," that is, options for other people to buy their stock if it reached a given price by a certain date. For a while, this approach worked beautifully, generating extra income for the retiree shareholders, but then Kresge became Kmart and the stock took off. Now, purchasers of the covered calls started to exercise their right to buy, and a number of my retiree clients, who had sold covered calls, were surprised to find themselves obligated to sell the shares that had been providing them with good income. Some complained I had promised them that there wouldn't be any risk that they would lose their stock or incur a loss. One client had a letter from me saying that they would face no risk. None of this would have mattered to my partners except that I had written that letter on First Omaha stationery, which was, I learned, a very serious legal no-no. In this case, it meant that the company had an obligation to pay off that customer's losses.

I was naïve enough in those days not to understand the legalities of keeping my businesses strictly separate, and to me it seemed silly to get upset because I had reached for the wrong box of letterhead. In any case, we were not on the hook for a lot of money. Dave and Bob, however, felt that I had put their reputations on the line.

Dave asked, "Are there any more of these?"

I didn't expect any, and I told him so, but it turned out there was another client with another letter. Then Dave was livid. He said, "I feel like I'm in a partnership with a guy I can't trust." He called me a "proven liar," and his face got dark red, the way it did when he was most frustrated and angry. I admitted my mistake, and I assumed the whole thing would blow over.

Only later did I see that to someone with Dave's brilliant mind and his natural aversion to risk, this was nerve-racking. He was smart enough to imagine all the potential risk, everything that could go wrong, and now he kept asking himself: If Joe did not anticipate the problem with these Kresge clients, what other hidden problems might the company have?

At our next meeting, I raised the possibility of paying a dividend. Tim McReynolds came to represent the Agri-Firm shareholders, which I hoped would show Bob and Dave that the shareholders had their own concerns, separate from mine. This was the fall of 1981, and he was at a new law firm. Tim told Dave and Bob that the shareholders wanted representation on the company board, and that Nebraska law was on their side. Apparently, if you had a certain percentage of ownership, you couldn't be frozen out.

Having Tim at the meeting seemed to me like a way to show Keith and the other shareholders that we respected them and took them seriously, but my partners were upset. Dave felt, as he told me later, that I was making a power play, trying to get myself a second vote on the board that I would control, so that when we three disagreed, I could force a stalemate. To them, again, it appeared a worrisome sign about my character: here was a guy who, if he lost a fair vote and didn't get his way, showed up with a lawyer.

The truth is that I did not want to give those shareholders a dividend, but it is also true that by now I felt that since I was president the others should let me lead. There had been some Saturday morning meeting around that time where it was clear Bob and Dave were going to oppose me again on something, and I took a break to use the john, thinking to myself that I should just let them have their way. And then, somehow, when I came back, I thought: *No. I don't want to back down.* Bob hadn't backed down when he had thought we should go to twenty-five-dollar trades. Now I felt that the company needed someone to take the strong leadership that he had given up. Bob had taught me so much, and I always believed he was smarter than me, but at this stage in our partnership he didn't share my vision.

What made them uncomfortable, I think, was the roller-coaster ride of risk, failure, and success. They felt I was too freewheeling—too much of a hustler, too aggressive, too loose with the rules, not buttoned-down enough. Toward the end of that week, they let me know that there would be a directors' meeting on Monday morning. They didn't ask me, they told me.

I called Tim McReynolds for advice. "We only have three directors. I think the two of them intend to vote me out of office. Is this serious?"

He said, "Joe, you're screwed. They can propose an election of officers, and once you're out, you would have to work for them, and they can fire you. But let me think about it. Maybe there's something we can do."

It was Friday night before he got back to me. He said, "I think we may be able to stop them. We have to go to court and get an injunction to enjoin the directors' meeting until after we hold a stockholders' meeting. Then, once Agri-Firm has a vote, we will propose adding a fourth director whom you control. Once we have that fourth director, if they move for a vote to remove you as president, the split will be two against two. With a tie, they have to stay with the existing president." I thought this was a genius idea. Of course, now we would be doing exactly what they had feared I would do.

Tim worked all weekend on the legal justification and the papers. At six on Monday morning, he telephoned me and said, "I'm going home to shower and put on a coat and tie. Meet me at the courthouse."

He presented his argument to the judge, explaining why it would be inequitable to allow a vote on removing the president before the shareholders' meeting, and the judge granted a restraining order. We posted the required one-hundred-dollar bond. Someone had to serve the restraining order on Dave and Bob, but Tim couldn't do it, so he gave the copies to me.

I remember walking into work like it was any other Monday morning. No one else on the staff knew the officers were in a fight. I asked Dave and Bob to join me in the little room where we held our meetings. I felt like a soldier going into battle—or, rather, I didn't feel much of anything. Just that fighting attitude: *I'm going to protect myself and what we've built at this company. If you want the fight, I'll bring it to you.*

I handed a copy of the restraining order to each of them. I suppose I explained that we were going to have a shareholders' meeting before anything else happened. The tension in the room was very high, but no one expressed any feeling. Bob deferred to Dave, and Dave said they were going to speak to their attorneys. Then they walked the document over to White, Lipp, Simon & Powers. Their lawyers apparently said, "Tim's right. You can't vote Ricketts out unless you have the shareholders' meeting first. He's got you." When word got back to Tim, he was quite proud.

Dave and Bob couldn't hold their directors' meeting. Now I wanted my shareholders' meeting. But they had called Ray Simon, one of the named partners, and lucky for them, he knew off the top of his head what they should do. He had them walk out of my meeting, so there was no quorum. That meant there weren't enough officers present to take a binding vote to add a fourth board member.

Once they walked out on me, I called Tim at the courthouse and asked if it was over. Had we lost? He said, "Do not end that meeting. Continue the meeting without adjourning, because the notice requirement for reconvening a continued meeting is less than the notice required to bring a shareholders' meeting. Anytime they send notice of a new directors' meeting, you can continue your meeting first, and in your meeting, you will move to vote on adding a fourth director. They won't want that, so neither meeting will ever take place. As long as the stalemate lasts, you'll still be president."

Now we were all stuck. Meanwhile, the exchanges were open, and the phone kept ringing. There was nothing to do but go back to taking orders for trades. I'm sure by now our other brokers and the back-room staff felt the tension. Can you imagine working together in one room under those conditions? Later, Dave would say that if he and I had continued trying to run the business together, one of us would have been dead, the other one would have been in jail for killing him, and he didn't know which he would be.

It wasn't that long before I received a letter from Dave. He said he felt like he was at a party where he wasn't welcome, so he was going to leave the party and put it behind him. He said he could see I wanted to take over, and that he would sell me his stock for an amount in the six figures. His only requirement was that I offer Bob the same deal.

Dave's planned departure left Bob in an unappealing situation. With three remaining blocks of stock—his, mine, and the group of my friends and family—he would become a minority partner. Around this time, Bob also got some bad medical news. He had heart disease and required bypass surgery. I'd never heard of a bypass before—this was still a new surgical procedure, requiring a special trip to the Mayo Clinic in Minnesota. I could see it scared the hell out of Bob. His father had died of a heart attack in his early fifties while working in his grocery store. Bob was now around sixty, working long days at an office with plenty of stress, and he thought this diagnosis was the beginning of his own approaching death. He came to Dave and me and explained, "I don't want to leave my family in the lurch. I don't want any of my capital invested in the business anymore." Now both of them wanted to be bought out.

I estimated that I would need as much as half a million dollars to buy their equity and ensure sufficient capital to keep growing the business. Legally, I couldn't borrow to maintain net capital, so I had to find a bank that would loan me all the money to buy out Bob and Dave. But I had no bank relationships. Guided by Tim, I began making the rounds of the banks with branches in town where Tim had connections. Omaha National Bank debated it for months. Douglas County Bank took a couple of months, then told us no. Packers National Bank took their time and told us no. The delay was agonizing. I suppose they all thought, *Here's a risky new type of enterprise we don't understand, run by an immature, inexperienced young fellow. Does it make any sense to give him our money?*

There were three main banks in town. Third largest was the First National Bank of Omaha. Their approach was more old-fashioned, and Tim felt it was worth a try because their chief loan officer, Jim Bonham, was considered the brightest banker around. Bonham insisted that I bring Marlene to the appointment, to help them evaluate the entire family's commitment to making the venture successful. They visited our office and took notice of the plain metal desks, the bare linoleum floors, and the other indicators of thrift and serious commitment.

When Marlene and I went to our meeting with Bonham, he listened carefully. His questions showed that he understood the business opportunity of discount brokerage and our company's very midwestern culture. When we finished talking, he excused himself and came back with his boss. I gave the whole pitch again. After less than an hour, they said that, subject to the usual verifications, they would give us the loan.

To complete the reorganization and buyout, I created a new company named World Securities. With a name like that, no one would mistake us for a merely local broker-dealer. World Securities purchased all the existing shares of First Omaha using our new line of credit from the bank. The deal provided for a three-year payout. Dave was happy with the deal he had gotten, which gave him a nest egg for the future. I would not learn for many years that Dave had a congenital heart defect and expected to die young, which, in fact, he did. His windfall from First Omaha took some pressure off and allowed him to enjoy his life more.

Once the conflict over management styles was past, Dave found that he still enjoyed the challenge of managing the back office of a growing business. To my surprise, he stayed on for another year and a half, and we got along fine. I had never wanted to force my partners out, only to build up the business. It made me happy to have Dave stay with us. At the Christmas party in 1982, he told me, "Joe, you're a better boss than you were a business partner. When we don't have to make joint decisions, we work better together."

Bob's bypass operation was successful, and he made a good recovery. His son was a doctor, so he had the word not only of his personal doctor but also of a trusted family member that his heart was repaired and he ought to live for a good long time. He began to miss participating in the business. Over the next few years, I would learn, he explored starting his own broker-dealer firm. From what I understand, he felt at first that he was too old to build another business from scratch, but Betty said she missed being a broker and that she wanted to be part of a new company.

By 1985, my brother Dick would come to work for me, and the

following year I picked him to be company president. Dick was the best choice to represent the company to the public, but my decision irritated some of the older employees, such as Elton Semke and Bob Carley; it was hard enough for them to accept me as the new CEO, let alone get used to my kid brother as president. When Bob Carley objected to following Dick's directives, I fired him, which seemed to come as a shock. He was not used to me as the man in charge. "You can't fire me!" he yelled. "I quit!"

Bob Carley went to Bob Perelman, and together with Betty they started a new firm called Perelman-Carley & Associates, a broker-dealer that would do what Perelman had liked doing all along: answering the phone and taking stock trades. Perelman began to contact his old First Omaha accounts and ask them to switch from my firm to his. I called him and said, "Hey, that's not fair. I paid you. I paid you hundreds of thousands for those accounts. You can't take them away, even if a few years have gone by."

He said, "Oh, but they're mine, Joe. I can take them anytime."

And that was how I came to sue the mentor I had loved.

Tim McReynolds handled the case. He followed my direction, but did not support my choice. Although he said it was petty to sue, I think he came to understand my motivation. I felt morally obliged. Bob had never understood that the business came before everything, and now he was creating direct competition to it. That meant it was up to me, again, to protect the company. I had to protect my relatives. I had to protect my friends. I had to protect my family. I had to show the people who put up the money for me that I was looking out for their interests.

I lost that lawsuit because I had not required Bob to sign a noncompete agreement. From that time on, although we both lived in Omaha, we never spoke again. We had been advised to stay away from each other during the case, and we maintained that distance until he passed away at the age of ninety-one.

Once, out hiking, I was surprised to see the stocky figure of Bob Carley coming toward me on the path. I could tell he was going to keep his head down and walk right by, as if I were a stranger.

I said, "What are you doing? You just can't walk by. You've got to say hello."

"Hi," he said. Then he walked on. Those were our final words to each other.

I saw Bob Perelman one more time, many years later, when Marlene and I were invited to the wedding of a young person who had worked for us back when Bob and I were partners, someone who never took sides on the lawsuit. Marlene and I were joining the receiving line when I said, "Wait—I see Bob and Betty up ahead."

He looked older and grayer, and also mellower. I felt that both he and I wanted to talk but were afraid of where the conversation would go and what might happen in front of all those people. We might have liked to pretend that our disagreements had never happened, that we could just sit down at the same table and talk like we used to do about any number of things: our families, the changes in the brokerage business, social issues. But, of course, it was impossible. We had to stay on different sides of the room. Had either of us opened our mouths, I was afraid of the angry remarks that would come out, and this was not the place. I would have had to ask him, first thing, "Why did you think you could do that? Why did you think you could take my clients?" We could never have managed to make small talk, not about the wedding or the weather. I looked at him up ahead of us on the receiving line and I said to Marlene, "Let's allow some more people to join the line first, before we step in." She knew what I meant.

It would have been interesting, though, to learn what Bob thought of my success. His firm had done pretty well, growing to about twenty employees, but it had topped out there, about the size of First Omaha Securities when he left us. He had fulfilled his vision, so different from mine.

At the same time, he knew my company had been wonderfully successful. It felt good to know that my company had kept growing and growing, just as I'd dreamed. It felt great. But I suppose anyone would still feel that curiosity, meeting up with their great mentor, to show him or her what they had made, to have him or her acknowledge what they had accomplished. It would have been wonderful if Bob could have said, "My God, Joe, I taught you so much, and what a huge success you made with it."

But for us, that was impossible. I doubt that Bob could even have acknowledged me as his student because I wound up making choices different from his. I can't honestly imagine him speaking to me with appreciation, which would have meant admitting he had been wrong.

That day at the wedding, we kept to our respective sides of the room. We kept our feelings to ourselves. But as Marlene says, "Don't you ever listen to country and western music? There's always somebody whose heart is breaking." This was one of those tragedies that just happen at some point in everyone's life.

CHAPTER 6

When I bought my partners out in 1982, I felt like Clark Kent when he got away from the crowd, slipped into a phone booth, and closed the door. I felt like Superman taking off. I still had a responsibility to our stockholders, but they believed in me—or if they didn't, they were relatives and close friends with enough loyalty to let me make my own decisions. I had to report to them truthfully whatever happened to the business, but I knew they weren't going to hold me back.

It was quite wonderful to work without any other decision-makers: to make choices on my own, to fail on my own, and to know that, win or lose, I would not have another company officer pointing a finger at me. The risks were all on me now, and that was how I felt most comfortable.

I was fortunate to take control of the company at the end of a prolonged bear market, when changes in the economy were increasing the number of stock trades and drawing new investors.

Although interest rates had skyrocketed in the late 1970s and inflation had risen close to 12 percent, after President Jimmy Carter had appointed Paul Volcker to head the Federal Reserve in 1979, and Ronald Reagan had been elected in 1980, the inflation rate had begun to fall. Volcker pushed for an increase in the federal funds rate and began to tighten credit. Breaking with precedent, the Fed let interest rates move upward freely. Before the end of 1981, the prime rate had peaked at 21.5 percent and the economy plunged into a prolonged recession. The unemployment rate rose to 10 percent. The already bearish market fell even further, as high-cost, low-profit manufacturing companies laid off workers in droves. Some companies went out of business, but those that survived through cost cutting became more efficient. Tax reforms championed by President Reagan, combined with a massive fiscal stimulus focused on defense spending, pumped cash into the economy. The short-term impact on workers was harsh, but Volcker did succeed in slowing the pace of inflation, which was falling steadily around the time I took control of the company.

At the same time, the increasing deregulation of global banking systems brought a flood of investment capital into the United States, which helped bankroll the activities of a new breed of corporate raiders. Savvy investors like Carl Icahn and T. Boone Pickens targeted many of the big conglomerates that had been formed in the 1960s that now had assets worth more than their market value. Fueled by innovations in the junk bond market, these corporate raiders launched hostile takeovers and leveraged buyouts that drove stock prices up. Popular movies like *Wall Street* focused on the success of these corporate raiders, igniting the popular imagination and making people want to try investing in stocks.

These new investors represented potential new customers for discount brokers, and we were all looking for ways to take more of the growing pool of trades away from the full-service brokers. The conventional approach was to offer a variety of extra financial services to retail customers. Like many of my competitors, we now tried to provide more than a plain vanilla execution of a trade. We introduced a Prime Money Account in 1982 and gave customers the ability to write checks or use a Visa card tied to their account. The company even launched a travel service that guaranteed the lowest possible airfares, though that didn't last long.

Beyond offering amenities, I kept asking myself, *How could the company stand out from the growing crowd of discount brokers?* I had so many ideas. All the places I went and the things I saw—a big-box store, a client's office—sparked possibilities in my head. *I could do that a little better. I see a way to be more efficient, more effective.* I knew most of my ideas would probably fail, but the ideas just came and came. Some days, it was exhausting, and I wished I could turn my brain off. Mostly, though, it was exciting.

Having the ideas come to my mind was only the first step. Next, I had to imagine what actions I would take to try an idea out. Any actions I took, of course, would affect other aspects of the company, setting off a kind of chain reaction. Maybe a new approach would bring in new customers, but the costs would be too high to make a profit, as we had found when we opened branch offices. Maybe another idea would make a profit, but would it earn enough return on capital to make it worth the effort?

Each idea required this kind of speculative thinking, and I could only do that thinking alone. I found the time after dinner. I might sit and think at home on our screened-in back porch—if it was raining, the porch was a pleasant place. On clear nights, I'd go for walks, looking at the trees. (Years later, I would still meet neighbors who would say, "You know, Joe, I used to see you walking through our neighborhood at night.") If it had snowed, I stayed downstairs in my basement office. There was no one else down there and no phone, so I could think. I never made notes to myself. I just let the ideas ferment until one was ready. I knew that if I thought long and hard enough, the moment would come—*Oh! That's the answer.*

Even the best speculative thinking, though, only gives you a plan. It won't tell you the results you'll get when you put that plan into practice. I still had to choose to risk our resources or not—run the experiment, learn by trying. I couldn't ask others in the business if a given approach would work because they had never tried it, either. I couldn't ask the client what they would like because people don't know what they like until they try it.

It was true that I could survey my customers—and I did, sometimes. In 1983, a survey would find that 90 percent of clients rated our service as excellent, and, even better, 80 percent of new customers came as referrals from existing customers. We were doing something right. But for decisions about what to do next, it was never as simple as interviewing the client, because clients mainly ask for more of what they like already, at a lower price.

Every new opportunity I saw obligated us to take risks, and tension over risk had been the source of a lot of the conflict with my partners before they left. Now, though, the risks were mine to take. Why wasn't I more afraid? To other people, risk seemed to mean fear, but to me, fear wasn't something terrible. What I wanted was not to live without fear, but to have freedom, specifically the freedom to take on a challenge and try to meet it. That felt incredible to me, the best feeling in the whole world, to try something new that might make me money, create jobs for others, and build lasting success. And if I failed, well, I had started from nothing, and I knew I could go back to nothing. I would still be me.

I was ready now to carry out some of the ideas that my former partners had vetoed, and I decided to create subsidiaries to test some of the different opportunities I had imagined and analyzed. I couldn't start all the subsidiaries at once, so I would pick one, try to develop a model for how it would work, then hand it off to someone else in the company to carry while I worked on another.

Our primary source of revenue was, of course, stock trades for individual investors. In late 1982, we rebranded that retail business as First National Brokerage and went looking for cost-effective ways other than advertising to get more customers. I had asked Tim McReynolds to look for ways we could partner with banks without breaking the rules, but I didn't know where that would lead.

Another subsidiary, First National Futures, Inc., was formed to offer retail trading in commodities. This was a different kind of investing from stocks. You speculated on whether the price of corn or pork bellies, for example, would go up or down in a limited period. One way it was different from stocks was that you had to sell before whatever commodity you had bought to speculate on was actually delivered to your door.

A third subsidiary, formed in 1983, evolved out of the company's clearing operations. It came about because our low commissions drew the interest of small broker-dealers who asked if we would clear their trades for them. These were often little mom-and-pop operations, good entrepreneurial people just getting started in the business who might only have one of their licenses and only perform four or five stock trades a day. Some of them would have been content to pay our twenty-five-dollar retail rate, but I told them, "We can do better than that—we can charge you a lot less." Word began to get around that we were a discount wholesale operation, and more small retail brokers sought our services. I thought this would be good for the company even if it didn't make much money, because clearing for others would build our capacity to clear more trades for a lower cost per trade. I imagined we would need that capacity when our retail operation grew. In the meantime, we could pick up a little extra revenue on the wholesale side.

We called the wholesale clearing operation Ameritrade Clearing. I don't remember coming up with the name, though later a lot of people would say they had suggested it to me. It was part of an ongoing effort to generate different names for subsidiaries that made a similar point: Our company's ambition was to broker trading on a national scale. Like "First National Securities," the name "Ameritrade" was a variation on the theme of investing across the nation, trading across America. We could have called the new subsidiary First National Clearing, but we were trying to separate the brands so if one would fail, it would not drag down the reputation of the others.

From this point on, the company would go through a lot of names, both for the subsidiaries and the holding company that contained them. The ambition reflected in the names grew from national to global—the holding company was World Securities from 1981 to 1987, when it became TransTerra, Latin for "across the earth." Names of subsidiaries were many and sometimes recycled. I will mainly refer to the company in the rest of this book as Ameritrade, because that's the name that ultimately stuck.

Everything about our operation was still small and informal. When we realized that we needed a controller to head our accounting department, I filled the position through personal connections. I spoke to Mike Naughton, my mentor at our accounting firm, and he talked to a fellow there named Tom Pleiss. Tom had started as a controller at another company but wound up in a staff position that didn't suit him. He had no experience at all in securities, but Mike felt he would be a good match for us as controller. He told Tom, "You just go down and see Joe."

I felt confident that because he came to us through Mike, this

Tom Pleiss would be not just an excellent accountant but also a hard worker who shared the ethic that we were all in this together and we would do what was necessary to get the job done. He came expecting an interview and found me at my desk. I shook his hand and told him, "Mike said to hire you. So, when can you start? And would you like a beer?" He was our twenty-fifth employee and an important addition.

Besides his accounting degree and work experience, Tom Pleiss had some carpentry skills that came in handy when the office needed more shelves. I can also recall him washing the windows. The company was still what we could call today a startup, only unlike today we had no shared understanding of what "startup" meant, and we certainly didn't have any Nerf basketball or Ping-Pong tables. We were making up what would now be called our startup culture as we went along.

Even though we were now executing big plans to become a national firm with multiple subsidiaries, our operation at that time filled just two rooms with a hallway in between. One room was retail, taking orders from customers. The other was the back office, processing trades. Ten or twelve people worked in each room. Everything about taking the orders from customers and confirming them with the market makers and other brokers was still done by talking on the phone and writing by hand, with no automation in the sense of the word today, transactions on computers. (At that time, RadioShack did sell what was called a personal computer, which saved data to a magnetic cassette tape. The total storage capacity of a typical machine was four kilobytes, equal to only two typed pages of text. No one was using those early machines for investing.)

In one way, though, we were automated. We had a conveyor belt similar to a supermarket checkout, though ours was narrower. On each side of the belt, Tom Pleiss built plywood cubicles for the brokers who answered the phones, took the stock orders, and wrote out the tickets. The cubicles were enclosed for privacy, but the cubicle walls had square holes in them. When an order came over the phone, a broker would write a ticket by hand, rip off the bottom copy to keep, and push the other three copies through the hole onto the conveyor belt. The ticket would ride about twenty feet to the Order Trading department, where three or four desks made the top of a T at the end of the belt.

The department was run by Judy Day and Judy Moore, and my wife, Marlene, handled the over-the-counter trades. Two women picked up the tickets for trades on the New York Stock Exchange and entered them into a terminal. Two more women picked up the trades that were handled by market makers and telephoned them to try to get the best price for our client before the price changed.

That conveyor belt was noisy as hell, like a threshing machine, a constant *nnnnnn*. Employees were always yelling over the sound: *I can't read your writing! You forgot to mark if it was an open or closed option transaction!* That noise went on until about 3:30 each day, when someone would yell, "Pull the plug!" and the conveyor belt stopped. The entire process, from the client's order to the final confirmation with the market maker, took just a few minutes, which we thought was very fast, though of course today it happens electronically in an instant. Circa 1982, though, we were innovators in high-speed automated trading.

Marlene enjoyed making those calls to the market makers. She spoke with the same guys frequently, so she got to know them all over the country. Not many women were doing that work, and she and the other women on the phones got called "honey," "sweetie," "baby," and who knows what else. They would reciprocate and call the men the same names. When one of the market makers was truly offensive, Marlene refused to give his company any more orders until they assigned someone else to work with her.

A lot of the traders were from New York and New Jersey, and they thought that all of us in Nebraska must be hicks from the sticks, that Omaha was a place lost to time. Sometimes a market maker would visit, and we had the feeling they were surprised not to see covered wagons drawn by horses. Once, when Marlene was slow getting a report to one of the market makers to recap that day's orders, she told him, "I'm sorry I'm late, but we just had an Indian attack. We're still pulling the arrows out of the walls." He didn't seem to question it.

Marlene and the women she worked with began to make a game of telling the guys from the East Coast stories and seeing what they would believe.

"Sorry I couldn't get back to you sooner," she said sometimes. "Nebraska's a corn state, so we were having a Mazola party."

"What's a Mazola party?"

"You know, everyone takes off their clothes and pours on the corn oil, and then we all just sort of squish together."

Quick-witted, friendly, she could spend five minutes on the phone and make a person feel she was their best friend. She had to call all the market makers, and she was a success as the head of over-the-counter trading.

All through 1982 and '83, I poured money back into the company, developing the subsidiaries by investing in new marketing channels, new lines of business, and additional advertising. By the end of 1983, we had grown from twenty-five to about forty-five employees. The more we tried to do, the more we needed to change and improve. The pressure was intense. As I wrote to my shareholders that year, everything we were doing was costing us money to expand facilities. We would probably have to relocate; we needed a new phone system; and we had to expand our computer facility. The abilities of our management group would soon be taxed to the limit.

My family felt the pressure at home too. Because Marlene was running the over-the-counter trading department, she was at the office a great deal. I was grateful to have her there, but with both of us centering our days on work, many things at home didn't get done. My daughter, Laura, says that what she remembers about the early 1980s was the long hours her parents worked and how tired we were.

I don't mean to suggest that the children were deprived. They always had plenty to eat and good schools to attend. We had a used car I bought from my uncle and a big enough house, but as the kids remember it, the house was in shambles. The oven door had broken, so we propped a chair up against it to keep it closed. The carpeting was wearing thin. The roof leaked in multiple spots, but I wasn't going to fix it. I couldn't do home repairs—my dad had fired me years earlier when I had tried to work as one of his carpenters—so if we didn't have money to spare then the roof was going to keep leaking. When it started to rain, everyone would grab buckets and pots. We all knew where the water came in.

Another wife might have made her husband feel like he had to quit trying to build his own business and go get a regular job that paid twenty grand more—but offered him far less of a future. But Marlene did not add to my pressure by telling me to make more money so she could have a better car or a bigger home. My son Tom likes to say that his mother was the rock on which the whole family culture was built.

At times, the kids felt that they were almost disadvantaged compared to friends in the neighborhood who had beautifully furnished homes, wore the latest fashions, and went on far-flung vacations both winter and summer. I would sometimes drive my family to a motel on West Okoboji Lake for a weekend, or for a visit with Marlene's brother Keith, who lived in neighboring Silver Lake, Iowa. I took the kids camping for a night or two. That was as close as we got to an extended holiday. Once, Laura, now a teenager, asked me, "Hey, Dad, can't we go on a family vacation, too?"

I answered, "Would you rather go on vacation or would you rather go to college?"

There were lessons like that for all of the children. Todd can remember asking me for sixty-nine cents to get a hamburger at Burger King with his friends, and how I explained that we already had meat and bread at home. Tom remembers that when he went to college and tore his new jeans, he wrote to his mother asking her to send him a new pair. She mailed him the new jeans. I included a bill.

We expected all the kids to be aware of the value of money and to learn commitment to their work. When Laura was in high school, rather than taking a job at a fast-food restaurant or the mall, she worked for us, first as a receptionist and then as a quote clerk, looking up stock prices for customers who called in. One day, before the markets had closed, the tornado sirens downtown began to howl. I told all the employees to head for the basement. Laura switched the phones to night service and started to leave her desk, but I stopped her.

"What are you doing?" I asked.

"Aren't we going to the basement?"

"There's no tornado in New York. The market isn't closed. We have to have somebody answering the phone."

At first, she laughed as though I was joking, but then the phone rang, and I sat down to take a call. Later, she told me that she had been shocked and a little offended. She thought, *You're going to risk your daughter's life so you can keep the business open?* But I think she came to understand that I was not afraid of tornadoes hurting her, because the likelihood of one hitting was remote, but I was afraid of missing orders. When her mother heard about it, however, she was not amused.

At the office and at home, we were putting everything we could into the company. We were developing the subsidiaries, taking good risks, and increasing revenues, but expenses increased at an equal pace. I still saw no improvement in the bottom line. Despite all our growth, I felt deeply frustrated. In a business administration class, the theory is that you must impose a timeline on a venture and if it doesn't show a profit within the set time, you give it up. I found, though, that business school practices would not apply until the company reached a certain size, and I felt it was too soon to give up on any of our subsidiaries and their innovative approaches. We had to keep trying to grow our top-line revenues and absorb the costs until we had thoroughly tested every idea—and, of course, that was a subjective judgment. I had no formula for when to quit, only vision, persistence, and intuition.

Once again, there seemed no choice but for me to make the decisions alone. It was my money and my future at stake, and I had come to understand that every situation looks different when you have your own money at risk. If you pretend to buy stocks with play money, as students of the market will do when they're learning how it works, you may find it's relatively easy to stick to a given system for investments. One day, though, you get to the point where you're making a profit on paper, and you feel ready to invest for real. Now you take your hard-earned savings and buy a real stock. That's when you discover it's altogether different when you've got your own real money at risk. Of course, everybody in the world will tell you what to do with it. Sometimes it's your mother. Sometimes it's your spouse. Sometimes it's the smart, well-educated people who work with you who say, "Oh, you'd be crazy to try that!" But with Ameritrade, even those people had to do what I told them because I owned the business and wanted to learn what would happen if I stuck with all my bets: Given a choice, which subsidiary would the customers prefer?

As the Ameritrade Clearing subsidiary began to grow, we found we had a lot to learn. Aside from one operation in Denver, there was no one offering wholesale clearing outside of New York or Chicago. We had to figure it out as we went along. One of our correspondent firms (the firms we cleared for) turned out to be extremely responsible. They never seemed to have an *i* they didn't dot or a *t* they didn't cross. I remember that Tom Pleiss, our new controller, sent them a letter congratulating them and expressing how much we appreciated doing business with them. The head of the company acted as if their excellence in operations was no big deal, but later, when we visited their offices, we saw that they had framed Tom's letter and hung it on the wall.

We shared ideas and experiences about clearing with the folks in Denver, but the rest of the industry seemed to have the attitude that we were doomed to fail. Omaha was no financial center, and people said we wouldn't be able to hire workers in Nebraska with sufficient experience. As soon as we had begun to do parts of the clearing process for ourselves, we heard people say, "You aren't from the big cities; you're out in Omaha, so you must not be capable of meeting the challenges of this business. You must be dumb." I remember Tom would sometimes say, "Well, we're from Omaha, so we're dumb enough to try." It reminded me of the old joke about C students: they're the ones who become millionaires because they're too dumb to understand that the odds are against them.

It was true that we could not find people to hire in Omaha with experience in wholesale clearing, but that became a kind of blessing because we could train people our way, make our own mistakes, and learn from them without having to fight against the culture of some previous employer. Also, because we were the only clearinghouse in the Kansas City district of the NASD, the regulators spent a lot of time with us. They were learning, too. I had no patience for dealing with those people, but Tom Pleiss kept me away from them and cultivated a good relationship with them. We gave the regulators what they needed to do their jobs well, and there was no hostility or suspicion between us.

As it turned out, I was not alone in recognizing a big opportunity in serving the wholesale clearing market. Out in California, two guys named William Porter and Bernard Newcomb founded a company in 1982 that they called TradePlus, a wholesale service bureau that would come to provide automated clearing services to various big brokerages including Fidelity Brokerage Services, Quick & Reilly, and Charles Schwab. As those brokerages created their own automated Internet trading services, TradePlus began to compete with them by offering online retail trades, and in 1991, under the name E*Trade, they became one of our biggest competitors.

I started phoning small- to medium-size retail firms, those doing from fifty to two hundred trades a day, soliciting their business. Had they heard that we were offering wholesale clearing? Would they like to understand what we charged? I was unable to win the clearing business of larger firms. Most larger firms were on the coasts, and between their location and their attitudes about the Midwest, they assumed they would do better using a clearing firm that was also located on one of the coasts.

The only larger firms that wanted us to clear for them were the penny brokers. In the over-the-counter markets, the lowest-priced stocks were not part of the electronic stock-pricing system. Their stock prices, which were often below a dollar—sometimes just pennies—were printed once a day on pink paper. These "pink sheets" listing "penny stocks" were sent out daily to brokers who subscribed, known as penny brokers. If you wanted to know how a penny stock's price had changed during the day after the pink sheet was printed, you had to call the market maker and ask.

To me, the penny brokers were inspiring. At that time, it was far harder to get capital for a new business than it is today. If some folks with a good idea started up a company in a garage, they might not have anywhere to get money to sustain the company as it developed. Penny brokers would issue a small amount of stock, maybe a million dollars' worth, and offer shares to the public at a very low price. The risks were high but so were the rewards if you bought stock in a company at the very beginning. Penny stocks were the angel investing of the time.

It was difficult, however, for the penny brokers to find anyone to do their clearing. The stocks themselves were by nature low value and volatile, and the businesses that issued them were at a high risk of failing. Established clearing brokers, careful to maintain their "white shoe" image of handling the most important and successful clients, didn't want to be associated with cheap stocks and failure, so they often refused to clear for penny brokers. Those firms that did agree to do the clearing, often located in Denver, offered poor rates and refused to accommodate the particular needs of dealers in low-priced stocks. The general attitude seemed to be: We don't have to put up with small-timers.

To me, though, the work that the penny brokers did seemed important, even heroic: connecting small, entrepreneurial businesses with the kind of investors willing to take a big risk for a big reward. There's a saying that the easiest person to sell to is a salesman, and when the penny brokers sold me the story of their business, I bought it. I felt proud to be doing something for the good of the American economy.

Also, when we met with some of these brokers, they seemed like nice-looking, nice-acting people in good suits, honest members of society who were working to take advantage of the free enterprise system. I wanted them to do well. I charged them less than I could have and tried to accommodate their particular needs because I believed they were true business pioneers. If some of them were late in paying us, or if they fell behind in their recordkeeping, I told my back-office staff to be patient. Also, I was excited about this growing revenue stream. For these reasons, I was slow to recognize that many of the penny brokers were corrupt.

Usually, there were three separate financial organizations involved in the issuing of stock: the investment bankers who put up the capital to fund the new stock; the market makers who offered the stock for sale, setting the bid and ask prices; and the broker-dealers who bought and sold shares to retail customers. According to regulations, these three functions had to be kept separate. Some of the penny brokers, however, arranged to combine the three functions, giving them the power to manipulate stock prices.

Several penny brokers in different parts of the country would collude to run up the price of a given penny stock. First, they would publish their bid and ask prices in the pink sheets. Then, they would call their established customers and tell them to buy that stock. That first day, the price might appear on the sheet as thirty to forty cents. The next day, it would appear as forty to fifty cents, and up it would go until members of the public—people with no knowledge of evaluating startup companies, just gamblers looking for a quick score—would see that the stock "looked hot" and start buying. Many of the companies that issued these penny stocks were tiny operations run out of a garage or bedroom, with big stories about plans for the future that were mostly fiction, stories the penny brokers had embellished. Once the public was buying the stock at the inflated price, the penny brokers would tell their preferred customers that the stock had finished its run and offer the preferred customers a new tip about an even better deal. As the original buyers all dumped their stock at once, the price would fall to zero. The whole scam was known as pump and dump.

The sudden collapse of these stocks did not appear suspicious because most startup businesses, as many as eight or nine out of ten, will fail. There was no obvious way to tell which failures were legitimate businesses that didn't work out and which were fake stocks that had been manipulated. Meanwhile, the penny brokers were running up the price of their next new stock.

One firm we dealt with in Denver was closed down by the FBI because they were a front for the Mafia. Another broker was convicted of killing a man. For a short period of time, we even cleared for Stratton Oakmont, the scammers later made infamous as the subject of *The Wolf of Wall Street*. We did it because I was naïve. Never in the bottom of my brain had it occurred to me that people would be that crooked, or that their version of the American dream would be to screw everyone else.

In fact, I was doubly naïve. I assumed that the regulators kept a close eye on our entire industry, like the adults in my town had watched out for us kids, and so I did not need to worry about bad actors. I failed to imagine that a firm would base its business on avoiding the regulators. The NASD would threaten lawsuits, then the penny brokers would delay and push back, and their resistance slowed the legal process and kept the regulators from doing their jobs. We needed better regulation and enforcement, and in time the NASD would be replaced by FINRA—the Financial Industry Regulatory Authority—but those changes were years away.

The deception was made easier because we were all using early computers to keep our records, and those old, slow machines often fell behind. Gradually, though, it became clear to us that some of our penny brokers were making trades all day long without talking to their customers, then telling us at the end of the day that they needed us to change the prices on the tickets after the market had closed. In this way, they hid their price fixing and made it look as though legitimate buying was what pushed up the price of their chosen stock. That was as improper as stealing. Of course, the penny brokers always had an explanation. They would tell us that innocent mistakes had been made, or that they had gotten overwhelmed by the volume or the complexity of their trades and they needed our help to set things right.

The pump-and-dump scams were putting my company at risk. When buyers of penny stocks saw their investment become worthless in a single day, they generally had not yet paid for their stock purchases. Regulations at that time allowed for three days before a customer was required to pay us, the clearing broker, for any trade they had agreed to make. If they didn't pay us, we were left to make up the difference.

One day, Bill Glasz, who was the vice president working directly with these penny brokers, told me, "We can't go any further with Stratton Oakmont. We've been bending over for them, but it's too much. I'm afraid they're crooks." I told him to tell the client that they were putting our company in danger and we couldn't clear for them anymore. We had been in trouble with the SEC in the 1970s, and the regulators were not going to be kind to us twice.

When we told them so, they promised to do everything by the book if we would keep clearing their trades. For a couple of months after they made their promise, they gave us no problems. Then they started to twist the rules again. We told them, again, that we were going to stop clearing for them, and, again, they promised to clean up their act. Finally, we told them: *We can't trust you. We know that in a couple of months you're going back to your old practices.*

It might seem obvious now, but it took time for the pattern to become clear. The NASD wouldn't get serious about shutting down Stratton Oakmont, for example, until 1989, and they would not put the firm out of business until 1996. However, this was still the early '80s, and I was naïve enough to believe, first, that there were few truly bad actors, and second, that any bad actors would get caught by the regulators. I also had confidence in the accountants I had hired to make sure we followed regulations and avoided a further run-in with the SEC, no matter what our clients did. And so, even after we ended our relationship with Stratton Oakmont, we went on clearing for other penny brokers, honest and dishonest alike, though I didn't know about the dishonesty. There was another guy in Denver I really got along with, whose operation turned out to be a complete scam, but it took a couple of years for me to see that. That's because clearing produced a good cash flow, much better than expected.

Cleaning up after the penny brokers took me on a few adventures. One day, Tim McReynolds flew with me to Las Vegas for court hearings with a penny broker who owed us money. We arrived on a Sunday so we could be in court on Monday morning, and we were not staying on the Vegas Strip, we were staying downtown. As soon as we got to our hotel, though, Tim left for the Strip to play blackjack. When I met him before court the next morning, I saw that the tall, skinny man's eyes were bloodshot. His clothes, which he hadn't changed since the day before, were rumpled. He had been out until four in the morning counting cards, he said, starting with $800 and winning $20,000. He didn't even have his briefcase with him. He pulled a thick stack of cash out of his coat pocket—his winnings—and asked, "Can I put this in your briefcase?" As I would discover, he was known at all the big casinos as a high roller, and any one of them would take him out for expensive dinners and fine bottles of wine. When we came to Vegas for hearings, as we had to do repeatedly, he would sometimes bring me to dinner as his guest.

Even after playing blackjack late into the night, Tim performed his duties in court as if nothing unusual had happened. Then he took back his stack of cash and went off to play blackjack again. By the time I met him at the airport, he had lost all the money. As I remember it, he had even lost the plane ticket I had bought for him back in Omaha. He asked me, "Joe, would you buy me another one?" As I recall it, I did. Tim, however, does not recall ever betting and losing a plane ticket.

Meanwhile, he had placed a different sort of bet for us that paid off in a remarkable change in the industry. I had retained him to solve the seemingly impossible problem of how to get the SEC to let us set up offices in banks. In November 1982, Tim got us a letter from the SEC saying that while they did not formally approve of what we wanted to do, if we went ahead with it in precisely the way Tim had described, they agreed to take no legal action against us.

That "no action" letter was a breakthrough for the entire industry. It gave agency brokers (brokers who sell to retail customers) permission to create a contract with a bank and advertise discount brokerage through that bank. The banks would send our ads to their customers, and, early on, an employee would sit at a desk in the bank to meet with those who responded to the advertisement and sign them up as customers. We would make the trades for those customers and pay the banks part of the revenue. It was permitted as long as the banks stayed out of the brokerage business, provided no stock recommendations or research, and used us as their agents for trading. In other words, Tim had shown the SEC that while commercial banks could not, according to regulations, act like full-service brokers, there was room in the rules for those banks to act like discount brokers. This was revolutionary.

Soon after we received the letter, I was at a convention of broker-dealers where an expert on a panel described how his company had partnered with a savings and loan in California without seeking permission from the regulators. The SEC had shut them down. The expert offered that as a cautionary tale for any other firm thinking of trying it.

Self-interest told me that I should keep my mouth shut because we now had an advantage that no other broker-dealer shared. However, I didn't like some so-called expert on brokerage speaking to my peers and giving them wrong information about our industry. I stood up in the audience, a room full of a couple hundred brokers, and said, "You can do it if you do it in the right way! I have received a no-action letter that will allow me to proceed."

The whole room was electrified. Ten guys stood up and rushed out, and I'm sure they were all attorneys looking for a phone booth so they could tell their companies to start working on no-action letters.

I hurried to use our first-mover advantage and build relationships with banks and savings and loans. By June 1983, we had established the Bancvest brand for investment accounts at commercial banks; we had also discovered that there was such intense competition between banks and savings and loans that we needed a separate brand that did not have the word *bank* in it. We came up with "Televest," because the clients of savings and loans would use the telephone to place their trades.

I began paying sales calls on these institutions, explaining that we were the first brokerage allowed to offer their customers the chance to open trading accounts at their branches. The customers would set up their accounts at their institution, but the accounts would live on our books. We would share some of our commission revenue with the banks.

It was a surprisingly hard sell. Bankers were used to the idea that brokers could not perform investment banking functions, and they did not tend to grasp right away the difference between investment banking, which involves bringing new stock or bond issues to market as a way for companies to raise money, and agency trading, which is buying and selling stocks for individual, retail investors. But as I signed contracts with a few banks, more bankers read about it in the newspaper. Gradually, they came around. I had high hopes for signing Citicorp, one of the nation's largest banks, but that never came through. Still, within a year, Ameritrade had partnerships in place with sixty-five institutions operating in 350 locations.

As this was happening, we still had all of our front-office people working out of one room. Calls would come in on different phone lines and the employees would have to remember to answer "First National Brokerage" or "Bancvest" or "Televest," or even "Ameritrade Clearing," depending on the line, to give the impression that these were the offices of different companies. It took some time as we grew to get the subsidiaries appropriately separated.

While we were doing that, the stock market took off. By the middle of 1983, the value unlocked by corporate raiders and the speculation fueled by new sources of capital created what the journalists called a "raging bull market." Initial public offerings increased dramatically as companies offered $8.7 billion in new stock to investors, a 378 percent increase over 1982. The discount brokerage industry, only eight years old, was now handling nearly 20 percent of stock trading. In November 1983, Bank of America offered $55 million for broker Charles Schwab & Company, and with that high-profile purchase of a discount broker, the press and the regulators started treating us differently. The responses to our advertising picked up. For the first time, it began to feel as though we would be recognized as an entirely legitimate business, as we rightly deserved.

I began to take home more money as salary. The change had started when Bob Perelman had left. Because he had been comfortable financially, Bob had always preferred to keep his wages, and therefore his taxes, low. Once he was gone, I felt a little freer in that respect. Now, with the booming market and our increasing success, my family felt the difference at home. Laura remembers that family finances turned a corner during her freshman year in high school, around 1983. Instead of buying a used Buick from my uncle, I bought my next car new. We rehabbed the whole house, replacing the stained carpet. Now the oven door stayed closed and the roof didn't leak. We began to take longer vacations. Peter and Tom went to college, and though tuition bills put pressure on the household budget, I was able to pay their way. I didn't want them to go through what I had to in order to pay for my schooling.

Then, in 1984, the market went sideways. Commission revenues dropped 20 percent. Fortunately, we were able to see the decline coming. Anticipating that we would need fewer people to open new accounts and take orders, we cut costs early by letting go of our most recent hires. As a result, while pretax profits in the brokerage industry as a whole dropped 70 percent, our earnings rose 8 percent. Even during a "raging bull market," we had kept to our commitment to keep costs low, and that commitment had kept us growing through the market correction.

In 1985, we consolidated our operations under the name Ameritrade. I had never been entirely comfortable with the name First National Brokerage because it so clearly aped the name of a bank. The name Ameritrade, though, was fresh and it was ours. We hadn't realized when we first came up with it that it was something special. Like our subsidiaries, we had to test it out for a few years before we recognized that we had a winner.

Ameritrade was now one of about three hundred regional brokerage firms around the country providing their owners with a comfortable living, taking home a couple hundred thousand dollars a year. A lot of leaders in the discount brokerage business seemed to think they had arrived at a solid resting place. Many who had been successful at starting a firm now sold to someone else.

However, I had no interest in selling, and I did not believe we were in any position to rest. I wanted to keep making our 30 percent return on investment year over year until I had a company big enough to pass on to my kids. I believed we still had a long way to go to establish something lasting. I couldn't see the future, but when I looked carefully at the performance of our subsidiaries, I did see that although we had somewhat improved our bottom line, we had not actually found a way to increase profits on the scale I had been seeking since 1975.

While we were signing up new accounts through banks and savings and loans, making use of our "no action" letter, the surprise was that those accounts were never big moneymakers. Discount brokerage was suited to people who felt ready to make their own investment decisions, but the customers we got through banks often wanted guidance from an investment advisor. Our revenue depended on doing a high volume of trades, but the customers we got through banks generally made a few trades and then held their stocks for the long term. Overall, we learned, people didn't seem to think of banks as places to do their brokerage business. Also, the culture of banks was too different from that of brokers; they moved some tellers to desks to open accounts for us, but the tellers didn't think like we did. It became clear that while the contracts I had arranged with financial institutions were worthwhile, they would never be a big source of revenue. This was another of those outcomes you could only learn by trying.

Similarly, the commodities subsidiary we had created, First National Futures, was a push. It added revenue but also added to our costs and overall risk, and it never seemed to be worth the time and effort. We shut it down and brought those employees to work for other parts of the company.

Our most successful subsidiary turned out to be the one from which we had expected the least, Ameritrade Clearing. While growth in our retail trading was nearly flat, wholesale clearing increased until, by October 1984, it accounted for almost 30 percent of our revenue. Of course, with clearing we were relying on commissions from the penny brokers, including the crooks who were spreading the word that the dumb, idealistic guy at Ameritrade would meet all their needs. Our big growth area was a ticking time bomb. What many in the industry took for a comfortable arrival was just a temporary haven, and the biggest financial crisis since the Depression was less than two years away.

CHAPTER 7

In the last quarter of 1985 and the first quarter of 1986, fueled by a corporate takeover frenzy, brokerage firms saw record profits. At Ameritrade, with strong cost controls in place, we reported the best six-month period in our history. It was wonderful. I bought a Jaguar with a beautiful old chassis for me and Marlene. What fun it was to drive that car, not just the beauty of the machine but also the meaning of it, like a championship ring to commemorate our team's winning season. We were achieving some financial success. *Look at us go!*

Success itself, however, put enormous pressure on our systems and our employees. As far back as 1983, I had written to my longtime shareholders, warning them of the challenges of growth. Now, if we were going to sustain the success that justified that Jaguar, every aspect of the company would need an urgent upgrade.

Outgrowing our old office space, we moved into what was known as the Douglas Building, a former Masonic Temple seven stories tall.

It had a ballroom/auditorium on the sixth floor and an illustrious history—the cornerstone had been laid in 1916 after a parade attended by five thousand Freemasons, many of whom celebrated the start of construction with a banquet at Freedom Hall. For us, though, what mattered was that the rent was low and the space extensive—there were entire empty floors available on short notice. There was an elevator and a nice old-time marble lobby still in good shape. We built a lunchroom and, in time, space for different departments, including a special room on the second floor with a raised floor for the Honeywell computer. The computer could malfunction if there was too much static electricity, so we had to keep the room humid. We got the humidity from the building's steam heat system, which meant the moist air was also hot. The women who worked with the computer in that special room wore sundresses and sandals, even in winter.

I thought the Douglas Building was perfect for our rapidly growing business, but to a visitor the site could be a shock. First of all, we were in downtown Omaha. Once a thriving area, by the 1980s it had fallen on hard times. Some of the surrounding buildings had been left vacant. There was gang activity in the area at night. Bums would find their way into our building and prostitutes would sneak in between johns, to clean up in the bathrooms in unused parts of the building. Some prospective hires who set up interviews lost interest when they realized where we were located. "My spouse won't let me work east of Seventy-Second Street," some told us. "That's not safe."

We had a guy who would walk the halls to make sure no one had come in who wasn't supposed to be there, but he left at six in the evening. Once, after he had escorted out the same homeless person a few times, we received a bomb threat. The police asked us to vacate the building, but I had a strong feeling that this phone call to the police had been made by the man we kicked out. I told the officer in charge, "I'm sorry, but we don't accept bomb threats during business hours."

Cathy Smith, who tended to the computer at night, brought a dog for protection, an unusually large Rottweiler with a tan muzzle. I would show up, forgetting the dog was in the building, and before I was close enough to talk to her, he would get between us, barking. That dog scared the crap out of me, but Cathy said he was a mama's boy, very loyal, and he kept her safe while the computer calculated trades and printed out all our records.

Pigeons roosted on the ledges outside the building, so the challenge walking into the building was to avoid their droppings. Once inside, even visitors unfamiliar with the different classifications of commercial office space could tell that this was not Class A. There was no wood-paneled entryway with an impressive welcome area for the receptionist, no fine art on the walls, no consistent design to the decorations or the furnishings, which were bought at surplus outlets. Some employees worked at used two-hundred-pound oak desks, others at government-surplus metal ones. The office walls were blue because Dave Kellogg had located a large supply of blue paint at a discount and hired some of the information-technology people to paint for us in their off-hours.

As a workplace, the building had many quirks. Hot in summer and cold in winter, its uneven temperature-control system could chill one office at forty degrees and heat another to eighty. Even while the women in the specially heated computer room wore summer clothes, other employees wore their winter coats all day. The air-intake vents were so huge and powerful they could suck papers off your desk.

The different functions of the company were in different parts of that big building, so to reach another department you might have to climb to another floor or walk down some dark, dank hallway. The IT folks were down on a lower floor with no windows, where reams and reams of computer printouts were stacked to the ceiling—that was "data storage" in those years. When they ran out of space, they began storing printouts in the ballroom upstairs, so someone who needed to check those records had to ride up in the rickety elevator.

Kurt Halvorson, an accountant who would join us in 1987 from what was now called Deloitte Haskins, still remembers his first impression of our offices. Twenty-five years old, he arrived for his first day in his best suit, with his shoes newly shined and his briefcase in hand. It was so early in the morning that the receptionist wasn't at her desk. He didn't know where to go or who to ask, but then by chance he saw me coming down the hall.

"Kurt, right?" I asked him.

"Right. Today's my first day."

"Oh, how wonderful. Well, follow me."

I walked him to his assigned office. When we opened what was going to be his door, three employees of the clearing operation were sharing his pale oak desk. In the clearing business in those years, the crowding was such that when the person working at the middle chair got up to use the restroom, someone else would occupy the chair, because the middle seat was where you could get your legs under the desk without banging your knees into the drawers.

"Hey, everybody," I said. "This is our new controller's office now, so you guys need to find another place to work." Once they left, there were still papers and a couple of typewriters on the desk. "Don't worry," I said. "We can stick those typewriters somewhere. We'll get this cleaned off."

Next, I led him down a narrow hallway stacked high with boxes. It was time for him to meet his boss, Tom Pleiss, the president of Ameritrade Clearing. Kurt tried to open the door, but there were so many people inside Tom's office that the door would only open about six inches. Somebody inside had to stand up and move their chair so we could get in. Kurt felt alarmed at first that the entire company was in disarray, a pressurized and barely disciplined chaos.

The remarkable thing was that people did come into this environment and feel: *Yes, this is the place for me. I want to work here*. They did not only tolerate it; they actively chose it. In a way, the crowding and the mismatched furnishings were what drew our growing management team. Mostly former "shoebox accountants," they knew the same lesson I had learned updating credit ratings when I was on the road for Dun & Bradstreet: one business could look impressive going bankrupt while another could look a mess but be thriving. They were used to finding the truth not by looking at the furniture and wall decorations but by studying the receipts often handed to them at the start of an audit in a shoebox, then tracing the cash flow to discover underlying financial truth, like a doctor studying an X-ray.

The accountants I was hiring for management positions recognized that in a company growing so fast, a dollar saved now on rent or furniture or even paper clips might be the dollar that helped ensure our survival in the short term. A dollar in profits reinvested in the business this year could be worth hundreds or thousands later.

That focus on thrift and reinvestment required patience and discipline. It also helped to have a sense of humor. I did want to do some basic remodeling in the Douglas Building, including replacing the carpet, but in keeping with our commitment to cost control, I wanted to avoid the expense of temporarily moving our people to another office space while the new carpet was put down. I didn't even want to pay the premium to have the carpet installed at night, so I had the carpet laid during the workday. I remember they were putting down glue near the area we called the Cage, where Carol Jeppeson worked on clearing and compliance issues, when an urgent matter came up and she needed to talk to me right away. I was on the phone when out of the corner of my eye I saw Carol come tearing through the Cage.

It was winter, and she was wearing a wool suit. Then she hit that wet glue and went down, bang, flat on her back.

I got off the phone.

"Carol," I asked, "are you okay?"

She was still on her back in the glue, but she said, "Yeah."

Another fellow, closer to her, came to offer her a hand, and she asked him, "Are you sure about doing that? Because you could end up down here with me."

He helped her up. By now a crowd had gathered to see if she was all right. Carol faced them and said, "You know, I do birthday parties, too."

There was a dry cleaner's downstairs, so one of the women called to find out what you do with a wool suit coated in carpet glue. They said to soak it in water right away. The women took Carol into the bathroom to help her out of her suit and she came out again wearing just her leather winter coat and whatever she had on underneath. Before she left to go home, she said, "It'll be just my luck if today I get stopped by the cops." Under pressure, it helped to laugh.

In addition to the strains we felt in keeping costs low, we faced another challenge: our computer system was struggling to keep up with our growing volume of trades. As the nearly ten-year-old machine churned through the day's transactions and then tried to update accounts overnight, it fell behind. One day's recordkeeping might not be complete until ten or even eleven the next morning, by which time the markets were open again, the phones were ringing, and new trades were being entered based on the incomplete records of the day before. At times, we got out of balance reconciling our records with the clearinghouse. We had no choice but to accept their version and move on. Later, at night or over the weekend, we had to recheck our records of the trades and funds exchanges to find the mistakes.

We wanted to keep increasing the number of trades we did, but the computer could not handle much more.

Back when David Kellogg had created our first system, we had learned that software was not a need you met once and crossed off your list. You had to keep updating software forever. Regulations change, interest rates change, and software system updates become a full-time job for a dedicated department. Now, we realized that our hardware had also hit its limit. No matter what upgrades and tweaks we could make to our Honeywell and its operating system, the old machine could no longer keep up. It might seem strange that this took us by surprise, but we had only ever owned one computer and we had no idea what we would need to replace it. What technology would serve our needs and last? What would we have to pay for it?

Many smaller brokerages avoided such questions by outsourcing their computing needs, relying on firms such as ADP, Automatic Data Processing. I was not going to be dependent on another company for something at the heart of our business. I wanted to be in control of our computing. But these systems were enormously expensive and complex. When AT&T and Quotron Systems teamed up in 1985 to develop a computer-based financial information system for Shearson Lehman/American Express, replacing "dumb" terminals with personal computers that would allow brokers the ability to simultaneously access market data, account information, and messaging services, they announced that a five-year contract for equipment, software, and services would cost between $150 and $200 million. It was an unthinkable amount of money, a massive ambition. They might as well have been announcing plans for the first private moon shot or a human colony on Mars.

Ameritrade could not possibly have afforded anything of that magnitude, and, given the pace of change in hardware and software, I worried that whatever I could spend, the system would be out of date as soon as it was built. Yet if we declined the challenge and fell behind our competitors, we risked getting left in the dust by an industry destined for fully computerized automation. Both the NYSE and the American Stock Exchange had developed automated execution systems for trades of a thousand shares. Meanwhile, Dean Witter Reynolds, Shearson Lehman/American Express, and Merrill Lynch all disclosed in January 1985 that they were close to launching proprietary systems that would automatically execute trades of up to a thousand shares in over-the-counter stocks. Nasdaq had created its Small Order Execution System that automatically executed trades of up to five hundred shares. The days when telephone orders for stock were taken by customer service reps, then copied by hand and entered manually into a computer, were coming to an end. Although that end came slowly and in stages, we couldn't deny it.

Finally, we settled on a West Coast computer company to design and build a system based on a thirty-two-bit-chip computer due to be released that summer. Their use of technology impressed us, but they had never built a system for a brokerage firm. Unfortunately, they went out of business before they could deliver. We lost money and valuable time.

Next, we went with a company based in Providence, Rhode Island, that claimed experience in the brokerage industry. But their experience was mainly with full-service brokers. They did not have a precise understanding of the needs of discount brokers. And to be honest, we didn't have a precise understanding of what we needed our computer system to do. We worked together, through trial and error, and when the Rhode Island company delivered software to us in early 1986, the result still wasn't exactly what we needed. Meanwhile, we had to keep running our business with our existing system, trying to squeeze out every last byte of processing capacity. As a result, by the summer of 1986, the computer's "clearing clerical-type errors" had cost us several hundred thousand dollars and threatened to undermine relationships with customers.

Throughout this time, I had kept in touch with Dave Kellogg, my former partner who had built our original computer system. After he had left us, he bought a software store, thinking he would build on his computer expertise and offer consulting services to small businesses. It hadn't taken long, though, for him to realize that he was not particularly good at managing a retail operation. He let that business go, and we started talking about my difficulties. We arranged that he would work for the Rhode Island firm as a subcontractor, helping to develop both a back-end system for processing trades and a front-end system for order entry and communications.

Dave had a gift, not just for working with computers but also for understanding what people needed from them. Unlike your typical information-systems manager in the 1980s, he wasn't some Wizard of Oz hiding behind a curtain of new technology. A collaborator rather than a turf protector or a guardian of the systems, Dave asked questions. He accepted suggestions. And, in addition, he had years of experience with the accounting, auditing, and regulatory compliance issues of discount brokerage. I hoped he could bridge the gap between what we needed and what the technology could deliver.

In Dave's wide-ranging conversations about our computing needs, he received a suggestion from Tim McReynolds, my attorney, who, along with his wife, had experience with programming. They were familiar with a computer system for managing law offices, written in a little-known language called MUMPS that was originally designed for use at Massachusetts General Hospital, then expanded for use in other settings by Dr. Donald Gall at the Massachusetts Institute of Technology. Tim and his wife were excited about MUMPS because, they said, it was both a language and an operating system in one, and in addition, its database was "hierarchical" rather than "relational." I was not especially interested in the technical details, but I was very interested in what Dave said would be their consequences: Relational databases slowed down as they got bigger, but this hierarchical one could maintain its speed at it grew.

Working with MUMPS, Dave and the Rhode Island firm found a way to overlay a relational database on top of a hierarchical one, to get better ease of use with no loss of speed. They felt that this was an innovation that could put us ahead of the competition, truly a better mousetrap: a system that could grow without slowing us down. It was also more cost-efficient—we would spend less on hardware to run this software than another approach that didn't use such innovative computer code. We concluded that we could buy a Data General Eclipse MV/20000 to run the new MUMPS-based software, a machine so sophisticated it could back up our data to magnetic tape. This computer wasn't vulnerable to static electricity like the old one, so we didn't need steam to maintain a high level of humidity. Instead, this machine required its own air conditioner to keep it from overheating. Boy, did I feel important when I stopped in that cool room with the raised floor and saw the lights flashing on our new computer—it looked as if we were running a nuclear research facility.

Buying that computer seemed like a chance to reach my longstanding goal of increasing our volume and revenue with only a minimal increase in costs. But Dave was still developing software in the new MUMPS language. The team was making progress, but I was deeply frustrated. The joke around the office was that you knew you had a sick computer system when the name of your programming language was a disease.

While Dave's team continued to struggle with the new computer system, and lost revenue continued to add up, we also felt increasing strain on the human side of our operations. The more trades and the more clearing we did, the greater the pressure on our employees and our management team to take on more responsibilities. If you stayed with Ameritrade, you would quickly find yourself doing more work and a wider variety of tasks than you had ever imagined. There were opportunities to work with new technologies and manage operations that no one else would have given to young, blue-collar employees with limited formal education. For some employees, this represented a life-changing opportunity that inspired dedication and loyalty.

Cathy Smith, for example, who took care of our computer at night with her Rottweiler at her feet, had come to us in 1978 when she was twenty-two. A high school graduate who had worked as a busgirl and at an insurance company, helping to print customer policies, she was our thirteenth hire. We needed her to input data as a teletype operator, but unfortunately, Cathy's fingers were slow. A teletype operator she was not. In a more conventional company, she would have been let go, but David Kellogg, who back in 1978 was still developing our first computer system, had noticed that although she had no formal computer training, she was mechanically inclined. She asked a lot of questions and took a lot of notes. Although she lacked the formal terminology she might have picked up in a college class, when Dave explained, she understood.

Half the challenge with the computer system in those years was keeping the hardware running. You could leave a computer slowly working on a big calculation and discover a few hours later that it had stopped. Cathy had an ear for when the bearings were going out on the big platter-size disk drives. She had an eye for when the number of pages printing out for a report didn't make sense for the job that had been programmed. I don't know how many times Cathy saved our bacon—she would drop in on weekends to make sure the system was running properly and that it would be up in the morning. It got to the point that she could call the tech people on the phone, describe the sounds the computer was making as it malfunctioned, and they could diagnose the problem and send a technician over with all the parts necessary for the repair. Cathy Smith worked from midnight to eight in the morning, or longer when needed, and we relied on her.

Another example, perhaps the most dramatic, was Carol Jeppeson. Hired back in 1975 to serve as a receptionist when we first launched the company, almost within hours she began to help with the recordkeeping for our trades. She took over our clearing operation in the 1970s, as I've described, because she was very bright, she understood the details, and she brought dedication and integrity to that complicated work. Carol had no college degree, but like me, as she liked to say, she bored easily. Driven to learn and to do more, she earned all the licenses she needed to become the finop, the financial and operations principal of the company.

Back in 1980, I remember, we'd had a client in New York that owed us about fifty thousand dollars, according to our records. However, they didn't see it that way. I was adamant that they had to pay us. They said I was wrong. The conflict was heading toward a lengthy and expensive court battle and the loss of a valuable business relationship. Instead, I told them: "What we disagree about is a matter of recordkeeping. There is a factual answer. So here is what we are going to do. You are going to pay for Carol Jeppeson to fly to New York. She will look at your books and she will tell you and me what is wrong. If she comes back to me and says you don't owe anything, we're okay. But Carol's got to look at it and decide." They respected her enough by then to agree to my terms.

Carol was from the small town of Council Bluffs, Iowa, the daughter and granddaughter of farmers, and she had not had the kind of life that ever takes you to New York City. As it happened, she arrived during the 1980 Democratic National Convention. The client couldn't find any hotel for her except the Carlyle, where the politicians were staying. After she left the client's office for the first time to go back to her hotel, her cab was stopped by security and the driver was told he couldn't go any farther. One of the candidates was conducting a news conference in front of the hotel and only VIPs were allowed. The driver told the police officer, "Apparently, you don't know who I have here in my cab." Carol looked around to see whom he had in his cab. The driver claimed that Carol was a diplomat from some country or other, and that got her past security and back to her hotel room. In the end, working at the client's main office, she found the evidence that demonstrated to our client that they owed us the money, and they accepted her findings and paid. She saved that relationship.

By the mid-1980s, Carol Jeppeson was essential to the company, working as both compliance manager and operations manager. We paid for her to study for her college degree. She was my right hand, our unofficial chief operating officer, the person called first when we had a crisis with a client. There was a penny broker in Colorado, for example, who appeared to be creating stocks with dubious value and then hyping them to their customers. The penny broker owed us a lot of money and Carol was concerned that we might never get paid. The head of that brokerage made himself hard to contact, so she left him this message on a Friday: "I need a hundred thousand dollars from you today. Until then, we will accept no more transactions from your firm. We will hold all your accounts starting right now, and there will be no activity until I get a hundred thousand dollars."

On Saturday, he called her at home. He told her, "You can't do that. You just can't do that."

"Yes, I can," she said. "I'm shutting you down."

"I'm going to talk to Joe Ricketts," he said.

"No, you're not," she answered. "You are not going to talk to anyone but me, and I will not do anything for you until we get that hundred thousand."

Sure enough, Monday morning, after chartering a plane, this client and his attorney were waiting outside the Douglas Building at seven in the morning to meet her. And before they left, we had the money.

At the same time that Carol was handling high-stress situations on the client side, she was also responding to personnel crises within the company. Very early one Easter morning, while hosting her parents for the weekend, she got a call from Cathy, who had gone into the office because our overtaxed computer system wasn't working through our recordkeeping properly. At that time, we also had a new systems person, a man who made sexually inappropriate comments on the job and made Cathy uncomfortable. At three o'clock on Easter morning, Carol told me later, Cathy called her at home, angry about this new systems guy and the quality of his work. Cathy was responsible and professional in her approach to work; she would not have called without reason. At the same time, it was almost Easter morning. Carol had her parents staying with her, and her mother was upset by the calls coming in so late.

A couple of hours later, still before dawn, the systems person called with his side of the story. Carol had to tell him to save it for Monday at work. His call had awoken Carol's mother again.

"Does this go on a lot?" Carol's mother asked. "You've been getting calls off and on all weekend."

Carol told her it did.

"How in the hell are you doing that?" her mother asked. Back in the 1970s, when Carol had taken over our clearing operation, she had suffered from migraines. Now, as she took on increasing management responsibilities, she enjoyed the work and she excelled at it, but she worried over living up to them with her characteristic conscientiousness and excellence. She developed ulcers. I don't think either of us understood at that time that people could get ulcers from the stress of work they value and enjoy.

The Peter Principle, a book about hierarchies published in 1969, had suggested that workers in a business hierarchy who do a good job will rise to a higher position and keep rising until finally they reach their "level of incompetence." Carol was never incompetent in any of her duties, but there was a point beyond which the emotional and physical toll became more than she could handle. She asked me repeatedly in the 1980s to replace her, but I didn't want to lose my right hand. I had to plead with her to stay several times, and she agreed.

Everyone who remained at Ameritrade felt the strain of our success. We grew so fast and promoted people so quickly that everyone lived with unexpected demands and escalating stress. My wife said that I was partly to blame. She complained that I scared people—even though I controlled my temper, I was a large man with a deep voice, and when things didn't go my way I would cuss. We were still a relatively small company—when I was angry, many people could overhear, to the point that my staff could judge how serious a problem we faced was based on the cuss words I used. It often fell to Marlene or Carol to smooth feathers after my yelling got someone upset.

In that respect, under the pressure of our success, I was facing my own version of the Peter Principle. I was not a natural leader. I had never meant to be a leader at all. I had only "promoted" myself to head of the company when my former partners had been unwilling to take on the position. I thought my true role was to figure out what we had to do next to make money. Once I knew, I expected those who worked for me to fall into lockstep behind me and execute my plan. Some of the time, for many of the people who chose to work with us, that was a plus. They knew I had a vision and that I was driven to achieve it, no matter how hard I had to push myself or others to get to the next level. But as a manager, I gave a lot of orders—and a lot of ulcers.

We did have some secret weapons, however, to help us overcome, even sometimes to love, the stress of our work. The markets closed at four on the East Coast, so come Friday, at three Central Time, the phones would shut down. After we completed all our book work, we closed and locked the office door. Then we went to the Rookery to tell our stories of the week's events and to laugh together. I loved to take everyone out for beer on a Friday. We shared some of the pleasure of surmounting obstacles and succeeding, which is one of the great pleasures in the world.

My son, Peter, who worked for us as a teenager one summer, stuffing envelopes and bringing bulk mailings to the post office, remembers that one of his young coworkers would bring a case of beer to the parking lot after work on Friday, and hang out with his car door open and music blasting from the stereo. Sometimes I'd stop and have a beer or two with the younger workers, like a happy hour, before I went to join the more senior staff at the bar.

A lot of the credit for making Ameritrade feel like a shared enterprise in those years goes to Marlene. A caring, nurturing person whose love held our family together, she brought that care and those softer, emotional skills to the office, so that a family feeling spread throughout the company. She baked birthday cakes for everyone, often shaped or decorated in some manner that was meaningful to the individual. Many people had not been celebrated that way on their birthday in years, if they ever had, and the recognition and attention meant a great deal to them. People looked forward to their birthday cakes and talked about them after. It gave a feeling not just of shared commitment and responsibility but also of caring and affection. Marlene knew how to make people feel special, and she did that for every single person at Ameritrade. When we finally grew too big for her to keep up with all that cake baking, she switched to a monthly donut day when we could acknowledge the birthdays of that month. I suppose some of the ways she made people feel welcome came out of her teaching, where she had wanted to make sure every child felt that they belonged in her class.

Besides the birthday gatherings, we also had summer picnics, Halloween parties, and hayrides. There were company football games on Saturdays in a big open field that was the future site for our expansion. I remember that when Peter worked for us, it was important to him that the company was not just a place to do your job but also that Ameritrade employees hung out socially.

And we had some unbelievable Christmas parties. One of my uncles, Eddie Galas, had a well-known restaurant in South Omaha, Eddie's Restaurant, and when we still had fewer than a hundred employees, I would host, and Marlene would make everybody gag gifts. I remember one Christmas, when Carol was feeling the strain of her many responsibilities, Marlene's joke gift to her was a barf bag. The gifts were another way to help everyone acknowledge all we went through together, and to laugh about it.

There was one young employee, Todd, whom Marlene liked to tease because he was from Iowa. We have a fair amount of humor in the Midwest about who is dumber than whom. In Iowa, they joke that if the southernmost Iowa counties seceded to Missouri, it would raise the average IQ in both states. In Nebraska, we like to rib the Iowans. One year, Marlene's gift for him was a T-shirt she had lettered. Todd had said he couldn't make it to the party, so she gave him the shirt in advance. Then he showed up anyway, wearing a suit for the other, fancier party where he was expected. Marlene gave him a bit of a hard time for not wearing his gift shirt to our party, and all of a sudden, he ripped open his dress shirt and revealed the T-shirt underneath, which read, "Me is a smart Ioweigan." I had rarely seen

Marlene speechless, but she was speechless. We were all cracking up. The spirit was just wonderful.

These moments were fun, and fun mattered more than you might think. Enjoying these times together, I believe, we all felt that we were in the same boat, and that despite the pressure, Ameritrade was a pretty great place to be. That kept us focused on achieving our shared goals. In the "raging bull market" of the 1980s, I became increasingly aware of how important it was to have that sense of belonging and purpose, and ways to find healthy release. Some of the other broker-dealers in the business did not, and their ways of coping with the stress were self-destructive. This was illustrated in movies such as *Other People's Money* and *The Wolf of Wall Street*, which showed stockbrokers destroying their lives with dope, alcohol, and sex, which was just another kind of drug. When I heard about those brokers in New York with their Quaaludes and their prostitutes, I thought they were lost.

It made a great difference that as a company we could let off steam *together*, that the culture was not every man for himself. It helped, as well, that our substance of choice was beer. Beer, whatever its drawbacks, is not dope. Marlene generally did not come out for drinks on Friday at the Rookery. She went home and got supper ready for the children. Often, I did not get home in time to eat with them. I might have had twelve beers on a Friday evening. I might have had more. I'm sure there were a few nights that it was only by the grace of God that I didn't have a car accident. But it was only beer and it helped me get rid of all my pent-up stress. I got myself home, and our family and our business could press on together.

The feeling we had at Ameritrade of an enterprise shared was not based only on parties and socializing. It was also financial. In the early 1980s, I created a profit-sharing plan that Carol Jeppeson administered. We issued our employees company stock, so that as the company grew in value, all of our permanent employees would benefit. They could not take the stock with them if they left—they had to sell it back to the company and take the proceeds—but as long as they were with us and contributing to our growth, they owned a portion of the return on our investment. I couldn't afford to pay big salaries because my business model was based on keeping costs low and reinvesting every spare dollar, but I could, in effect, promise that if they helped me execute my model and we achieved the success I envisioned, they would enjoy it too.

I was first inspired to create a profit-sharing plan by Cathy Smith, our failed teletype-operator turned computer-whisperer. Seeing that young woman in her twenties devoting such long hours to the repetitive, tedious, essential work of keeping our computer running, I felt grateful. I didn't want to have to replace her. She was loyal, always on time, and worked nights and weekends. In those years, also, there was a lot of talk in the national news about whether the social security system would fail. It occurred to me that if Cathy stayed with us for her full career, as I hoped she would, there would not be enough social security for her to retire on. I hated the idea that the people who devoted themselves to our company might be destitute when they came to retirement. I thought, *I'd better have a retirement plan for these young people.*

Later, my willingness to reward employees with a share in the company's success surprised University of Chicago business school professor Mark Mitchell. In the mid-1990s, when Mitchell looked at the company's financials for us, he told me, "You're being very generous to these employees." I believe he meant that we could have gotten away with offering less. But I told him: Your business will never do better than the people you have working for you. You have got to treat them right if you want them to stay with the company. That was doubly true in Omaha, which did not have the large pool of workers with experience in the securities industry that you might find in New York or Chicago. Most of my employees were trained in their skills and expertise within Ameritrade. To lose one was, therefore, doubly expensive, because we would have to spend money finding a replacement and then training that new hire.

As it turned out, Cathy stayed with us, overseeing our computer system, for more than twenty years. Before she left, we had to ask her to write a manual of everything she knew for the team she left behind. Even so, when the system would break down and our tech people were working on the repair, you would hear the old hands say, "Cathy would have had it fixed by now."

Profit-sharing, personal recognition, fun, and a belief that we were all in this together helped relieve the intense pressure of our growing company, but they were not a cure-all. Carol Jeppeson told me again that her job as my right hand was becoming too much for her.

"I need to get out, I just really need to," she said in 1987. "I'm getting to the point where I know everything around here."

One of her great strengths had always been that, as she said, she bored easily. She always wanted to learn the next thing, take on the next project—an essential quality if you work for a driven entrepreneur. But by this time, she had helped to both create and oversee compliance for so many aspects of our operation that she had become the one person who knew and understood all the rules. Even when we hired other people to shoulder some of her burden, it still fell to her to be the ultimate authority on compliance. "I'm still the finop. I'm still . . . everything. I have to sign off on everything. I do not want to become this old lady who sits in an office and tells everyone else, 'You can't do this. You can't do that.' " Carol had grown with the company by learning and innovating and improvising, but now what the company needed was not for her to explore and master new areas of the business, but to be the authority figure who enforced the rules. It went against her nature, and I came to realize that our success and the changes it required were burning her out, just as the new direction I had wanted to go in in the 1970s seemed to burn out Dave Kellogg and Bob Perelman.

Carol was still completing her degree in night school at the University of Nebraska, and there, in a statistics class that was a prerequisite for applying to MBA programs, she ran into Bob Slezak, another of the accountants at Deloitte Haskins who had participated in our yearly audits. He had always had a notion that he might work for us one day. Carol told him that we were looking for an operations manager, and they chatted in class for a few weeks. Finally, Carol said, "Do I need to hit you over the head? Would you be interested in applying for the job?"

"Would I?" Bob said. "I sure would!"

His first day was in March 1987, and once he started, she left. She said that her husband hated her quitting because they would miss company parties. Later, I felt very sad because Carol and other early, essential employees such as Judy Moore, a key manager, should have gotten rich when the stock in the profit-sharing plan went public. I wrote them checks for the value of their shares when they left, but we were still a private company then and the stock was worth far less. They had received bonuses for their performance, but the work was too stressful for them to stick around to reap the full benefits. You have to stick around.

By the spring of 1987, the '80s bull market was showing signs of weakness. It got my attention when Warren Buffett, legendary investor and Omaha native, decided that the market was overpriced and moved $700 million into medium-term, tax-exempt bonds rather than equities. That summer, on the heels of a third-world debt crisis, Citicorp announced the second largest loss in corporate history. Meanwhile, interest rates had been rising for nearly two years along with fears of a return of inflation. Amid these disturbing trends, Alan Greenspan replaced Paul Volcker as chairman of the Federal Reserve. Greenspan continued Volcker's anti-inflation policies, persuading the Federal Reserve Board to raise the discount rate in September, a move that was quickly followed by central banks in Japan and Germany. The increase in interest rates unsettled investors.

In August, the Dow peaked at 2,722, with shares trading at an average of nearly twenty times earnings, but as new fears of a worldwide credit crunch rippled through the markets, share prices stalled. Now, in 1987, not only had the market reached an all-time high but trading volumes were skyrocketing, and as we tried to handle a greater number of trades than ever before, we acknowledged that our old computer system was on the verge of collapse.

Fortunately, by the fall of 1987, the MUMPS-based system that David Kellogg had been developing with the firm in Rhode Island was at last ready for a trial run. We had planned on extensive testing, but as the old system began to fail, I felt we had no time for tests. We hired temps to complete the slow task of transferring the company's data from the old Honeywell machine to the new Data General Eclipse MV/20000. For a month, the company ran both systems simultaneously and the new computer limped through each day's activities, more or less keeping up, but there were many problems still to resolve. Dave warned me that his crew was holding the system together with Scotch tape and baling wire. They worked around the clock, and when they were too exhausted to continue, they would crash at a hotel a few blocks away. As soon as they could get up and take a shower, they came back and somebody else went to crash. For two or three weeks, the team worked without stopping.

Today, many people are familiar with the concept of beta testing software. You start using a new program that doesn't work quite right and you learn from the experiences of the customers who try it out first. But our new system wasn't a single offering we were testing out on a group of willing, self-selected guinea pigs. This was the main system for our entire company. Every one of our customers depended on it. As the accountants put it, "There is a nontrivial chance that the system will not perform as needed." Meaning: *If this doesn't work, we're out of business.* Even so, with the old system breaking down, I felt we had no choice.

It was September, and we were reaching the end of our fiscal year. We knew that with two computer systems going, there might be some difficulty gathering all the data we were required to report, so the company moved its year-end closing date from September 20 to the last Friday in September, giving us a little more time to submit the required reports. But when that date came, Dave couldn't get the month-end closing results he needed. He had not fully vetted the program he had written for closing out each month, and now he found that it didn't run.

We faced a choice: Do we ask the regulators for permission to break the rules, or do we act without their blessing and seek forgiveness later? We decided to act and live with the consequences. We informed the SEC and the NASD that we were going to wait an extra week, and that we would close out our year on October 2. Of course, this alerted them that we were having difficulty fulfilling our regulatory obligations. Once again, there was the possibility that they might shut the company down.

For the next week, we had all hands on deck, trying to fix glitches in the system, clean up our data, and generate the required reports that would balance the books. A lot of this work was done manually. There was a cloud over the entire company. "Then one day the sun came up," Dave would say, "and everything was all right." Avoiding a repeat of 1976, we filed our reports correctly by the adjusted due date. Soon the new computer was keeping up with our trades. The new system was a success.

We were so proud. We felt that we had bought the entire computer industry and that the new system would last forever. Dave Kellogg's system not only met the needs of the business in 1987 but its basic infrastructure continued to serve the company for nearly a decade, providing Ameritrade with critical competitive advantages. In time, we would be trading as many transactions on our one relatively small computer as Schwab was reported to be trading on eight computers nationwide—and they had to sync up their computers long-distance to do it. Our system kept our costs down for years. Later, we made an investment in a computer firm called CSS Corp, and their programmers threw tens of millions of dollars into their efforts to build a much bigger and more ambitious system. But they were never able to replicate the functionality that Dave gave us as an inspired amateur.

While the company was focused on the transition to the new computer system, Bill Glasz, then our vice president for trading, became concerned that there was a new and dangerous degree of risk in our clearing for other brokers as a result of our margin policies, meaning our policies regarding stocks that customers purchased with money we loaned them. The rules required the customer to maintain a certain percentage of equity in their account. For example, if the customer put five thousand dollars in an account and borrowed another five thousand from Ameritrade, then the total equity in the account was ten thousand. If the "maintenance minimum" was 25 percent, then the customer was required to maintain a minimum total equity of cash and stocks in that account of 25 percent of that original ten thousand, or twenty-five hundred dollars. If their stocks went down enough that the value of the stock plus any remaining cash did not meet that minimum, the customer was required to add either cash or stocks to that account to maintain the minimum. When we warned them that they were getting close to the minimum, we notified them in what was called a margin call. If they fell far enough below, we had a legal obligation to sell their stocks for them, whether they approved or not.

Our margin policies—the rules that allowed investors to trade partially on credit—had been designed with individual investors in mind, and basically, we operated on an honor system: If someone placed a trade, we trusted that they would fulfill their financial responsibilities as a result of that trade, whether it resulted in a gain or a loss. Bill Glasz raised the alarm that there was too much risk of these bets going wrong and the customer refusing to pay back the money we had loaned them. But between the shift to the computer system and the unrest in the markets, we did not do more than talk about Bill's concerns.

The markets overall were experiencing volatility like we had never seen before. In October, Congress opened hearings on corporate securities and the activities of corporate raiders like Ivan Boesky, Carl Icahn, and James Goldsmith. The Democratic caucus of the House Ways and Means Committee agreed to add new anti-takeover provisions to the tax laws, a move that would put a damper on junk bond financing and suppress the kind of merger and leveraged-buyout activity that had fed the market fever of the mid-1980s. According to some market analysts, this move triggered as much as a 10 percent decline in stock prices over the next three days.

There was also financial uncertainty resulting from the collapse of OPEC, which had sent the price of crude oil tumbling in 1986. On October 15 and again the next day, Iran fired missiles on oil tankers owned by Americans or flying the American flag. Also on the sixteenth, when markets in London were closed by the Great Storm of 1987, the Dow fell 4.6 percent. Some traders were sure that come Monday the market would rebound, but Friday was only the prelude.

October 19, 1987, would become known as Black Monday. From the opening bell, our phones began to ring nonstop with orders to sell, sell, sell. Customer service representatives scrambled to keep up. Someone came to my office to alert me that the Dow was dropping like we had never seen. When I came out, I saw our customer service reps standing in a daze, looking at the quote machines and not believing what they saw.

The phones continued ringing. As the market was inundated with sell orders, the systems brokers relied on nationwide began to fall behind. The ticker tape and the reporting of trades could not keep up. Confusion reigned. Without accurate price data, we couldn't correctly handle our customers' stock options. Some of the good brokerage houses that provided us with the flow of orders we processed for customers were so overwhelmed that they couldn't answer their phones. One hundred percent of their customers were calling to sell. We had never had that happen before. When brokers didn't stand by their bids, prices went into free fall.

The strategies designed by the regulators to manage risk in a sudden sell-off assumed that prices might drop by at most 5 percent in a day, but the sell-off quickly crossed that barrier. Many of us had our own stock portfolios, and we watched as a quarter of our wealth in equities evaporated in a day. It was like a disaster movie. The plane was going down, the pilot had passed out at the controls, and those people in the cabin with some experience had to come together to save the plane from crashing.

The sell orders seemed to come in waves. As one round of sell orders drove prices down, more margin accounts at every brokerage fell below their maintenance minimums, legally obligating those brokers to sell stocks in many of those accounts, which created another wave of sell orders. When a wave hit, we didn't have enough staff to answer the phones, so I sat down with the others and began taking orders. Tensions were incredibly high. The automated systems were overwhelmed, and we could not always get reliable stock price quotes. We wrote down many requests by hand, knowing we would have to enter them into the system later.

Prices in general had come down so far that Ameritrade might already have been broke. Had we known how low our net capital had in fact fallen, we would have been obligated to report it to the SEC and the NASD, who should have shut us down. But we weren't actually sure where we were. We were just praying and holding our breath to get the market closed.

By the end of the day, the Dow had fallen exactly 508 points to 1,738.74, a decline of nearly 23 percent. The volume of trades was enormous, and we were very, very fortunate to have the new computer system in place to process those trades. But the market had gone down so fast that the computer had not been able to keep up with all the recordkeeping. Many people worked late that night in our margin department, going through the trades that hadn't been automated. Our clerks had to relay the information by symbols for each stock on their Quotron terminals, write down the closing price for that stock, and hand it to a data-entry person who would enter a trade at that price into the computer system.

We were not done with pricing all the day's trades until around ten that night. Only then, when we had all the price information in the computer, could we start the system updating the customer accounts to tell us which ones had fallen below their maintenance margins. By now it was getting very late. We still needed to get the margin calls out so we could close the books for the day. Those staying to work on the calls were not due back until ten the next morning, but those like me who were expected back for the opening of the market would have to return by eight. When I felt I couldn't do any more useful work, I went to Tom Pleiss to get one more report on the company's overall financial situation. I could depend on him to tell me exactly where we were exposed to financial risk. He understood what was happening in the market, and I could rely on him to give an honest report, the worst of it. Then I said, "I'm tired. I don't have any more energy. I'm going home to sleep. I'll be back first thing tomorrow." I knew I could count on Tom to call me if things somehow got worse overnight.

Someone said maybe we shouldn't open the next day at all, but I said, "We'll open our doors. We'll go on and we'll get through this. We're behind now in our records, but the market will slow down and then we'll get caught up."

I went to get my coat. Some of my employees looked shocked that I thought I could sleep when we still didn't know how much money we had lost, what our net capital was, and whether we were in compliance. If we knew we were out of compliance, then we had the legal responsibility to shut ourselves down. I did know that threat was real, but there wasn't anything more I could do about it.

At that moment I could only think, *Joe, get ahold of yourself. Think clearly. It's true that you might go out of business, but if you do, it's not the end of the world. If they shut you down, you'll still go home to your wife and the kids. You will feel bad for a couple of days then you'll go find a job. So, don't let your emotions run away with you. Take it easy, calm down, get some rest, and later, when we find out where we are, then we'll know what to do next.*

The margin department sent out our margin calls in the form of FedEx letters telling customers they didn't have enough equity in their accounts. We had our books balanced in time for the market to open the next day, based on the information we had at the time. If that information turned out to be wrong, we knew we might still be in violation of the net capital requirement, but all we could do was follow the rules and make use of the information that was available to us at the time.

Kurt Halvorson still talks about that morning—it was only six weeks after he had left our accounting firm to join Ameritrade. Twenty-five years old, with a pregnant wife at home, he came in the morning after the crash to sit in his pale-blue office with its mismatched furniture and ask himself, *Why exactly did I leave the safety, security, and comfort of public accounting for this?*

The crash had happened so fast that it caught everybody off guard—including the regulators. We weren't certain about our calculations of our net capital, and they were too busy with the unfolding crisis to come and ask us. Meanwhile, we were all very lucky—not just our company but also our country—that Federal Reserve chair Alan Greenspan directed the major banks to open their coffers and allow broker-dealers to take short-term loans to get through the crisis. That averted a true meltdown of the market. We were so close to beginning another depression, but the next day, the market took a big jump up almost as fast as it had gone down. Some of the people to whom we had sent letters saying that they were below the maintenance margin now found, by the time their letters were delivered, that the value of their stock had recovered enough that they didn't owe us money after all. Some customers whose stock we sold by legal obligation were similarly surprised that by the time we completed the sale, the price had recovered. Of course, it was still likely that Ameritrade had been in violation of the requirements for some hours, but in that we were no different from the rest of the industry. The regulators let it go.

For the next few days, we worked to get our records in order, to get margin calls issued, and to liquidate customers' positions so we

1

I was born in Nebraska City, Nebraska, a town of about seven thousand, in 1941. The town formed my first ideas of success, based on the store owners I clerked for and the doctors and dentists I met in town. Many of the small-business owners who employed local kids like me took it upon themselves not just to train the young people who worked for them to do their tasks correctly but also to help shape their character.

2

Nebraska City as seen from above in 1949, when I was eight. In the summer, my mother would pack me a lunch in a sack and I was free to walk to the park or to a place in the woods that was good for playing and fishing. At the same time, I was aware that many adults in town knew who I was and would report inappropriate behavior back to my mother. That experience of great freedom plus responsibility for my actions was the perfect foundation for a young entrepreneur.

3

Marlene Volkmer and me in our St. Bernard's Academy yearbook photos. We met in high school and got married in 1963, when we were each in college. Marlene was the stronger student, but I was ambitious and willing to work as hard as necessary to succeed.

4

Marlene and me with our growing family back in Nebraska in 1969, after I completed the Dean Witter training program and became a stockbroker. Pete and Tom are dressed like twins; Laura was one. We were visiting someone out in the country who had the money to buy film for photos. I had money for only one nonessential, and that was beer.

Back in Omaha in 1969, we attended a performance of *Fiddler on the Roof* with friends, then came home, put the soundtrack album on the turntable, and had a few drinks. With a red baseball cap standing in for Tevye's cap and a tan sash around my waist for a prayer shawl, I danced and sang along to "If I Were a Rich Man," feeling proud of my new career and optimistic about my future riches. But America was in for two long bear markets. It was a terrible time to become a stockbroker.

5

6

We worked so hard in the 1970s and '80s that no one took any photographs at work. Someone did manage to take this photograph of Bob Perelman, my first partner and mentor, and his wife, Betty, who worked with us, at a Christmas party in 1985, ten years after we founded the business. The party was at Eddie's Restaurant, run by my uncle Eddie Galas in South Omaha.

7

Working such long hours under so much pressure, we relied on our Friday evenings out for drinks and our office parties to let off steam and give everyone the chance to share and celebrate the challenges we'd overcome. Here Dave Kellogg, my partner and the creator of our first computer system, wears a fire chief's hat at our Spring Party in 1983. Dave put out a lot of fires for the company.

8

Also at the Spring Party in 1983, employee Todd Burbridge shows off the T-shirt Marlene had made for him to tease him about his supposedly inferior intelligence on account of his being from Iowa and not Nebraska. Sharing these personalized gifts, along with the cakes Marlene would bake for birthdays and the drinks I enjoyed buying my employees on Friday nights, was remarkably important to people. They felt recognized and remembered, like family. We needed that kind of closeness if we were going to spend so much of our time working together.

9

Our first big marketing success came in 1975, when we offered stock trades for a $25 flat fee to customers who called our toll-free number. But our second big success came in 1985, when we became the first company to offer trading by touch-tone phone—you dialed into our computer and entered your buy or sell information by pressing buttons on the keypad. Here's my brother Dick, showing the world that if you had a touch-tone phone, you could call in to make trades for only three pennies per share on our Accutrade system.

10

The family posing at a Halloween party in October 1995. Although the company was growing fast, we stuck to our party tradition. Left to right: Marlene Ricketts (nun), Joe Ricketts (nun), Curt Conklin (Hamlet), Pete Ricketts (pirate), Todd Ricketts (Robin), and an unidentified bear.

11

Tom Pleiss, Larry Collett, my brother Jim Ricketts, and me posing with a trade show display for a back-office data system. We tried to sell it to other brokerage firms under the World Data brand in the early 1990s, but I don't believe we ever sold one. There were so many products we offered over the years and so many approaches to marketing that went nowhere; there's no way to know what customers will prefer until you give them the chance to show you. But we all look proud of that shiny new personal computer with its five-and-a-quarter-inch floppy-disk drive.

12 13

Left: We spent millions developing Accutrade for Windows, anticipating that this state-of-the-art PC-resident software would be the most powerful computer-trading method ever offered to the public. However, it was cumbersome to install. We mailed each potential customer a stack of eighteen three-and-a-half-inch floppy disks, and the customer had to install the software correctly and then learn to connect their PC to our computers via modem. In comparison, trading on the Web allowed customers to access our computers directly, without all the difficult setup. The newer, cheaper, more user-friendly upstart disrupted the expensive state-of-the-art. *Right:* A publicity photo taken at the Ameritrade headquarters in Omaha in the early 2000s shows me riding high. By this point, I owned more than a couple of suits, and my pants weren't worn to shiny.

14

The growing success of Ameritrade in the 1990s gave me the chance to discover one of the great loves of my life: traveling the country by motorcycle. Here, my high school friends Jerry Gress and Dan Gude and I pose in 1998 on our new Japanese bikes at the start of our first trip to the Sturgis Motorcycle Rally in Sturgis, South Dakota. It rained for the first three hundred miles of that trip, making us wonder if biking was really for us, but by the time we got home we were hooked, and I bought myself a custom-designed Harley-Davidson.

15

With proceeds from the sale of Ameritrade stock, my four children, Tom, Todd, Laura, and Pete, purchased the Chicago Cubs in 2009. While I had given up my dream that my children would one day take over the company and run it after I was gone, Ameritrade earnings made it possible for my children (seen here at Wrigley Field during the 2016 World Series) to come together to manage a business, keeping in close contact and resolving their differences together, very much as I had hoped.

16

Among my entrepreneurial pursuits after leaving Ameritrade is building a business around bison meat, which makes the most delicious steaks and burgers but has less fat than chicken. Here Marlene and I pose as we celebrate the 2005 bison roundup near my ranch in Wyoming, where each bison is directed through a chute for inspection and health care. It's a festive day, and we invite family and friends.

17

Hiking in 2015 near the Hoback River in Wyoming, where I've put up a lodge so people can come fish for trout. Having stepped back fully from Ameritrade but remaining restless, I've focused on philanthropy, including the Ricketts Conservation Foundation, the Ricketts Art Foundation, and the Cloisters on the Platte Foundation, and on new entrepreneurial endeavors.

could meet all of the settling trades in the market and meet our capital requirements. We all felt terrible pressure, because we knew that if we had one more day with a decline like we had seen on Monday, we probably could not stay in business. However, I don't think the management team let themselves think very long about the possibility that we would fail. By this point, I had hired five accountants who were Haskins & Sells alums among my senior management. They had been brought up in the same culture, with a strong focus on accuracy, transparency in disclosure, and an analytical desire to understand why events were happening. They were loyal to me, and their overall attitude, which came through so clearly that week, was that if we had a problem, they were our problem-solvers, and they would work that problem until it was solved. Just as we were fortunate to have the new computer system in place, we were equally lucky when the crisis came to have a management team so united in its culture and its commitment to the company.

Although some clients were fortunate and saw their losses erased, others who had bought stocks on margin—with our money—couldn't or wouldn't take responsibility for stocks worth far less now than they had paid. I overheard my brother, Dick, on a call with a penny broker in the Southwest whose total equity in his account had fallen to less than what we had loaned him in his margin account. He owed us a great deal, but he told Dick flat out, "I'm not going to pay you."

"You don't have a choice," Dick said.

"I told you. I'm not writing that check."

The longer the conversation went on, the angrier my brother got. This was a big, wealthy customer who felt he could push us around. Normally, if a customer refused to pay us, we could sell the stocks in the account and compensate ourselves with the proceeds, but the penny stocks in his account were now worthless.

"There's nothing you can do about it," the penny broker said, taunting my brother.

Dick was a shareholder in the company, one of the original investors who had given me money in 1975, and this penny broker's arrogance pushed him over the edge.

"You know what I can do?" Dick shot back. "I can send Guido to get our money. Do you understand what I'm saying? When he comes to your house, you'd better be able to give it to him."

The customer wired us the full amount the next day. But I said, "Oh, Dick, you can't do that. Because the next time you threaten to break someone's legs, the customer isn't going to send you the money. He's going to report us."

We did take some financial hits. Even with the market bouncing back, we lost about half a million dollars the day of the crash. Nevertheless, we all dug in and got to work in order to try to reestablish the accounts of our clients who had margin debt outstanding, to try to work with them to meet their margin calls, and to try to make sure that our correspondent brokers had not boarded up shop and left. Because of round-the-clock work by Ted Serflaten (running the margins area at that time, smoking two packs of cigarettes a day), Bob Slezak, Tom Pleiss, Bob Fowler, Kurt Halvorson, Mary Fay (who had taken over the customer service department just one week before), and so many other hardworking people, we got through it.

There were three factors that allowed us to survive when a number of other firms did not. The first was the new computer system. We had built it to handle the strains of growth, not because we anticipated a market collapse, but having built it, we were prepared to handle a huge increase in trading volume, and that kept us in business.

The second was our human capital, the dedication and vigilance of our employees.

The third is a little harder to explain.

Bob Slezak called it dumb luck. It was not luck, of course, that we had recognized that we would need greater computing capacity and a bigger, yet still-unified management team, but it was luck that we had those in place on the day we needed them most.

Kurt Halvorson would say the third factor was the Divine hand.

To me, the difference between those two is not always clear. When I look back, I feel that I've been lucky all my life. You could say the good Lord likes me. But, you know, it's one of those things: the harder you work, the luckier you get.

CHAPTER

8

The most painful result of the Crash of '87 for us was the lay-offs. Before the market declined so extremely, the company had grown to more than 150 employees. Now, I had to cut that number in half. I felt that I owed it to those who reported to me to notify them myself, in person, one by one. Oh, that hurt. We had done so much to build a family feeling in the company, and now I was taking this group that had worked so hard together and had such fun at the end of the week, and I was breaking it up. Some employees wept.

After delivering the bad news to one person, I had to sit down and compose myself before I could speak to the next. Because I had not been born into money, I knew what hard times meant. My employees had felt comfortable buying cars with bank loans. Many were taking out mortgages and starting families. The loss of these jobs would change families' plans, affect spouses and children. It had always been a point of pride for me that this business I had built was helping to bring prosperity to some of my neighbors. I knew that

Ameritrade gave some of our young people a reason to stay in Nebraska rather than seek work on the coasts, as so many others did. I knew that workers we let go could not simply walk down the street to apply for a comparable job elsewhere in town. There were few comparable jobs in Omaha. Those jobs were far away, and that was a wrenching situation for anyone. I remember telling Marlene, "I have to do this, but I would rather cut off my own arm."

As a business matter, we had no choice. Our revenues were down in all areas, but the biggest change was that we had stopped clearing for the penny brokers. Many had abandoned their stocks completely during the downturn and simply disappeared. Some tried to come back, but the regulators were wiser now to their tricks and shut more of them down. Some penny brokers that did survive hadn't dealt with Ameritrade properly, and we refused to work with them again. All told, we probably lost 75 percent of our wholesale clearing business.

At the same time, for our individual accounts, we had new credit policies both inside and outside the company. The old rules had anticipated at most a 5 percent drop in the market; the new rules assumed the drop could be as much as 30 percent. Credit was now reduced in margin accounts, meaning that clients could buy less stock than before against the same amount of equity, and this change further decreased both the number of trades we were doing and the interest we made on the money we loaned customers in their margin accounts. Before the crash, we had sometimes allowed a customer who asked for it an extra day to respond to a margin call, but now we strictly enforced the rules.

Our next two years, fiscal '88 and '89, were loss years. To meet the net capital requirements while our revenues were down, we had no choice but to reduce costs, and our main variable cost was payroll.

That was how I came to tell about half my employees that I didn't need them anymore.

I was often asked about the lessons we drew from the crash, but beyond the many technical changes to protect us from excessive risk in future downturns, I was left not so much with lessons as with two questions I couldn't answer. First, if we couldn't bring the wholesale clearing business back to what it had been before, could we make dramatically more money on the retail side? Second, was there something wrong with our approach to hiring and promotions? If fast growth led to mass layoffs, I never wanted to grow that fast again. And yet, I wanted to grow very fast. Could I change our operations to strike a better balance between my obligations to my shareholders and my obligations to my employees?

I engaged a consultant who advised me to attack that problem by hiring a human resources manager. Marlene agreed, but I told her, "The last damn thing I need is a human resources person. We're doing fine." I meant that we were still a small company—now half as small as before. We still needed to watch our pennies. I did not want to spend those pennies on executive salaries for an HR manager or similar executive positions, such as a marketing manager or general counsel. I always had the fear that our trade volume could dip down again, leaving us unable to pay expensive executives. I always wanted to get a little bit more strength in the business operation, a little bit more viability before we made commitments to establish executive positions. For the time being, I felt, hiring was a function we could perform for ourselves, just as we built our own bookshelves and painted our own walls.

An exception to my policy was Bob Slezak, who we promoted to become our first-ever chief financial officer and treasurer. Bob had been hired to replace Carol Jeppeson and oversee our operations. After the crash, he was heavily involved in shutting off some of the unreliable broker-dealers and establishing procedural changes to better monitor and manage risk. He guided our efforts not just to eliminate the possibility of error, but to streamline the company, make it more efficient, and eliminate the multitude of folks we hired in Purchase and Sales who were there only to enter and reenter the same data. He had a special gift for looking at the numbers and creating financial forecasts to show me the results we could expect if I made this or that change in our spending on advertising, payroll, and so forth. When we were doing five hundred trades a day, he was already projecting how we could reach a thousand.

If Bob gave me a projection with a result I didn't like, I could ask him to change it in this way or that, and he would find yet another new approach. His forecasts were a huge help to me as I tried out different strategic approaches in my mind. For all these reasons, as I talked it over with Tom Pleiss, I felt Bob had proved himself, so we made him CFO.

Even Bob, however, had come to Ameritrade not through any formal human resources process but through our small, casual web of business and family connections—a recommendation from my mentor, Mike Naughton, and a chance meeting with Carol Jeppeson, my right hand, in a university classroom. I felt we were doing fine with an informal approach that directly addressed one of my biggest needs: loyalty. Some of my first hires, employees whose salaries I had paid while they got their licenses, had soon left to work elsewhere. I had realized I needed people who were not going to leave me. Looking for loyalty, I had hired some of my siblings and some of their spouses and their children, as well as cousins and people Marlene and I socialized with, who were bound to us by friendship.

I had hired my brother Dick, four years my junior, who was a natural salesman, with the charm and authority to handle customers when they had a complaint. He would advise others in the company how to take care of a customer who was unhappy with the way their trade was executed or the timing of a margin call. I hired my brother Jim for his management ability. I first hired my younger sister, Mary, because she needed a job in the summers during college and it was fun to have her around. Later, she came to work for us full-time; then she had a health problem that made her want to change her whole life, so she moved to California. When her health improved, she happened to get a job with a big discount broker on the West Coast, and then she returned to us with valuable experience. I loved them all. I felt they were people I could trust, and, as the eldest child in the family, I felt some responsibility to make sure they could find good jobs—as long as they would perform at the same level as nonfamily.

Dick had worked out so well, in fact, that in the mid-'80s, when I needed to keep my attention on launching and growing our different subsidiaries and replacing the computer system, I had made him president. Although I was capable of managing an operation and selling what we offered, what I most wanted to do and what I did best was figuring out how to make the company grow. It was a great help to me to have Dick oversee the day-to-day retail trading operation and act as the public face of the company, speaking for it and selling it to the world, so that I could focus on longer-term business strategy and marketing. With his charm and management ability, I knew he could do it. I felt that it was going to be a fantastic career for somebody, and I wanted my brother to have it.

We had also been well served by many employees who were not actual family but came from within the circle of those we knew and trusted. Back in the mid-'80s, for example, when I had first started to bring home a little more money, Marlene had decided to remodel the living room and she needed it painted. Her good friend was married to a CPA who had gotten laid off when his company was acquired by a larger firm. That had left the husband, Bob Fowler, in a bad position, because he was far enough along in his career that he was used to making good money, and accounting firms generally don't hire at the level he had reached. They hire kids out of college.

Bob was unemployed for a while and his family was hurting. Marlene said to me, "Joe, do you mind if I ask my friend's husband to come over and paint our living room? I saw the work he did at their house and he has great attention to detail."

In this way, Bob came to work for us essentially as a favor. We were paying him, but it was a favor that he used his talents and integrity and his willingness to work hard to do such a good job on our living room, better than we could have paid anyone else to do. When I came home for lunch, as I often did, he joined us at the lunch table and so I got to know him. I had mentioned to Marlene that the company needed some part-time help doing the accounting and she suggested I offer Bob the position. Once he joined us, the company kept growing. The part-time need became a full-time need. Bob took it on, and what he did for us as an accountant was incredible. He was a tiger for accuracy and detail, and he worked nine days a week—Saturdays and Sundays on both ends. It felt as if every time I came into the office, Bob was there.

Another of those successful accidents was Mary K. Fay, who had graduated from a community college across the Missouri River in Council Bluffs, Iowa. She started at Ameritrade in 1983 as a clerk in the dividends department of the clearing division. Within a year, she was promoted to department manager, even though she didn't have a management degree. Sometime later, she felt that one of the women who reported to her had been treated roughly by my brother Dick. He was not an easy person to take on, but she complained to him, and in response he told her, "Anybody who can stand up to me can stand up to a customer." Dick recommended Mary for a position in customer service, a department she would come to run, doing excellent work. Later, she became an operations manager, with both a manager of trading and a manager of customer service reporting to her. We had had no idea, hiring her as a clerk, that she might be capable of all that.

With successful hires like these in mind, I did not see the point of taking on an HR manager. But then, through that same informal hiring process, a human resources manager sneaked in through our back door. My wife had, I believe, ninety-eight first cousins, and one of them, John Hohman, married a woman named Susan whom I didn't really know. We saw her at a reunion of the Heng family, Marlene's mother's family, a summertime picnic lunch held in a park. A lot of larger families held their reunions in parks in order to have enough room. As I drove my family home, Marlene told me that Susan had lost her job right after their son had been accepted to Stanford. Could we find a position for her? I can recall gripping the steering wheel and saying, "I can't hire all your relatives just because they don't have jobs! That's exactly the wrong way to hire someone—because they need the work. We have to focus on what the company needs."

Nevertheless, at Marlene's suggestion, Susan submitted a résumé. She was a grown woman with three children in school, but I offered that she could take the place of one of the college kids who had been working for us answering phones and giving out stock quotes for $4.28 an hour. She agreed to take the job, with two conditions. First, that she would continue to look for something that paid better in her field, which was human resources. Second, that the supervisor in the quotes department had to approve of her. Susan wouldn't accept a job she had gotten by using her relationship with Marlene to jump the chain of command. She wanted the hire done properly. That was a sign of things to come.

Susan Hohman was the daughter of an army colonel who was relocated almost every year. Growing up, she had lived in twenty-one different homes in the United States plus one in Saigon, Vietnam. Often, the order to move again came in October, after school had started and the other kids had already found their friends. She had learned how to arrive late, size up the formal and informal rules of a new school and a new town, and determine how to make a place for herself within it. She liked to say that her entire life had been training in understanding people and organizations. She had intended to study human resources work in college, but instead she married early and took a ten-year-plus break to stay home while her children were small.

From the day she arrived at Ameritrade in 1986, given a place at a long table full of clerks with Quotron terminals and telephones, she studied how the quotes department was run, asking questions about our reliance on a fee agency for temporary workers. Sometimes, she learned, her supervisor would simply hire the last person the agency sent over to interview on a Friday because we were that desperate for someone to answer the phones Monday morning. Bill Glasz remembers seeing Susan's focus and organization early on and telling her, "You're going to develop an empire here." She was a natural leader.

During a break, Susan came to my office and told me she could rationalize our system for hiring and promotions. I told her to keep answering the phones and giving quotes, but that in her spare time she could start the work she had described. She agreed.

Susan spent weeks interviewing everyone in the company to figure out what they did. Often, she discovered, staff had been promoted so quickly that they couldn't clearly explain their job responsibilities or how they were qualified to fulfill them. Soon she began to work with a faculty member at the University of Nebraska, Omaha, to introduce a critical-thinking appraisal test, and beginning in late 1986, every employee under the Ameritrade umbrella went through that process, including me.

I didn't realize she lacked a formal background in human resources, but I would not necessarily have held that against her. After all, I was the one running the business, and I did not have an MBA. What mattered to me was that when she talked to me about our staffing situation, I understood her. We communicated comfortably. Once, she met my mother, and right away, Susan told me later, my mother said, "I know it's really hard working for my boys. I know they're really hard to work for." But Susan did not feel that way. She saw working with me as an opportunity. Like Carol Jeppeson had been with clearing, like David Kellogg had been with the computer system, Susan Hohman was entrepreneurial in an area of the company we urgently needed to develop. She identified problems herself, taught herself to invent solutions, made mistakes but admitted them quickly and learned from them. We got along very well.

Susan believed that if a person could read, write, think, and count, and if they were willing to work hard, then we could train them to do what we needed. We shared the view that one person of talent can do the work of two to three average workers, which keeps your payroll costs down. I wanted our employees to be energetic, ingenious, and willing to take a risk—entrepreneurs in their approach if not in their job description. (If they were only going to put in their hours and go home, then let them go work for the government.) And, as Bob Slezak liked to say, the Ameritrade worker was an egoless person who woke up every day with the best interests of the company at heart. Susan set out to hire for that combination of talent, drive, and commitment to the company.

To find such employees, Susan increasingly sought out and relied on objective assessments to test applicants. Her interest led us to work with Selection Research Inc. (SRI), a Nebraska-based company founded in 1969 that developed structured psychological interviews to identify individuals whose talents fit with a defined role in a particular organization. (In 1988, SRI acquired the polling company founded by George Gallup in the 1930s and took Gallup's more famous name.) Her use of formal assessments made hiring, which was already a challenge, even more of a challenge. She told me that she was hiring only one out of every eleven candidates that went through her assessments. But she said, "Joe, if we hire talent, if we hire the best, we can go to the stars." I don't think she knew exactly where the stars were, but she had a clear vision of how to find the people to take us there.

Part of her vision was to make Ameritrade a more broadly desirable place to work. She pushed for us to raise our compensation. She told me that even the fee agency that provided our temporary workers would complain when she called them: "Oh, you're Susan Hohman from Ameritrade. You're the one who wants the preppy workers but won't pay anything." I told her we could not afford big increases in pay, and she said, "All right, then let's start with small increases." She told me we needed to find a better building for our offices, "because this place doesn't breed excellence."

We also instituted a dress code. Men could wear only white, long-sleeved, 100 percent cotton shirts with ties. They weren't allowed to have facial hair. I had read that people with beards were perceived as being less trustworthy, and I wouldn't have any unshaven men. Women couldn't wear pants—they had to wear skirt suits, and anytime they left their desks, they had to wear the suit jacket.

I agreed with Susan's focus on excellence and merit. We also agreed, without ever talking about it directly, that other factors sometimes considered in hiring had no place at Ameritrade. I did not favor job candidates with degrees from big-name colleges because they often seemed to be focused on guaranteeing comfortable careers for themselves rather than expecting to work hard to help their company thrive.

It didn't matter to us if an employee was a man or a woman, what their ethnic background might be, or what they did in their private life. In the Midwest in the '80s, part of the hiring process at some companies still depended on your background—was the candidate's family English? German? Irish? Or was it something else? There were still towns in Nebraska and Iowa where an English person wanting to marry an Irish person or a Protestant wanting to marry a Catholic was unacceptable to their families, a "mixed marriage." But the values my parents had taught me were that you judged people by the quality of their work and the content of their character. Did they keep their word? Did they give their all? Those were the things that mattered, I had been taught, and I had taken those lessons to heart.

When I was a boy, there had been a family that moved into our neighborhood with a son around my age. His name was Tom, I think. He was introverted and easily frightened. He got picked on by everyone, including me. One December night, we were all going caroling. You stood on people's front porches and you sang for them. A few of us picked this boy up and pretended we were going to throw him over a porch railing. We scared him tremendously. Then we lowered him most of the way down and dropped him maybe six inches, to frighten him a little more. Well, somehow, falling only that short distance, he broke his ankle. Our fathers all heard about it. The nuns at school heard about it, too.

I came to feel ashamed that I had been part of that cruelty. My father had taught me that you don't go along with the crowd because the crowd, a lot of the time, is wrong. You don't abide by other people's value systems—you must think about and build your own.

That night was the last time I went along with a bullying crowd. When I went to college there were some boys who were said to be homosexual, and a lot of the other students avoided them and made fun of them. Nobody would sit with them in the cafeteria, but I would sit at their table. I spoke to them. It was kind of scary at first—I didn't know how a boy who liked other boys would act. I didn't know what people might think of me for talking to them. But by that time, I was independent. I didn't give a [expletive] what anybody else thought.

Of course, acting on these values was not always easy. Once, when I was a young man, my father heard about a couple in our community that was getting married. I remember him asking me, "How would *you* feel if your daughter wanted to marry a black man?" And I thought, *Oh my God, my dad is prejudiced. His idea is treat others equal but don't mix. He's teaching me one thing and thinking another.*

I realized then that these things are not easy at all. Eliminating bias is hard work and doesn't always come naturally. But I knew the essential values of my family and I tried to stand up for them in my life and in my company. Frankly, we had a difficult enough time finding competent people. We couldn't afford to restrict hiring for reasons that were not relevant to the work.

It was in this spirit that Susan Hohman, who first joined us at $4.28 an hour, became our head of human resources. Tom Pleiss and I found that we were happy with her hires, which freed us to focus our attention on other areas. After the Crash of '87, she helped me determine who was essential and whom we could lay off. She would become one of the pivotal people who shaped Ameritrade.

After the crash, when I stepped back and considered the company's overall situation, I saw that our basic strategy and financial promise had not really improved since we first offered the twenty-five-dollar trade back in the mid-'70s. Our advertising brought us customers, but despite all the innovations I had tried since then, we still had not achieved true economies of scale. We increased our revenues, but as we opened more accounts and completed more trades, our expenses went up in proportion to our income. If we were ever going to grow beyond being just a regional operator in the world of discount brokerage, as our names promised—First National Brokerage, TransTerra, Ameritrade—I had to find a way to bring in new accounts without the added expense of a lot of new staff, and the added risk that in a downturn we would again require mass layoffs.

There was a lot of talk in the business press at that time about how the future of banking was in personal computers. Any day now, we were told, everything in our lives would be handled through personal computers. It seemed that the future of the brokerage business, too, lay in the direction of computerizing what had been handled until now by clerks with telephones, paper and pencil, and "dumb" data-entry terminals. But when I looked into computerizing our trading, I found that the personal computers of the 1980s were slow and clunky. To connect a PC to our system at Ameritrade, the customer first needed to install special software from a floppy disk, which took time. When the customer wanted to check a stock quote or make a trade, unless they had a phone line dedicated to their computer, they had to dial in on a phone line with a modem, wait to establish a connection, and then use awkward software with a pre-Windows operating system. The Internet back then was still only a Defense Department system used by research scientists; no one was banking online. I don't think many Americans even knew the word *online*.

I experimented for about a year, trying to put in a computer-based system for accessing stock quotes and placing orders, but the approaches we tried were too difficult to use. Then, one day, I was making a phone call to another business. The phone rang and the call was answered not by a receptionist but by a recorded voice asking me to use the keypad on my touch-tone phone to spell the last name of the person I was trying to reach. That got me thinking.

I went to talk with the guy in charge of our technology. Could he build a software system that would allow customers to call in and use the keys of the touch-tone phone to request stock quotes and place orders? He said it had never been done before, as far as he knew. I think the suggestion took him by surprise because I wasn't asking him to do it with computers, but in a way, that was my advantage: I had no special interest in computers. My interest was in giving my customers more freedom in their trading. Did he think he could do that with a touch-tone phone? He said yeah, he could do it.

I asked him how long it would take and what it would cost, and he came back to me later with an estimate—I think it was half a million dollars and six months. Of course, he had no idea what he was talking about. No one had ever done this before in the investing business, so we had no idea what it would take to create a system that was easy to use.

He got to work. When I was roughly $600,000 into it, he said, "Mr. Ricketts, we need another couple hundred thousand, another couple of months, and then we'll have it done." After that, he needed some more. Where do you stop? We were learning by trial and error. The only way to get it right was to first get it wrong. So, I just kept going, putting more money in. Finally, I lost my patience and fired him and hired somebody else, but then it was the same thing again every few months until I was in for a few million.

I had faith in the idea because I could picture the future benefit so clearly. We might spend a lot to get set up, but once we did, we would have an automated trading system that could grow and grow without requiring me to hire more people. With most of our costs behind us and limitless possibility for growth, our profits could rise not in steady proportion to our costs, as they had always done, but exponentially. For that, I was willing to place what was for us a big and risky bet.

While spending far more money and time than I had anticipated on the touch-tone phone project, I began to do some research on its marketing. I organized focus groups of five or ten customers at a time and described the service and how they would key in their requests for quotes and orders. The letters ABC were on the 2 key, while DEF were on the 3 key. To generate the ticker BF, for example, you would have to press the 2 key twice and then the 3 key three times. It was that easy, I said. I only talked about the service and not about any other considerations, such as price. Then I asked: Would you be interested in trying that?

The response was, overwhelmingly, no. Customers in the focus groups asked, "Why should I learn a new method that works off a touch-tone phone when I can use that phone to call and talk to a broker?" They already had a simple stock-trading system that they liked. "I dial the 800 number and reach the broker I know personally, who gives me good service. Why change?"

Hoping for a different response, I sent a note out to all our customers along with their quarterly statements, explaining the new service we were developing. *Was this something that would interest them?* I asked. I was ignored.

Between the discouraging market research I had done and the increasing cost of getting the system up, my anxiety was very high. Millions of dollars into this project, it looked like I had a loser. My son Todd, when he tried out the touch-tone system, said, "It sucks." He didn't find it especially easy or appealing to use. The reasonable move was to quit and cut my losses.

But again, I benefited from the independence my family had taught me. You don't go along with the crowd, because the crowd, a lot of the time, is wrong. I wanted to give this touch-tone approach the chance to prove itself, just like you give a person the chance to show their talents and their character, and never mind what others say about them.

Maybe I'm just a stubborn, egotistical son of a bitch. My son

Tom says I'm pathologically independent. It's true that I think I'm right until proven wrong. That's part of it. But another part, the unusual part that I can't explain, is that when everybody tells me I'm wrong, my comfort level goes up. If the world is going in one direction and I'm going in the other, I take it as a sign that I must be onto something good. I feel excited, happy, relaxed. Precisely because I'm all alone, I imagine how valuable it will be when I reach the treasure and no one else even suspects where it's buried.

I don't know where that part of me comes from. My commitment to the touch-tone project, though, was not simple stubbornness. I believed then what I believe today: People feel better when they take control of their own choices. As a boy, I would sit still in church when my mother told me so, but I yearned to be outside and free. This touch-tone technology, I felt, was a way to offer more freedom. Customers could make their own trades by themselves exactly when they chose, with no middleman. If they didn't realize yet that they wanted this freedom, it was because they were focused on what was familiar. As Henry Ford once observed about developing the Model T, if he had asked his customers what they wanted for personal transportation, they would have answered, "Faster horses."

I was trying to anticipate what human nature would prefer for stock trading before anyone had experienced what I had to offer. For that reason, even in 1988, when the tech people finally got the touch-tone system working, I was afraid no one would give it a chance. I needed a breakthrough advertising concept, something that would motivate people to learn the unfamiliar system and try it out.

On the wholesale side of trading, we paid brokers so many pennies per share traded, but no one had ever offered that to retail customers. I decided to startle the world into giving its attention to our services by offering a trade for just three cents a share. I got an image in my head of my brother Dick, smiling in a good suit with a touch-tone phone in one hand and three pennies in the other, showing that three cents was all you had to pay him to trade one share by phone. I hoped it would be a little campy, a little fun, to show the pennies, and also easy to understand. We hired a photographer to take the picture and a professional designer to structure the ad on the page, and they got the effect I was after: a charming, prosperous-looking man you could trust to trade your stocks at a lower price. A simple and exciting offer.

We also needed a name that would help everyone understand that the touch-tone service was separate from our usual retail offering. I didn't want to spend money on a marketing firm to name it, so I organized an employee pool. We asked everyone to submit their suggestions for names, promising the winner a gift certificate for two, dinner at an Omaha restaurant worth twenty-five bucks, which in 1988 bought a pretty good dinner. Out of the suggestions, we chose Accutrade. Customers seemed a bit leery of this automated system with no person to keep an eye on it, so we liked the "accu," which reassured that the trades would be accurate.

We ran the print advertisement in the back of the *Wall Street Journal* and a little in *Barron's*. The response was huge. So many people who saw the ad were intrigued enough to spend the five minutes learning how the touch-tone system worked. They began to use it and our business began to grow fast. And of course, we were the first to come out with a touch-tone service. Schwab, the biggest of the discount brokers, didn't introduce theirs until 1989. E*Trade never did it at all.

With the launch of Accutrade, we grew tremendously. By September 1991, for the first time, Ameritrade had annual revenues of almost $10 million. The company's nearly $56 million in assets included $22.4 million in capital reserves (to comply with federal regulations) and $23.2 million in receivables from customers and brokers.

Between January and December 1992 alone, the number of employees grew from 125 to 142, bringing the company almost back to its pre-crash size. At the close of that fiscal year in September, return on equity reached 56.8 percent—almost double my goal of 30 percent per year.

Looking back, I can see that although we developed the touch-tone system more than ten years after we had launched the company, in terms of the significant steps in our development, this was just the second major inflection point. The only other thing like it, an exponential change in our progress, had been the original advertisement in 1975 offering to trade a hundred shares for a twenty-five-dollar commission. That first inflection point established that we could survive as a regional business, but this second one in 1988 gave us the means to compete nationally.

With results like that, my minority stockholders began to pressure me either to pay dividends on the stock or go public. Neither, I felt, was going to happen in the near term. Over and over in my letters to stockholders, I made it clear that we were in a risky business and that I intended to keep on taking risks that might make others uncomfortable. I would not sacrifice opportunity, I warned them, just to satisfy shareholders who felt more risk-averse. If they weren't comfortable, they should sell their stock to me. According to the bylaws of the corporation, I was the only market for company stock, and I was ready to pay three times the book value to anyone who wanted to sell. If they stayed for the ride, however, they shouldn't complain when it got bumpy.

When I offered to buy them out, they shut up and enjoyed dramatic growth. The nation was emerging from a recession, and in the securities industry as a whole only large investment banks enjoyed better pretax profit margins than discount brokers. In this period of industry-wide success, Ameritrade outpaced most of its peers. As the bull market continued between September 1992 and September 1993, the company's total assets grew from $93.3 million to $151.2 million. Revenues increased from $15 million to $23.8 million. Most important, consolidated net income more than doubled from $1.64 million to $4.14 million, with a 94 percent overall return on equity—more than three times my yearly goal.

Expanding so fast, the company was nearly bursting out of its downtown offices. We purchased a corporate office building on the southwest side of Omaha just off Interstate 80 and moved into this new space the first weekend of December 1993. As soon as we moved in, we had to put a great big double wing on it, a two-story wing. We had a new computer room with space for all our servers and a separate room for our printers, because they made so much noise. The printers had ink ribbons like typewriters, and the print heads were drums that spun at 3000 rpm, with hammers timed to the metal letters and numbers on the spinning drums. Printing out our reports made a huge racket, quite impressive. It was a very, very exciting time.

Not everyone at the company, however, enjoyed our success equally. The more we were able to automate and computerize our operations, the less we needed the people who helped us sell stocks and call market makers the old-fashioned, telephone-based way. Marlene loved working the phones, but now she moved to writing directions for how the automated systems worked. The fun was out of it. After Todd stayed home from school for a few days with an illness and Marlene stayed home with him, I told her I didn't need her to come back to the office. She never worked at the new building off Interstate 80. I don't think she ever forgave me for automating the OTC trading department.

By now I was in my fifties. I was independent financially and finally felt I could relax and enjoy myself a little. I hiked the Appalachian

Trail for a week by myself, enjoying the chance to think without interruption while taking in the luxury of what nature provided, but it was too strenuous to carry all that equipment and water by myself. The next time, I went back with my wife and Jerry Gress, my old high school friend who had lent me money for the business when I was starting out. Jerry and I would hike the trail for the day and then come out to a road to meet Marlene and other friends who had been exploring small towns and going to antique stores nearby. They would pick us up in the car and take us back to the hotel to clean up. Then we would go out to dinner, sleep in beds with fresh sheets, and do it all again the next day. Those were very pleasant times.

One afternoon, as Jerry and I came out of Shenandoah National Park, we saw a rally of Honda motorcycles, a sort of outdoor convention where bikers exchange stories, ideas, and equipment. There were hundreds of motorcycles. Back when we were young, Jerry and I had wanted to ride, and now I saw that lots of the people on bikes had gray hair and wore tennis shoes. The next morning, at a pancake house, I asked a guy with gray hair if he'd been riding all his life. He was a barber, retired. He said, "No, no. I just started a few years ago." And I thought: *I can do that too*.

I told my brother Dick, who liked to ride, and he said, "You ought to get a bike."

"Find one for me!" I told him, and he did. Jerry got one too, but we had no idea how to ride them, so we took lessons. I practiced on a small motorcycle of Dick's, just trying it out in my neighborhood where there wasn't a lot of traffic. I took the whole summer to do that before I got on the big one Dick had found for me, and then I discovered that riding was the most fun thing in my life. I loved that combination of control and freedom. Because we were in the Midwest, we could find roads through beautiful countryside without much traffic. It was wonderful to get out in the country and have that feeling—*I'm fifty miles outside Omaha. I can go anywhere. I can do anything!* I loved it, just loved it.

I would be wrong, however, to make it sound as if now, at last, Ameritrade found smooth sailing. We simply were not in that kind of business. Our profits soared in the early '90s, but once again, we nearly shut down. This time it was the result of a lawsuit.

The case first came to light in September 1993 when officials in Columbiana County, Ohio, called the FBI to help them find $6 million that was missing from the county's bank accounts. As the investigators unraveled the story, they discovered that the county treasurer had turned to his son, who was not licensed as an Ohio securities salesman, to invest over $10 million in county funds. The son was indicted and accused of falsely representing that the funds were safely invested in certificates of deposit and US Treasury notes.

Instead of investing them safely, the son had opened a brokerage account with Ameritrade under the name S&S Investments. He invested the county's money in various high-risk instruments including call and put index options, and lost around $3.5 million in the market. He also opened brokerage accounts with firms in Detroit and Palo Alto and used more than three hundred thousand dollars in public funds to buy himself a condominium, a Jaguar, jewelry, and vacations. He eventually pleaded guilty to fifty-nine counts related to securities fraud and theft. Sentenced to nine years in federal prison, he was ordered to pay $4 million in restitution to the county.

I learned about this mess late on a Friday afternoon. Tom Pleiss and Bob Slezak had already dug up the facts before they pulled me into a conference room and revealed the bad news. Their faces were white, their dispositions dire. They had reviewed all the relevant rules and they believed we were going to be held responsible for the county's millions in losses. If we had to pay out that much money, they knew, the company would fall out of compliance with the net capital requirements. If we had a net capital violation, of course, the company would be shut down. They looked like ghosts that afternoon because they were expecting that we would all lose our jobs.

After talking the situation through, I gave everyone their marching orders: *On Monday morning, we're going to work up the necessary reports to document our involvement with the customer, and we will bring in such and such attorney to work with us. Double-check that we understand the challenge correctly, then on Monday we'll take care of everything. And for now? Everybody have a good weekend.*

As I headed toward the door, Bob and Tom looked stunned. Bob asked me, "Joe, do you understand what we're facing?"

They claim to this day that when I left the conference room I was whistling. I suppose they had expected me to curse, scream, yell—I don't know what. They say I walked out cheerfully, and they stared after me, mouths agape.

The truth is I wasn't actually whistling. I knew, though, that if I gave in and showed my fear, that fear would spread through the company, undermining the feeling that we were a great company, growing like mad, worth ten or twelve hours a day of devoted work. It was up to me to act as the leader, to show that all was not lost, and to not let them see I was afraid, though I was. I felt fear, but not to the extent they did. I remembered when the SEC shut us down in '75, and I felt as though we were in another situation like that, a bad situation but one we could survive.

In facing my fear, I had one advantage over them: they were CPAs, trained to worry about every possible risk. I was an entrepreneur, so I had learned to live with risk. Risk was with me all the time. I knew by then that when a crisis comes, all you can do is roll up your sleeves, do your work, and then get some rest and try to enjoy your downtime. Sometimes the outcome comes down to luck, but the harder you work, the luckier you get.

We went into the lawsuit with serious concerns. First, details had come to light that made Ameritrade look bad, such as records showing how the county treasurer's son had moved funds to a separate account, then instructed us to wire it to Caesars Palace in Las Vegas so he could gamble and carouse with it. The reality was that we had been in the dark, but some of the small details made it sound as if we had been in cahoots with the embezzler while he partied with public funds.

Second was the amount. My entire approach to running the business was to reinvest excess cash. So, we had no rainy-day fund for this sort of crisis. If a jury had awarded the county several million dollars, that would have been a death blow for us. Even if we were victorious in a long court fight, the story could cast a shadow on our reputation, making it harder in the future to secure capital or to take the company public. The consequences of both losing and winning could bankrupt us.

You may ask, why was this Ameritrade's problem? Why should Ameritrade be responsible for keeping customers from harming themselves or their fellow citizens in Columbiana County? If we had been a casino, we would not have had to worry. The guy could have played craps until he lost everything and that would have been understood as his problem, not ours. But a brokerage is not considered to be morally equivalent to a casino, and it operates in a different regulatory structure. The regulators had created that structure based on the model of a full-service brokerage, which provides stock recommendations for its customers and therefore has an obligation to know their customers and consider what is in their best interests. As discount brokers, however, we did not give recommendations. Our way of doing business gave us no chance to get to know our customers. We simply processed their trades. I felt that rules designed for the full-service brokers should not apply to us, but it was unclear how we would be viewed in the courtroom.

I could also see that this lawsuit was going to be a road game: the poor people of Ohio would be the plaintiffs, in Ohio, suing the heartless brokerage giant from far away to the west. Of course, we were not in fact the giant in our business, and we had not acted heartlessly: The embezzler had made all the right moves to make it look as if the money belonged to him. We were certain we had done nothing wrong, but less certain we could win the hearts of the wronged people of Ohio.

As the case began to move forward, it became clear that the government was at least partly receptive to my position. They weren't simply going to hold us to the old standards for full-service brokers. That meant the case would be long and complicated. The county concluded it wouldn't do them any good to wage a long court battle, and they offered to settle. On December 30, 1994, I agreed to pay $1.5 million. It was a heavy price, but we were able to pay it and still meet our net capital requirements. We had no better choice than to count ourselves lucky to remain in business.

As Bob Slezak would say, "That was a stomach churner."

CHAPTER 9

I always kept one eye on the possible threats from our competition, especially Charles Schwab & Company. Back in 1981, the San Francisco company's revenues had been $41 million dollars. By 1985, they were nearly $200 million. The nation's largest discount broker, by 1986 Schwab had 1.4 million customers, three times its nearest competitor.

Schwab was referred to as a discount broker because they charged lower commissions than the full-service brokers, but their commissions were not as low as ours. A large number of physical offices added to their costs. Their big advantage was being located in California, the state that is one of the biggest economies in the world. Also, as a subsidiary of Bank of America, they had shared in B of A's gilt-edged reputation and had access to that company's deep pockets. They spent $20 million a year on advertising. Because they had so much marketing power, I was concerned that they could put us out of business.

Had I been Charles Schwab, seeing some upstarts out of Nebraska survive the crash, take off again with a newfangled touch-tone service, and steal their market share, I would have gone for the kill. I would have dropped my commissions to match Ameritrade's pricing or even a little lower. That would have significantly reduced our growth. In time, a larger company would have come along and swallowed Ameritrade up.

It was either eat or be eaten, and I imagined that Schwab could have had us for dinner. I didn't know what the thought processes were at Schwab or big full-service brokerages like Merrill, but over time I concluded they did not consider us a serious threat. They held their commission rates high enough that we could grow and prosper as the low-price alternative. We went on picking up new customers all over the United States. It is possible they didn't take us seriously because no one believed a significant financial player could come from the Midwest.

Of course, there would have been benefits for me in selling Ameritrade to a bigger company as Schwab had done, but I had no interest in selling my company at any price. I wanted to be the one to buy others, to become the eater. That was part of my character. I could see clearly in my mind the day when Ameritrade would become the biggest broker in the country, as measured by the number of trades, and I said so freely. To everyone I told back then, though, even my top management, I think that goal was unimaginable. Had they been perfectly candid, they might have said I was getting fuzzy in the head from too many long motorcycle rides. That didn't concern me. If anything, it made me feel better.

I realized, however, that if we were going to become number one in trades, we would need to change the focus of the company. I already had my basic systems in place: advertising would keep us acquiring accounts while automation and computerization would provide economies of scale. Now, I needed to shift the emphasis from keeping us running to achieving exponential growth, and these changes would have to begin at the top.

By early 1991, my brother Dick had been president of our brokerage business for nearly five years. He was a natural salesman and an effective manager of a trading room, and he had been great as the face of the company in our marketing efforts and our communications with the media. But he was not an entrepreneur, not an innovator for a company evolving into something new. As he himself said, "My brother is very creative. I am not." The more changes I made in the company as he had known it, the less comfortable he felt. The tension was taking a toll on our relationship, and I was worried that the split could become permanent. It was difficult for us both because of the love between us.

In the spring of 1991, we decided together that Dick would leave Ameritrade. He owned about 7 percent of the company's stock, and I did not have the cash to buy him out. We agreed to a multiyear payment schedule that would liquidate Dick's equity by 1995. I knew that using company cash to buy my brother's shares would slow our growth, but I felt there was no other choice. Dick left Ameritrade a financially independent man.

I could have taken over the duties of president again, but I knew I would never be a great president because I didn't care to be one. I felt the same way about sales: although I was a good salesman, it bored me to sell the same story over and over again to different prospects. Nor did I want to go back to giving all those interviews to the goddamned financial media. I wanted to spend my time marketing to the broader public—to use my ingenuity to find ways to increase revenues and profits by taking big, strategic risks. That was always what I had enjoyed the most, and in my experience, no reward under heaven will motivate a person as much as doing the things you most like to do, those things you were born to be good at. Looking back, I see that I was lucky that my gifts and the needs of my shareholders aligned: it was better for me and them if I stuck to what I did best. At the time, though, I only knew that I was happy to be doing it.

One day I went to talk to Susan Hohman, my head of human resources. "I've got my systems in place," I told her. "Now I need excellent people, people smarter than I am who can help me grow this business. Can you find me those people?" We had never talked about hiring that way before. For years, I had provided the entrepreneurial impulse and had filled all my top management positions with accountants to make sure that the risks I took didn't get us in trouble. Tom Pleiss, Bob Slezak, Kurt Halvorson, and Bob Fowler—they had all started as accountants, and they were essential to the company. If they told me they were against something I wanted to try, I took them seriously. Tom Pleiss used to say, "My job, Joe, is keeping you out of jail." However, in hiring so many accountants, I had overdeveloped the company's risk-management function. The accountants were wonderful at their jobs, but as is often the case with great accountants, they were control people, not marketing people.

I asked Susan Hohman to help identify a new president, someone who could lead the company with more of a focus on marketing. She knew we were getting beyond her abilities, so she went back to the folks at Selection Research Inc., the Gallup company that had provided our assessment tests, for guidance. The name they suggested was Joseph Konen.

The son of a machinist, Joe Konen had grown up in the suburbs of Chicago. After earning an MBA in finance, he went to work for General Foods, then to the equipment manufacturer Allis-Chalmers for eleven years, and later to SRI, which brought him to Nebraska. He had taken responsibility for capital planning, divestitures, and acquisitions. He had the sales skills we would need and an attitude to match. "Accountants," he told me, "couldn't sell sex to sailors."

At Allis-Chalmers, Konen had observed that in office work, unlike in factory work, there were huge differences in the productivity of individual workers. One reconciliation clerk might reconcile three bank accounts in a day, while another could consistently complete twenty. Konen became interested in how to identify high-performing workers and how to recognize and reward them for giving their best performance.

I hired him to take over Ameritrade Clearing, our wholesale side, from veteran Tom Pleiss. I needed Tom in the role of controller so he could keep telling me the truth about our financial situation and make sure I stayed out of jail. My hope was that Joe would learn the business and then take over as president of the entire company.

When he arrived at Ameritrade Clearing, they averaged about eight hundred trades a day. If one day they had to clear a thousand, it seemed to Konen, people hung their heads unhappily because they had extra work to do. They preferred the slower days, but of course, we wanted them to do more work, faster. Konen established bonuses for individual performance and for raising the average number of trades per month. He kicked off the new approach with a high-energy meeting for which he persuaded me to dress up in a football uniform. He dressed as a cheerleader, if I remember correctly. He helped change the culture so that employees now felt that doing more trades than ever made it a good day.

Unlike me, in other words, Konen liked managing. He was interested in getting better at it and he did it better than I could. He was even good at managing me. I had acquired a reputation for micromanaging, which surprised me because it was not my image of myself. I believed that once you hired good people, you should leave them to do their work their way, and not check up on how many hours they were at their desks or how they chose to allocate their time. However, there were occasions when I discovered that an employee wasn't fulfilling specific responsibilities, and then I would give an instruction like, "From now on, I want you to spend half your time on this." Konen was helpful because he could follow behind me and explain, "Don't take Ricketts word for word. He doesn't mean you have to count up your hours and spend half of them on this particular task. He means that this task is important. He wants you to get it done. Focus on that."

When I had an idea that Konen thought was wrong, he tended to say, "Well, you could do that if you want to, Joe. Here are the pros and cons, and if that's truly what you want to do, we'll figure something out." I appreciated that he weighed the costs and benefits for me and then waited for me to make my own decision.

In October 1994, I made Joe Konen president and chief operating officer of the entire company. Even while he was president, he had a funny saying about his role, though I probably didn't hear him say it until much later. He would say, "Ameritrade? That's Joe Ricketts's baby, his daughter. And me? I'm not the president. I'm the guy dating her. If I treat her right and bring her home early, I can stick around for a while."

At the same time that we were hiring new management, we were again feeling the strain on our computer system. If we had a rush of orders, our system might get backed up so that orders were not executed at the time the customers had put them in. If we executed at the wrong time, we had to give the customer the price from the exact time the order was placed and eat the loss.

In addition to that front-office problem, the computer system was also struggling on the back end. The overnight processing that made sure we put the trades into customers' accounts and tracked the movement of their dollars was having an increasingly hard time keeping up. Our lagging recordkeeping was an ongoing source of uncertainty, a drag on our growth, and it raised the concern that the regulators would tell us we were doing more trades than we could handle and require us to cut back.

We also had conflicts with customers around system crashes that interrupted online trading. When our online system was down, I preferred that customers use the touch-tone system, because it eliminated the high costs of live customer service. But when the system was down, many preferred to speak to a live person. In that case, I insisted they pay the higher rate, because their call was costing me money. That irritated our customers, who felt they had only called in because our computer system had let them down. The whole situation would lead to arguments about whether they had to pay the higher fee, and arguments with customers were the last thing we wanted. Slowly I was forced to admit that despite the extraordinary quality of the BOSS system that Dave Kellogg had built us in the 1970s, we needed a replacement.

I spent a lot of 1992 studying the options for a new clearing system with a new back-office data processing system, but technology was changing so fast that finding the right replacement felt almost impossible. Way back in 1965, Intel cofounder Gordon Moore had predicted that technical innovations would lead to a doubling of computing power every two years, and Moore's Law became a torment to me: the computing power I had purchased in 1977 for $700,000 was, in 1992, worth less than $50,000. Everything I could buy today would be outdated in a year or two. This is the kind of problem that wakes an entrepreneur up at two in the morning.

As a business matter, if you're going to put a lot of money into equipment, you have to raise your prices enough to pay for it during the time you use it. But I was not doing enough trading volume to pay for the systems I was considering before they became antiquated.

What do you do in a situation like that? You must assume that you will increase your trading volume at a faster rate, so that you can earn enough to cover what you will spend. But when you plan around an assumption like that, you are essentially betting your future on a guess about achieving growth. That's a nerve-racking guess to have to make. Wasn't there another solution?

Researching the problem further, I met Bill Simpson, a consultant well known for developing a major computer system for Citicorp. I hired him to evaluate the existing systems on the market, but he saw the same problem I did: everything available was already too old, and developing a new system would be too expensive, $4 or $5 million, he estimated. Then we had another idea: What if we built the new system not just to serve Ameritrade, but to sell to other brokers as well? There were lots of brokerages that needed better computer systems, but hardly any could afford them. We came up with the notion to start a consortium of brokers who would all put in seed capital to develop a next-generation computer system. Once we had the basic system in place, we imagined, each company could tailor it to their own needs. In the brokerage business, companies that compete in the marketplace will sometimes cooperate in other areas—on our approach to regulation or investment banking, for example.

I had high hopes for this consortium, but the project drifted without firm deadlines or measures of accountability. Nearly two years and $3 million later, we finally admitted it was never going to work. Our systems still strained to keep up. We patched and upgraded them as well as we could, but I worried about how long we could go on that way.

By 1995, the stock market was booming again, driven by low interest rates and a relatively cheap dollar. Broad increases in American productivity, fueled by investments in new technology, allowed companies to do more with fewer people, which fed corporate profits and encouraged mergers. Market forces, changing economic theories, and activist investors put pressure on regulators and Congress throughout the 1990s to restructure the financial services regulations created during the Great Depression. The banking industry continued to push for repeal of the regulatory barriers erected by Glass-Steagall, and they were able to win victories that resulted in a substantial blurring of what had once been a bright line between the commercial and investment banking systems. This offered new business opportunities for brokers, including relief from some of the operational burdens of regulation. With all these factors in play, stock prices soared. The Dow Jones Industrial Average broke 6,000 in October 1996 and then 7,000 in April of '97.

Part of what lifted the market was a generational change in investing. The World War II generation, whose careers had developed during some of the most prosperous years in American history, was beginning to transfer its wealth to the baby boomers. As boomers themselves turned fifty, many became increasingly concerned about their retirements and started pouring money into stocks and mutual funds in their IRAs and 401(k) plans. With their nest eggs invested, many of these boomers became avid watchers of the market. They fed a growing media industry providing business and stock market news. As financial journalist Roger Lowenstein observed, for the first time "people talked about stocks in their homes and offices and wherever they went; they could scarcely escape. A little electronic ribbon began to appear at the bottom of the television, to flash across the windows of banks, to flicker in airport waiting rooms: the ribbon that was the ubiquitous presence, the daily barometer." With the explosion of information on investing, more people felt prepared to make their own investing decisions—a trend that reinforced our market opportunities, and we looked for ways to expand our marketing effort to reach them.

We hit on the idea of producing a half-hour television show at our offices called *Independent Investor* that could carry Accutrade's advertising to the growing population of self-directed investors. The thirty-minute segment featured stock pickers bantering about specific stocks or investment sectors. We were the underwriter and our ads ran during commercial breaks. The first couple of shows aired in 1992 on CNBC as paid programming, but eventually the show was syndicated in over eighty markets. We also forged a joint marketing effort with *Louis Rukeyser's Wall Street*, a popular financial advice newsletter sent to nearly 30 million Americans.

One of Joe Konen's first hires was Michael Anderson, a sales and marketing executive Konen knew from Majers Marketing Research who scored exceptionally well on the SRI assessments. Anderson took over as director of marketing and sales for Ameritrade Clearing when Konen became president of the whole company. Mike had a great sales sense, and he and I became the national salespersons for Ameritrade, though this came as a surprise to Mike. One day he was sitting beside me on a plane, squeezed in like sardines on a Midwest Express flight to New York, and I said, "You know, Mike, we need to make new television commercials for Accutrade."

"Is that right?" he said.

"You and I are going to be in the commercials."

"We will?" Mike asked. "What will we do?"

"We'll be like those two guys who advertise wine coolers."

"Bartles and Jaymes."

"Yeah, those guys."

For the first commercial, Michael came into the little studio where we shot the half-hour investing show, and I said, "Are you ready to go?"

"I'm pretty sure," he said. "Where's the teleprompter?"

Rick Davis, who was shooting the commercials for us on-site, said, "Oh, there's no teleprompter."

"What?" asked Mike.

"You were supposed to memorize your lines," I said. "I know mine."

"Nobody told me," Mike said. He had to learn his lines quick.

We would shoot a commercial with almost no rehearsal, and unless there were big glaring errors, we had it edited and then *boom*, there it would be on CNBC. The cable news network was new, and it let us reach the market of educated investors. Because advertising rates weren't high, we could afford to run our spots eight times a day. That was how we started getting our name out nationally. Altogether, by the middle of 1993, I was investing nearly $400,000 a month in advertising, but even that sum was below my target. My goal was a million a month, but I didn't have the cash to do it until 1995. I felt sure that with enough advertising we could conquer the world, but I still had to worry about keeping enough cash to meet the net capital requirements.

Soon, as we grew, we found that we had new competition. In January 1994, the Sherwood Group, one of the old-line, full-service brokerage firms, launched a new subsidiary in New York named National Discount Brokers, offering a flat fee of thirty dollars per trade plus a three-dollar handling charge for orders up to five thousand shares. For larger trades, the company added a penny a share for the entire order. In response to this new low commission, many other discounters dropped their prices, beginning what the *Washington Post* called "The Duel of the Discount Brokerages." I recognized the competitive threat, but I did not want to cannibalize Accutrade's margins by lowering my price when some of our established customers were still content to pay three cents per share with a forty-eight-dollar minimum. Instead, I decided to create a new brand to compete head-on with National Discount Brokers.

I had an idea that the best person to lead this new subsidiary might be Peter, my eldest son, though at that time none of my children worked for Ameritrade.

I had not been especially close to any of my kids when they were younger. I understood parenthood to mean that it was Marlene's job to raise the children and mine to provide for them financially. When I took Pete to start his first year at the University of Chicago, I was proud that he had been admitted to such a fine school. I remembered how jealous I had been as a kid of those classmates whose parents had paid their way through college, and I felt that Peter must understand that I had showed my love by working hard to earn his tuition so he didn't have to pay his way as I had done.

In the moment before I left him in his dorm room, I felt a swell of emotion. I said, "Goodbye, Pete. I love you." It's possible that was the first time I had said so out loud.

"Love me?" Pete said. "You don't even know me!"

It was true that we hadn't found many ways to get to know each other. As a boy, Pete had adored fishing, but it never interested me. I had no hobbies to share with him. Vacations bored me. And although I had coached each child for one year of Little League, I did it mostly because Marlene and the kids pressed it on me. I had no feel for baseball or being a Little League dad. My youngest son, Todd, still reminds me that when he was in fourth grade, I was the only coach for his team who didn't vote for him to play in the all-star game. Marlene reminds me that I didn't make it to Tom's high school graduation or Todd's college graduation.

Fathers in my family had always been stern and proper, and functioned as the disciplinarians. Mothers I knew growing up would say to a misbehaving child, "Go to the corner and wait till your dad gets home." My children had known me as the man who left early in the morning and came home expecting obedience, hard work, and honesty.

Once they grew up and left home, however, each one, in turn, going to college in Chicago, I had the chance to get to know them differently. I would travel there for business and invite them out for dinner or a drink. Sometimes they brought along friends. I enjoyed treating the young people to steak at Lawry's The Prime Rib, or oysters at the Cape Cod Room in the Drake Hotel. After the meal ended, I would keep the drinks coming, and we would joke around and laugh. Tom remembers a night we wound up sitting in a booth at McDonald's for a late-night snack. Doing an imitation of the guy in the *Super Size Me* film poster, I filled my mouth with french fries until they were sticking out from between my lips, and just went on talking as if nothing unusual was going on. Everyone laughed. I relished those chances to visit with my kids and begin to know the adults they were becoming.

My brother Bob also lived in Chicago. He was a great guy and took a lot of pleasure in spending time with my kids. I always knew there was something different about Bob, but I could never put my finger on it. He had gone to seminary high school and planned to be a priest, but then he made a different choice, serving in Vietnam and becoming an artist. When my kids were still teenagers, he talked to them as though they were adults, as though their thoughts mattered. Laura remembers how Bob would ask her opinion of women's lib, Title IX, and whether women should serve in the military, hot-button issues not discussed in my house because Marlene was very conservative. Bob was the kids' favorite uncle.

He was also gay, which our brother Jim says he always knew, but I didn't see it. Bob only came out to the family because he contracted AIDS. He called me from a hospital in 1983 and explained his situation. I remember that I had only recently learned about AIDS from a cover story in *Time*. I said, "My God, Bob. You're going to die."

He said, "No, I'm going to fight it."

Our mother couldn't understand that her son was gay. She did not accept that men could love other men. She said, "We don't tell anyone."

We had an aunt in Illinois who had been like a second mother to Bob, but when she found out, she told him, "I never want you to come back to my house again." I remember another member of my family saying, "Bob's gay—what are we going to do?"

I said, "Didn't you hear what Bob said? He's dying. He's family. Who cares if he's gay? We're going to take care of my brother."

My mother felt ashamed of Bob. I did not. I told anyone whom I believed cared for Bob and could help him. My mother didn't need to know whom I told. But I was afraid. AIDS was new then and still mostly unknown. At the time, scientists were not yet sure how it spread. When my brother Dick and I visited Bob in the hospital, he was in quarantine.

Bob was treated and then sent home with the knowledge that he might only have a year to live. The local doctors we brought him to see were afraid to treat him because they thought he might be contagious. Finally, we found a doctor who lived down the street who was willing to have him as a patient. That doctor lived up to his Hippocratic oath. Many years later, I attended his funeral and told everyone gathered there that his willingness to treat my brother was a true demonstration of character.

Bob passed the next year, in 1984. I was glad at least that my kids had seen me offer my brother compassion. I did not abandon him. Your kids pick up on what you do, not what you say, and this was a way I could show them the meaning of family.

In those years, my son Pete earned an undergraduate degree in biology from the University of Chicago and started work in a protein biochemistry lab. When he realized he didn't want to be a bench scientist, he looked around for a job and landed at Lexecon, an economic consulting firm providing economic expertise in legal cases. Then he went back to the University of Chicago to get an MBA. The summer between his first and second years, as Ameritrade began to look at growing by acquiring smaller competitors, he came back to Omaha to do some analytical work for Bob Slezak, our CFO. After Pete got his MBA, he worked in direct marketing at Union Pacific, then at an environmental consulting firm, where he was frustrated to receive little training or performance evaluation.

"They don't track how many opportunities we brought in versus how many we closed," he told me. "How are they supposed to judge whether we are any good at our jobs?"

Pete was not brokenhearted when, during a down cycle, the consulting firm laid him off. I told him, "You know, you're twenty-nine. If you're going to come back and work for the company, this would be a great time."

I was very excited to have one of my children join what I had always hoped would remain a family business. I was also very clear about my rules. As I had told them all: *You can come work for the company when you turn thirty, but you have to work for other companies first and then start at whatever level you've attained already. If you've worked as a janitor, you come to the company as a janitor. If you've earned a certain level of salary, you come to Ameritrade and receive that salary.*

Pete agreed to join the company. Before moving back to Omaha, he took a six-week vacation to Australia, because new hires at Ameritrade received only one week of vacation their first year. His first day, I walked him to Mary Fay's office and said, "This is my son, Peter. Would you find him a job?" The suddenness of the request surprised both of them. Mary Fay put him to work like any other new associate who needed to learn the retail side of the business, in a front-line position answering phones and looking up stock quotes on the Quotron system—the same small Quotron terminals he and his siblings used to play with when they had visited the office as kids.

Pete also took calls confirming that stock orders had filled. When a customer called in, he would put them on hold, set the phone down on the desk, walk over to a drawer of paper files and dig through them alphabetically, looking for the customer's name. Then he would pull out the trade ticket and see if the confirmation ticket was stapled to it. If so, he would walk back to his desk and read them the confirmation, then hang up, walk back to the drawer, and refile it. Even though by now we had an automated trading system, with some customers using the touch-tone system and a smaller number dialing in on modems to use our pre-Windows, DOS-based software, many customers still traded the old way. Pete started from there.

While he worked the phones by day, Pete studied at night and on weekends for his securities license exams. Once he passed, I came to him with a proposition. I asked him to assemble a team and spend the next six months launching a new broker-dealer subsidiary to compete with National Discount Brokers, the deep discounter that had set off the price war on stock trading. Our new brand would be Internet-only, no phone number at all, meant for customers who knew what they were doing and did not need customer service. My original name for the company was JP Securities, for Joe and Pete, but Pete picked the name Ceres, after the Roman goddess of agriculture, because her statue sits atop the Chicago Board of Trade Building.

As Pete took on this first management role, we had some conflict. There was a meeting at which he disagreed with me in front of a roomful of people. Afterward, I took him aside and said, "Don't ever do that again."

"What are you talking about?" he asked.

"Don't ever disagree with me again, not in front of other people.

It's disrespectful. If you have a point of view, give it to me one-on-one, off to the side." This was poor management on my part, but as I've said, I didn't know good management. For years after that, Pete would joke that I wanted to fire him and that he was lucky to have his mother to protect his job. The reality, though, was that we went to lunch together every day we were both in the office. Pete would say later that the choice to work with me was the second-best decision of his life, after marrying his wife. It was a blessing for both of us.

By the time Pete had Ceres ready for business, others in the industry were competing with National Discount Brokers by offering a twenty-five-dollar flat trade. The *New York Times* ran a headline: "The Cheap Get Cheaper." To take back our place as the low-price provider, Ceres entered the market offering the lowest price in the country—eighteen dollars per trade. We expected that at such a steep discount, it would take several years to build up a large enough client base to make the new company profitable, but the results astounded us. Geographical location had not mattered much for the touch-tone service at a minimum of forty-eight dollars a trade, but for Ceres, at eighteen, it seemed not to matter at all. Wherever in the country people had money to invest, Ceres signed up clients. Especially on the East Coast and in California, technologically sophisticated people were seeing our ads on CNBC and dialing in with their computers on their 9600 baud modems. I had never really heard of Silicon Valley, but it was making Ceres a success. Bill Glasz, slated to take over managing the new company now that Pete had gotten it up and running, may have described it best: "Ceres took off like a scalded-ass ape."

Our competitors, meanwhile, were bringing their own innovations to market. In 1995, I learned that Charles Schwab had bought Mayer & Schweitzer, a Nasdaq market maker that provided our clients the chance to buy or sell over-the-counter stocks. From the founding of our company, we had relied on market makers like

Mayer & Schweitzer to maintain inventories of stocks and to continuously update the prices for which they would buy (or "bid") and sell (or "ask") those stocks. The difference between their bid and ask prices, known as the spread, was the source of the profits they earned, a cost we had to absorb when we did business with them. Schwab's purchase, I realized, would allow Schwab to own the middleman and keep the benefits of the spread, and this vertical integration of operations and profits could free them to lower their commissions to match ours or go below. For the first time, they had the means to undercut us on price and take our customers.

I wasn't the only one to see this threat. Larry Waterhouse, the founder of Waterhouse Securities, Inc., shared my concern, as did other heads of discount brokerages, including Don Buchholz, the CEO of Southwest Securities, who had been a collaborator with us on the failed CSS project. We looked into the possibility of creating our own market maker, but the cost was too high. Regulations required a minimum investment of $20 million.

We began talking with Walter Raquet, a senior officer at Spear, Leeds & Kellogg Specialists, a brokerage that would later become part of Goldman Sachs. An accountant who had worked for many large broker-dealers who were market makers, Raquet was unusual in that he was an entrepreneur, an instigator. In conversation with him, the possibility emerged of forming a consortium of many discount brokers to start our own market maker. If we worked together, I came to understand, our collaborative market maker could achieve the same benefits as Schwab's, and that would allow Ameritrade to keep our prices below theirs.

To make this approach successful, we realized, we would have to create a next-generation market maker, fully computerized and automated, that used rule-based algorithms and not human experts to make decisions over order flow. It was the kind of innovation that would never get tried by a traditional, full-service brokerage because they were too committed to established ways of doing business—and to the people they had always paid to do business in those established ways. Walter Raquet brought into the conversation Kenneth Pasternak, a partner at his firm and a technology expert, who had a vision of creating a system that would need the same number of employees to process twenty-five thousand trades or two million.

The key would be to combine computer technology with our willingness to work together. We wouldn't be violating antitrust laws because we would go on competing with one another for clients, even as we collaborated in creating a shared, high-tech market maker to service those clients. It was a revolutionary idea, possible because the founders of discount brokerages were nonconformists, like me, and got some happiness and satisfaction out of doing something new. These were the sort of men who wore a suit and tie but acted irreverently. They didn't worry about doing what was expected or about buttering anybody up. In another era, they might have been out in the wilderness, trapping beaver for fur. We were rivals, but we came together to do something we all believed was important. I found it exciting to be part of this project even as we all kept our emotional distance. No one wanted to get too close and give away their business secrets.

At a meeting at Waterhouse's office in New York City, I told Walter that I had a serious concern about moving forward. "I can't be a part of this if you're going to continue to work for your current employer while you set up a business that's going to compete with them."

I knew this might be a deal breaker. Walter and Ken were both accustomed to seven-figure salaries. Ken was in line to become CEO of Spear, Leeds & Kellogg. They were not at a point in their careers where they needed to take any risks to have financial success, yet I was asking them to take a big risk.

"I'll quit," Walter replied. He was that type of person: no hesitation. I knew then that he was on our side. I came to appreciate later that they were both unusual men. Walter's father had been a firefighter. Ken was a child of first-generation immigrants, Holocaust survivors, who had gotten a master's degree in education and taught business in high school. He had started his career at Spear as their librarian. Both were inclined to prove that they could build a business their way, even though they had not gone to top-name schools or come from families with connections to the world of finance. Ken agreed to quit the firm as well and joined us a few months later.

Walter knew the community of retail brokerage firms and they all knew him, so they were inclined to listen to his sales pitch to invest in our new firm. He started putting together the organization that would collect the $20 million necessary, according to regulations, to establish an inventory of stocks for sale. The funds were to be held in an escrow account until a certain date, and if Raquet didn't reach the target of $20 million by that date, the funds would all have to be returned.

Ameritrade contributed $2 million in the form of a secured bank loan. It was a lot of money for us, a considerable risk. Everything seemed to be going according to plan until Walter called me on a Thursday to say he was coming up short. He had raised $19.5 million, and he needed another half a million by the next day.

"Will you lend me half a million so we don't have to give all the money back? I know I'm going to get it from another party by Monday."

"No," I said. "I'm not going to give you that. The rules are the rules."

"But Joe," he said, "it's all going to go away."

He kept selling me and pushing me. He would not let up. Of all the hard-asses he could have called, I must have been the most promising, somehow. Finally, when the entire deal was almost out of time, I said, "Okay. I'll tell you what I'm going to do. I'm going to get the cashiering department to wire it to you. After that, Tom Pleiss is going to notice that the money is gone and he's going to be all over me because I'm wiring out unsecured funds with no contract to protect us. He's going to argue that I'm putting the company at risk of coming up short for the net capital requirement. I'm going to tell him that on Monday morning you're going to send that half million back to me or else I'm hiring Guido to break your legs and kill you."

I was talking tough, but what it meant was that I had chosen to trust Walter with half a million dollars because he had given me his word. I can still remember how angry Tom got when he learned about it—typically, one of my employees would be afraid to get angry at me for being irresponsible, but Tom told me in no uncertain terms that I'd made a mistake. He felt I was wrong to have given up the cushion of funds that safeguarded our compliance with the net capital rules, let alone to have wired so much money without a contract. His honesty and ferocious protectiveness where the company was concerned made me respect him even more than before. Tom was a man of character; he didn't back down at all.

With my money, Walter hit his target of $20 million. He closed the partnership agreement with all the participants over the weekend. That Monday, his other funding came through and he returned my half million just as he had said. It all worked perfectly. That, to me, was the frontier spirit come alive—the odds are long, you know you can't meet every challenge alone, so you come together to meet a shared risk, secure that each person's word is their bond. There used to be a lot of trust in the brokerage industry, trust which made possible shared risk-taking, a group of us hanging by our fingernails together, not sure if we would succeed or fail. Those were thrilling times.

The consortium, known as Knight Securities, began operations at the end of July 1995. Before the end of the year, impressed with what I saw, I doubled my investment to $4 million. As partner firms funneled trades to the new company, our trading volume multiplied. Within a year, Knight ranked seventh among broker-dealers on the Nasdaq.

My youngest son, Todd, saw that growth up close. He was in Chicago in business school, and I called Ken, the technology wizard who had worked with us to launch Knight, and asked if he could give him a summer internship. Todd asked me, "Dad, what do you think they will have me do?"

"If they let you empty wastebaskets," I said, "you should be excited."

Todd started as an assistant to the traders on the floor and returned to a full-time position managing trading-floor operations and helping the company prepare to go public. On his first day in the summer of 1996, he told me, they did fifteen thousand trades. On his last day, they did eight hundred thousand.

The partner brokerages such as Ameritrade that funneled business to Knight benefited from the company's earnings and payments for order flow. By January 1999, the value of Ameritrade's initial investment would increase more than 2,000 percent, to $166 million. Just as important, the success of Knight Securities contributed to the financial efficiencies of our trading operations. It was wonderfully successful, and my satisfaction went deeper than making money. Ever since 1975, when the full-service firms had tagged us with the "discount" label, they had tried to make it sound as if what we offered was bargain-basement, a cheap product that wasn't for the normal investor. By starting a market maker, though, and getting it into the top ten, we shocked the industry. By demonstrating that "discount" brokers were now mainstream, we showed just how powerful and legitimate we had become.

Once we got Knight going, I pulled away to focus my attention on other projects. I saw the other partners at the board meetings, and they introduced me to the new board members they brought on, but otherwise, we stayed separate and apart. We all felt good, like the men my father had worked with, because we were succeeding, building our businesses, but there was no need for me to be further involved. Larry Waterhouse, Don Buchholz, and I put up the starting money and engaged Walter so that he could make the venture succeed. Then I stepped back.

By the mid-'90s, after we invested in Knight but before we made any money from it, Ameritrade's management did not anticipate another major investment for a while. Between launching both Ceres and Knight Securities, pouring $5 million into Accutrade for Windows, paying off the lawsuit in Ohio, and repurchasing the company stock from my brother Dick, all while maintaining our net capital requirements, we were fully extended, financially speaking. Even so, Mike Anderson, director of marketing and sales for Ameritrade Clearing, came to talk to me about a highly unusual brokerage he had visited in a professor's New York City apartment.

Keith Aufhauser had earned a PhD in economics at Harvard, writing a dissertation that defied the conventional explanation that slavery in America collapsed due to economic factors. Keith argued instead that new technology introduced in the British Caribbean in the nineteenth century had sustained slavery's profitability, and that the institution was brought down not by economic necessity but by social activism. It was a maverick position for an economics graduate student to take, and on the strength of his work he became a professor at Queens College and a visiting fellow at the Institute for Advanced Study in Princeton.

Meanwhile, he was dating a woman named Ruby, later his wife, who was studying to become a broker for Prudential Securities. Born and raised in China, Ruby needed help with her English-language study materials. Keith wasn't fluent in Mandarin, but he knew enough of the language to translate for her. By the time Ruby was ready to take the exam for her brokerage license, his head was so full of the material that he figured he might as well take the test, too.

To his surprise, the NASD required that an applicant be sponsored by a brokerage house, but unlike his wife, Keith had no corporate sponsor. He decided to start his own brokerage so he could sponsor himself. Now, instead of one test, he had to take eight or nine, but he passed them all. In 1981, he hired some former students to launch his brokerage in a corner of his father's small welding-rod factory in Plainview, which he also managed.

The couple got married and lived in a residential high-rise in Manhattan. With a two-bedroom apartment but only one bed, he made the second room into an office for the new business, K. Aufhauser & Co. His former students placed trades for a relatively small group of high-net-worth individuals, many of whom were his friends. The company grew, and when another apartment went up for sale in his building, he decided to buy it and move the other brokers there. This violated the rules of the residential building, but no one complained, and the landlord didn't seem to mind.

To build up business, Keith began to offer the lowest trading prices in the country. In 1990 *Fortune* and *Money* christened him the cheapest of the discounters, and his trading volume started to explode. He realized that he could either pay his increasing income back to the government as taxes or he could reinvest them in the company. He spent his profits on amusing, informal ads in *Barron's* and *Investor's Business Daily*, featuring cartoon sketches of a bull as a Scotsman and a bear as a Texan with a big lasso necktie. When CNBC was still in its infancy in the early 1990s, he took advantage of the broadcaster's relatively cheap advertising rates, as I had done. Aufhauser's volume kept growing. By the mid-'90s, when Mike Anderson brought the company to my attention, they had fifteen thousand accounts.

K. Aufhauser & Co. was a retail broker. They cleared their trades through Pershing, one of the big wholesale brokers. Mike paid a sales call to propose that Ameritrade Clearing could give Aufhauser a better deal on clearing than they got from Pershing. When Mike returned, he told me that K. Aufhauser & Co. was the strangest firm he had ever seen. Twenty brokers were working out of that little apartment with wires everywhere. To cross the room, you had to step around desks and equipment. People had to pull out their chairs to let you through. There were even employees working on the patio. It sounded like a business after my own heart.

From the founding of Ameritrade, we had acquired new accounts by advertising. We calculated the price we paid for each account by dividing the number of new accounts in a given period by the amount we spent on ads. In the '90s, however, we found that it could be cheaper to buy smaller competitors and take over their established accounts. It was all the same to me whether we spent our money on ads or acquisitions, but we had never bought a firm as big as Aufhauser, and there was no path to follow. I told Keith I might be interested and then turned the challenge over to my management team.

As my team looked closer, they found a second reason to like this unusual company. Keith had studied industry leaders like Schwab, Quick & Reilly, and Ameritrade to learn how to automate trades. All three had touch-tone and computer dial-up trading systems, but Keith soon found that the banks of telephone modems these systems relied on were unreliable. Too often, he realized, his brokers would do a trade worth a twenty-five-dollar commission, then spend costly hours on the phone trying to make the client's modem work.

Unlike his more successful competitors, though, Keith had come from academia, where professors increasingly relied on a worldwide research-sharing system developed as a collaboration between universities, the Defense Department, and defense contractors: the Internet. They were among the first to register an Internet domain name, www.Aufhauser.com. He and a programmer named Terry Thorson set up an elementary order-entry screen. On August 24, 1994, the company became the first discount brokerage to trade stock over the Internet using a proprietary email system called WealthWEB. These orders came in as email messages, not what we think of as online trading today, and Aufhauser didn't receive many of them, but they advertised the hell out of their capability to do so; in that way they built a reputation for being on the leading edge of brokerage technology.

I didn't have any expertise in the Internet. I didn't own a computer myself until Pete bought one for me and one for Joe Konen and had them installed on our office desks. Pete told me, "You don't have to use it, Dad, but I want people to come to your office and see the computer, so they know we're a technology company."

He was right. I didn't use that first computer. Never learned to turn it on. It would be years before I began to receive email, and for a long time I would write out my notes for my reply by hand and give them to my secretary to type up on the machine. Pete, though, had gotten interested in computing in school. Omaha was a test market for cable modems, and he was an early adopter of high-speed computer connections. One day, he attended a demonstration in Omaha on the use of a website called Piazza. A fellow showed everyone how he could make his computer in Nebraska access a German website—in German! Pete told me he thought it was the coolest thing. He wasn't looking at it as related to business; he just liked it. I told him, "This is something people are going to use. I want our customers to be able to trade over this Internet from their personal computers."

"But why, Dad?" he asked me. "Nobody has any of those!"

How did I know right away that we had to offer online trading? Because of our experience with the touch-tone phone service.

It's a funny thing: When I tell the story of the touch-tone service, people often seem to respond, "Ho-hum." It sounds like quaint, old-fashioned stuff, antique phones with big, square plastic buttons. But at the time, it was a breakthrough in technology and also a fantastic lesson for me about why technology matters. When we first introduced the touch-tone service, I had thought I knew the reason people would bother using it. Price. I thought they would tolerate a new technology to get a lower-cost trade. Once we introduced it, though, some amazing things happened. We found customers putting in orders over the phone with incredible speed. I could not imagine moving my fingers that fast.

I called some of them up and asked how they worked the touch-tone buttons so fast. They explained that they were not touching the buttons at all. Customers were building themselves little software systems that automatically played all the tones to send an order at a given price.

Now I understood. The sophisticated customers didn't tolerate the newer technology because of the lower price. They preferred using the new system because the technology offered the chance to take more power and more control for themselves. That was what they loved. They wanted *freedom*—and they would probably have paid a *higher* price to get it. I had missed out on revenue for my company. From that point on, I doubt there was anyone who believed in Internet trading, or any new trading technology that increased the customer's power and freedom, as much as I did.

But how to make online trading work? As we explored the possibilities, we had found that most people who traded online did so through a subscription service such as CompuServe, Prodigy, or

America Online. We tried to negotiate partnerships with those companies, but our larger competitors had already beaten us there, and in any case, those services were awkward to access and retained a great deal of control for themselves over what a customer could do. Now, though, when I saw Keith Aufhauser's approach to online trading, which didn't require going through a middleman subscription service, I thought it might be worth buying the company just to get his trading system. That gave us two reasons to make an offer.

We had acquired competitors before, smaller ones, so we thought we knew how to value the order flow and how to assess the accounts. Keith wanted $7.6 million for his business, a tremendous amount of money. I didn't have the cash and I didn't want to give up the stock, so I went back to First National Bank of Omaha. They had confidence in me by then, after all these years of success, and they made the loan, but even so, we were extended about as far as we could go.

Not only were we risking the $7.6 million we paid for K. Aufhauser & Co., we were also risking our own operations, because we barely kept any cash on hand to solve any problems that might arise either with the new acquisition or with our own company. I only dared to buy Aufhauser because I trusted the competence of the people who worked for us. I felt sure that my exceptional team could merge two businesses with two different clearing firms and two different methods of accounting without making any costly mistakes.

To manage the company's cash flow, Joe Konen, president of the company, froze spending wherever he could. No new hiring. No raises. He canceled the company's participation in the annual Securities Industry Association convention and forbid employee travel unless it was absolutely necessary. It choked us, financially. Konen compared it to the moment in a poker game when you not only bet everything you've got but borrow to bet more. He said, "Ricketts shoved all the chips out on the table and asked for a marker, too." I didn't feel good about putting those restrictions on my employees or myself, but in a broader way, I felt wonderful. A sensation often comes over me at a time of high but purposeful risk as if nothing can go wrong. It's almost euphoric.

My executive management team had estimated conservatively that the savings from combining Aufhauser's operations with our own would pay off the bank loan in two and a half years. With so much money on the line, we decided to send several senior executives to New York to manage the integration. My first choice was Mary Fay, who had started as a clerk in our Dividend and Reorganization department, then moved to a management position at Accutrade and continued to rise. Quite a while before the sale went through, I asked if she would care to go out to New York to run Aufhauser during its transition, and stay out East for another two years and get her master's degree.

Mary spoke to her husband, and they agreed that they would move to New York for four years. Then, when the deal went through, she told me there was a complication. She was three months pregnant. She still wanted to run a subsidiary, but she didn't want to leave Omaha with a baby coming.

I told her congratulations, and then I said, "You know what? Let me get back to you." I sat down with Joe, and we figured out that we could have Mary Fay stay in Omaha to take over Ceres Securities from Bill Glasz, who had recently taken over for Pete. Mary would still get a subsidiary to run without having to uproot her life. Bill would go to New York to run Aufhauser. He agreed, and he took a team of about ten, including my brother Jim.

The value of our purchase of K. Aufhauser & Co. was in their customer accounts, so the transition to Ameritrade had to happen in a way that did not give Aufhauser customers any reason to close those accounts and go elsewhere. We signed off on the purchase on a weekend, and Monday morning Ameritrade employees were answering Aufhauser phones, but still saying "Aufhauser." To the customers, the experience of placing a trade was just like it had been before, with a few new voices on the line. Customers saw no other changes for a few months until they got a notice that said, "We no longer have Pershing to do our clearing. We now have Ameritrade, so you will see that your monthly statements look a little different." Three months later we did the cutover: on Friday, the phones rang in New York City, but Monday morning they rang in Omaha. It all went smoothly, and the team credited Keith and Ruby Aufhauser for a tremendous amount of help.

Once we started clearing their trades, we made a discovery. Pershing, Aufhauser's former clearing firm, had been making more money off Aufhauser's trades than Aufhauser made. In this brave new world of discount brokerage, Keith hadn't understood how valuable his order flow was because he was only getting the retail piece of it. Now, Ameritrade got both pieces, first making the trades for customers and then clearing those trades with the market makers. And because our back-office systems were now mostly automated, we could process the added trades with little increase in cost. The new order flow from Aufhauser increased our total operations by one-fourth, which did wonders for our bottom line. The profits paid off our $7 million bank loan not in two and a half years, as we had estimated, but in one.

Now we realized that we could be very successful as a consolidator in the business, growing by acquiring our competitors. In an eat-or-be-eaten industry, we had learned to be the eater. Only the big ones were going to make a lot of money, and now we knew how we could become one of the big ones. We realized that we could set our sights much higher—if we had access to enough capital.

The catch was that we were not the only ones who saw the chance to grow huge. The day after we closed the deal to buy K. Aufhauser & Co., Keith called to tell me that a prominent private equity firm had contacted him. They had said, "We think Internet trading of stocks is going to be big, Keith, and we want to buy your company and put millions of dollars into it."

"I just sold it yesterday," Keith replied. "But there's a guy on the West Coast, Porter is his name, I believe, and he's got a little company called E*Trade that's starting to do what I was doing. Maybe you can go and see him."

Keith was just being a nice guy. He made the suggestion and they listened. That private equity firm poured millions into developing and marketing Internet trading technology with somebody else who had the vision and knew what to do, and E*Trade became one of our fiercest competitors.

CHAPTER 10

The Internet is still the Wild, Wild West of trading," a spokesperson for Charles Schwab & Co. told the *Los Angeles Times* in March 1995, explaining that the company did not want to jump into the new online trading market until it had addressed security concerns. If Schwab saw itself as unready to brave that Wild West, well, Ameritrade was not afraid. The frontier was where we came from, and we sensed the beginning of a new gold rush. With Aufhauser's domain name, it seemed, we had staked our claim, and with their Internet technology, we felt sure we had all the tools we needed to dig for gold.

When we looked closer, however, we found that the technology I had been so excited to buy wasn't worth a damn. True, an Aufhauser customer could use the website to place an Internet order for a trade, but when that order appeared on the company's computer screen, a clerk had to print it out on a dot-matrix printer, walk the printout over to the "dumb" terminal that communicated with the clearing company's order system, and type in the information, just as if the order had come from a customer calling over the phone. This so-called Internet trading was smoke and mirrors. It was held together with bubble gum and Scotch tape. And it wouldn't pay. Receiving an order online rather than over the phone would not save us any money. We were making a great deal of money from Aufhauser's accounts, so the acquisition was paying for itself and more, but it seemed we had been wrong about their revolutionary technology.

The head of my IT department scrutinized Aufhauser's website and reported that it wasn't worth keeping. He said it wasn't even worth another thought. A functional Internet trading website that didn't rely on human clerks would be far too expensive to develop, he told me, and anyway, Ameritrade was already working on something better: a version of Accutrade, the touch-tone phone system, that would run instead on software built for Microsoft's Windows operating system.

In 1995, Windows came preinstalled on most personal computers. We had already spent more than $2 million developing Accutrade for Windows, and I planned to spend millions more on advertising. Ours would be the first online investing system to offer individual investors programmed investment and basket trading, services that were usually only available to larger institutions. Our software also incorporated a tax-lot accounting system to help the investor understand the tax consequences of buy/sell decisions and track the dates of purchase and sale, as well as the cost basis of a security. The new software would be our big step forward, the be-all and end-all of trading software—if we could get it to work.

We hoped to launch in the fall of 1995. While one team, which included Pete, built the user interface for Windows, another designed the back-end system that would connect with Ameritrade's internal software, the current version of the BOSS system that Dave Kellogg and his team had first launched in the '70s. This was "middleware," software that would act as a translator between the personal computers of customers calling in and Ameritrade's mainframe computer. We called it the AccuWin server.

By August, the new system was ready for its first round of internal testing, but progress was slow. There were bugs in the Windows program and complications in the interfaces among the different parts of the system. That winter, as eighty company employees helped with the beta testing, we continued to find bugs in the software.

Meanwhile, earlier that year, Pete had attended the Spring Internet World conference in San Jose, where the latest Internet developments were presented. Microsoft founder Bill Gates was warning that the Internet might make Windows obsolete. In a now-famous memo entitled "The Internet Tidal Wave," written in May 1995, Gates had asserted that Netscape's new browser for the World Wide Web threatened to "commoditize the underlying operating system" and therefore posed a fundamental challenge to software created for Microsoft's Windows. I could not judge if that was true or not, but what Pete had learned gave me another reason to explore web-based trading. As it turned out, this was the beginning of the death of Accutrade for Windows. Before we even got it to the marketplace, it was already at risk.

What might come next? The answer came unexpectedly, through my second son, Tom, who had lived at the University of Chicago with a bright, off-the-wall young man named Curt Conklin. Once, I had visited their room and discovered they had painted it black, with white footprints climbing up the walls.

"Why is everything black?" I had asked Tom.

"Oh, Curt and I are having a party tonight," he said as if that was an explanation.

The two young men were inseparable, and Curt often came back with Tom and Pete to Omaha for holidays. Marlene affectionately called him "my little pervert" because of his irreverent take on the world. Laura joked that he was the creative son Marlene and I never had. He made himself part of the family, and I felt I could trust him.

Curt had come to college intending to study art, but after graduation took a job first in an investment bank and then in a large commercial bank. Disillusioned by the formal and hierarchical nature of those banks and by the cutthroat behavior of some of his colleagues, the young man left banking and went to work for the client he had most admired as a business, the restaurant group Lettuce Entertain You. In the mid-1980s, the company employed over two thousand people and had annual revenues of $40 million.

Curt lacked an accounting degree, so he couldn't get hired on the business side. Instead, he accepted a low-wage position welcoming customers as a day host at the restaurant Maggiano's Little Italy and set out to prove he could be useful. He worked long hours. When customers at the trendy restaurant, one of the busiest in Chicago, wouldn't wait where management wanted them to before they were seated, he designed a large host stand that kept waiting customers in place. The stand was copied in many of the Lettuce Entertain You restaurants. When orders backed up because the new digital-screen system was slow and not intuitive, he redesigned the system. He turned his low-wage job into an education in customer service and sales at the moment that new, clunky, digital tools were being introduced—essentially, a crash course in customer service and digital marketing when no such classes existed yet.

When Ameritrade needed someone to help us imagine what online stock trading might look like, Pete suggested we ask Curt to move to Omaha and run the marketing department of one of our subsidiaries. Curt had no interest in moving to Nebraska, but he agreed to come for an interview as an excuse for another weekend get-together with my sons. When we offered him a job with a healthy salary increase, though, he changed his mind and moved to Omaha.

I gave Curt a cubicle outside my office so we could test out strategies for direct marketing to specific groups of customers. He would talk to me about the Internet because he enjoyed playing around with it. I had no one with any background in online commerce, and here was this young kid who understood both marketing and online technology. In July 1995, I made Curt Conklin Accutrade's first director of Internet services.

Each of the subscription services, such as America Online, CompuServe, and Prodigy, demanded that Ameritrade and other brokers make an exclusive deal with them, giving them the right to all our online customers, which I could not accept. That left us mostly boxed out of the leading online trading sites.

Curt and Pete had another idea. They wanted to rebuild the Aufhauser website to allow people to do online trading without going through one of the big subscription services. Rebuilding the Aufhauser site to make it pay, however, was going to require two different types of talent. First, we needed people who knew the technology and could develop it. However, when Curt and Pete talked to the IT department about web-based trading, they got nowhere. None of the formally qualified technologists in the company wanted anything to do with the project. It seemed that no one in my IT department could conceive of how the Internet would be useful to our company.

I think it would be hard for anyone who didn't experience that moment to understand how new and unexplored online technology was in the 1990s. We knew that someone would have to write some kind of software to make it possible to conduct stock trading on a website, but who would do that? Where did you find them? What were the words to describe the kind of programmers we required? We were fortunate that we had access to the people who had built the original Aufhauser website, and who could refer us to programmers who would understand what we needed. In that way, our decision to buy Aufhauser gave us one of the keys to online trading after all.

Second, we needed creative people who could imagine how customers could use technologies in ways they had never done before, and that was where Curt came in. Ingenious, creative, highly energetic, he helped us tell our developers what to build and what to do.

For only $75,000, Ameritrade relaunched the Aufhauser website in November 1995, months before the far more complicated Accutrade for Windows was ready. We used our AccuWin server software as the web-based interface with Ameritrade's internal BOSS trading system. You might say it was serendipity that we had already created the middleware for Accutrade for Windows, so we had it ready to use with Aufhauser's website, but once again, the harder you work, the luckier you get. By the end of the year, the new subsidiary, with Aufhauser as its name, was executing about a hundred trades a day.

The difference between this new approach to online trading and what had existed before was profound. Until then, Internet-based stock trading was dependent on desktop software. To gain each new Accutrade for Windows customer, we first had to supply the customer with software—eighteen floppy disks—and then get them to install it correctly and learn its commands on their computer. When they were ready to make a trade, they had to connect by modem to our computers at Ameritrade. Many people new to trading found all of this confusing and time-consuming, and a lot could go wrong between the day the customer received our software in the mail and the first time they successfully transmitted a trade to our system. However, with the transition to browsers and the Web, that friction in our relationship with our customers went away. All the customers needed was their keyboard and their screen, and we could process their trades entirely electronically, without the need for clerks to print and reenter the data. The following month, the company launched a similar website for Ceres.

Curt and Pete took this big step forward virtually on their own. All email communications from visitors to our trading websites went to Curt, personally, because he was the only Ameritrade employee with an email address. Within months, he was logging onto his email at six in the morning and spending the next eight hours answering hundreds of questions from customers: "I clicked on this, and then that happened. What do I do next?" We had a clunky set of digital tools, and he was figuring out how to make them work as simply as possible for users who were sometimes hesitant to turn on their computers at all. After answering the emails, he moved on to the rest of his responsibilities. Those long days helped him build a solid understanding of the online customer experience.

As we looked for ways to attract online customers that didn't require us to rely on the subscription Internet services, we forged an agreement with an unusual web-based personal finance and investing site. David and Tom Gardner, brothers who had been English majors in college, had started an investment-advice newsletter with a friend in the summer of 1993 called the *Motley Fool*, naming it after a quote from Shakespeare's *As You Like It*. They targeted novice investors with plainspoken, intelligent, and humorous advice, but met with little success until Tom mentioned it in the personal-finance chat section of America Online. Then the brothers were flooded with inquiries from across the country. They set up a message board, and by February 1994, the *Motley Fool* had become the most popular personal-finance site on AOL.

On this new frontier of Internet marketing, things were done differently. Our legal contract with the *Motley Fool* guys, which I still have, was only three paragraphs long. We promised that Accutrade would pay them five thousand a month, beginning "on the day that

Accutrade receives its first expression of interest from a Foolish customer." The ninety-day agreement would be marked by three payments "at normal intervals . . . let's say one at the start, the second one thirty days later, and the third thirty days after that." The text continued: "This is a binding deal. You can't get out of it. Neither can we. We're pretty reasonable. If you don't like something we've done, let us know, we'll do our best to change it. If we screw up, we'll extend the agreement at no charge for the same number of days we screwed it up."

In conclusion, the agreement noted, "We're exploring this medium just as you are. This is not your typical document, but then again, this isn't your typical advertisement. We hope (and expect) that it will work well for both of us." I remember Pete saying to me, "Dad, don't you wish all our contracts could be like that?" There was that frontier spirit again—honest, idealistic, amazed to be part of a new world. The *Motley Fool* guys proved to be great partners for us.

America Online, however, was not happy with our arrangement. The Internet provider had exclusive agreements with other broker-dealers, and Accutrade wasn't one of them. Those broker-dealers put pressure on AOL, which put pressure on the *Motley Fool*. AOL threatened to sue unless they buried our ads at least three clicks into the company's site, but our new partners wouldn't back down. Finally, AOL decided to create a marketplace for many brokers rather than to continue exclusive relationships with only a few. Accutrade got great accounts from the site.

The technology that transmitted customers' touch-tone and online orders was as new and as improvised as that marketing arrangement with the *Motley Fool*. Mike Anderson remembers talking to a young employee, Chris Northern, who had more experience with computers. Mike said, "I'm still trying to understand this whole online trading thing. Does it run on one of those big IBM mainframes? What model?"

"No, Mike," he said. "It runs on a PC. It's in the tech closet in back."

"Wait," Mike said. "The front-end system for all of Accutrade is running on one personal computer in a closet?"

"Yeah," he said. "You want to see it?"

Chris Northern unlocked a door, and inside a five-by-ten storage closet Mike saw a computer—not a laptop, but a tower and monitor on a narrow desk, with a folding chair for whoever needed to work on it. Behind the computer was a huge bundle of wires and phones plugged into the wall, bringing in our touch-tone and online orders. To access the wires, you had to ask the person at the computer to get up and move out of the way.

"What happens if it dies?" Mike asked.

"Then no one can trade touch-tone or online," the younger man said. "I guess then I'd probably go out and buy another one."

"Maybe you ought to buy one today," Mike said, "and put it on the floor here in case we need it."

We all still expected that when Accutrade for Windows was ready, it would prove to be the online trading product of the future. After more than fifteen months in development and an investment of just under $5 million, all the debugging was finally complete. The new software went into production in mid-February 1996, with plans to begin shipping in March.

We sent a mailer to more than a million people offering the software for free, and eighty thousand accepted the offer. We also began promoting the use of Accutrade for Windows on an early handheld device developed by Sharp known as the Zaurus. It was like a rough draft of a smartphone but without the capacity to make calls or take photos or video. In addition to trading software, the device offered a time-management calendar, note-taking software, letter-writing functions, an address book, and modem and fax capability. Customers who signed up for this service paid a flat fee of eight hundred dollars a year for commissions, and they could make unlimited trades. The company loaned them the Sharp Zaurus to use as long as they maintained their account.

At every step, we faced uncertainty. We had believed that we had paid too much for K. Aufhauser & Co., then found that Keith Aufhauser had asked too little for his company. We believed that the value of that acquisition would come primarily from his retail accounts and technology, yet we saw far more profit from wholesale clearing of his trades. We invested millions in Accutrade for Windows, while our IT department showed no interest in the online trading system that would change the entire industry. The important lesson is that all these possibilities were not right or wrong answers. They were ideas, and what the free enterprise system lets you do with ideas is test their value by developing and bringing them to market. Free enterprise is a kind of science where the results are measured in dollars. You have to run the experiments to get the results.

These were still very early days for online trading. In the summer of 1996, securities bought and sold on the Web accounted for less than 1 percent of all daily trades. Proprietary software, like Accutrade for Windows or subscription services such as America Online or Prodigy, made up another 4 percent. Nevertheless, the *Los Angeles Times* reported in June that "the Internet is taking Wall Street by storm." Forrester Research estimated in August that there were 650,000 online brokerage accounts, up 50 percent from 1994. They predicted the number would rise to 1.3 million by 1998.

I felt sure that estimate was low. To me, the potential market looked enormous. Across the country, only roughly 1.5 million customers used deep discounters like Ameritrade. Another twelve to fourteen million relied on lower-priced brokers like Schwab, Quick & Reilly, or Fidelity Investments, but these companies maintained branch offices with high overhead, so I did not believe they could ever effectively compete with deep discounters. Another forty-five million people were still using full-service brokers. Adding these together, I saw an opportunity to win the business of close to sixty million existing investors who were overpaying for their trades and missing out on the ease and speed of online trading, not to mention all the Americans not yet trading. However, the chance to win these customers would be short-lived: Once an investor got comfortable with one online broker, I believed, it would be difficult to get them to switch. This was a true once-in-a-lifetime opportunity.

Competition intensified. Among the online traders, advertisements focused on price and efficiency. Schwab charged customers thirty-nine dollars for an online trade, more if the customer wanted to talk to a broker. E*Trade let customers buy or sell up to five thousand shares of a company listed on the New York Stock Exchange for just $14.95. Although online trades represented only a tiny fraction of the eight hundred thousand trades made per day on the major exchanges and Nasdaq, E*Trade had doubled the volume they'd processed only six months before. We started a new brand, All-American Brokers, to offer online trades for twelve dollars—the best price for an online trade, as reported by the *Wall Street Journal*. However, we knew that wouldn't keep us ahead of them forever. E*Trade closed 1995 with total revenues of $23.3 million, less than our $35 million. Nevertheless, the company's growth had been meteoric.

The surging volume of trades strained everyone's systems. In May 1996, E*Trade had to pay $1.7 million to customers after the company's computer system crashed for two and a half hours. Customers also complained to the online bulletin boards that E*Trade was slow to open accounts and at times provided sporadic or even inaccurate confirmation. Charles Schwab also earned a black eye in July when the *Wall Street Journal* reported that the company's entire mainframe computer had gone down for fifteen minutes while the market was open. Schwab employees manually handled trades placed during that period, but the company's reputation suffered. The *Wall Street Journal* reported that Schwab and other brokers offering online trading weren't sure how their systems would perform during surges of trading activity. The article noted, however, that some companies, including PC Financial Network, Lombard Institutional, and Ameritrade's four discount brokerage brands, "have been able to sidestep such problems by continually expanding their systems to handle more and more orders."

How had we done it? In a sense, we had benefited from the failure of the CSS consortium to produce a replacement for our outdated computer system. That failure, drawn out over more than two years, forced on us an essential discovery: Technology moved so fast now that it was pointless to think anymore of replacing one outdated system with an entirely new one. System updates had to become continuous, a never-ending function performed by an entire department. We never really replaced Dave Kellogg's BOSS system; we just kept building additions. By this time, we could handle ten thousand trades a day, but we were already talking about adding new hardware and software to triple or quadruple that capacity.

To win the race to attract and serve the huge market of online customers, I realized, would take massive investments both in technology and advertising, far more money than we had spent before. Even our unusually high annual return on investment would never generate all the capital we needed. I had imagined that Ameritrade would go public someday, but now I realized we had no time to waste. Best guess, we needed $100 million for advertising and another $100 million for technology. I thought those guesses were high, but they turned out to be low. I was exactly right, however, that we needed the money immediately.

Some of our competitors got the capital they needed when they were bought by banks with deep pockets. Toronto-Dominion, Canada's fifth-largest bank, acquired Waterhouse Investor Services. The following year, Fleet Financial would buy Quick & Reilly. However, I had no interest in being swallowed up by a bank.

Independent companies made their own efforts to raise capital. In June 1996, E*Trade filed papers to make an initial public offering of stock. We knew we had to do the same, though it meant the end of my dream of passing Ameritrade down to my children as a private company that they could run when I was gone. It was a painful decision but, in a sense, an easy one. Going public was our only chance to survive and compete as one of the biggest brokers.

I felt that I would be willing to make this move when our net income reached $1 million a month. The company finished its fiscal year in September with earnings of $11,158,345. Early in 1996, I directed Joe Konen to begin quiet conversations with investment banks about the possibility of an initial public offering.

Our first conversations with investment bankers did not go well. Nobody was really stepping up. We were perceived as too small. Finally, Credit Suisse First Boston showed some interest, and after they made their underwriting proposal, we agreed to move forward. The bankers were pleasantly surprised to discover how clean we had kept our books. I had been meticulous, for all these years, about keeping my personal funds and expenses separate from the business. I had known there would be public scrutiny one day, and more than that, running a clean business had always seemed a duty.

We took some further steps to prepare for an IPO. The holding company was reincorporated in Delaware, and the name was changed from TransTerra to Ameritrade Holding Corporation. Three months later, on December 6, the company filed its registration with the SEC.

I went out for a beer with my childhood friend Jerry Gress, who along with his wife, Pat, had loaned me four thousand dollars in the 1970s to invest in the business. I had never paid them back. In the early '80s, I had sent him a letter saying that because I couldn't afford to return the money, I would give him a share of company stock for every dollar he had given me. With the IPO approaching, I met Jerry at a lounge in Omaha that we liked called the Interlude. I explained to him that in the process of making the initial public offering, the bank would have to multiply his shares because the bankers didn't want us to open the stock at a very high price per share. His four thousand shares would now become 192,000 shares.

As we drank our beers, I said, "Your shares are going to be worth a lot of money, Jerry. You know what I'd like to do? After we go public, I'd like to present you with a check for a million dollars. Would you mind that? It would show people what could happen if they stay loyal to Ameritrade."

"Hell, no," Jerry said. "You're just blowing smoke. It's not going to be worth a million bucks."

As the date of the IPO approached, I began to think more than usual about indulging my personal interests. One morning I walked into Susan Hohman's office and confessed that with some of the money I would make from the IPO, I was going to buy a custom-made Harley-Davidson.

"That's the last thing I would have expected," she said. Susan seemed stunned.

Before we could offer Ameritrade stock to the public, Bob Slezak and Joe Konen and I had to sell investors on the idea of Ameritrade as a public company in what was called a road show. Throughout

February 1997, we crisscrossed the country visiting more than sixty institutional investors, making a case to include Ameritrade stock in their mutual fund, profit-sharing plan, or other form of institutional investment. Marlene had often teased me that I was the only man she knew who tapped his fingers impatiently during his own speeches, and I quickly grew impatient with this. It was exhausting to give the same speech day after day to people with limited knowledge. I got to the point where I could have delivered the other two guys' presentations for them, word for word. I felt I could have been more engaging if I could speak off the cuff, but the investment bankers insisted we stay on message.

The analysts who listened to our presentations seemed to have little understanding of our business beyond the idea that we were another new dot-com company looking for cash to grow a big customer base. Many insisted to me that what customers really wanted was to buy stocks from a full-service stockbroker, as though we had not been proving that idea wrong for twenty years. They did not grasp our potential, and they priced our shares too low. I reached my breaking point when I learned, very close to the time of the offering, that the bankers would not honor our verbal agreement about the number of shares to be sold to friends and family. Livid, I walked out of the final negotiations.

"Do what you want," I told Joe Konen and Bob Slezak. "Close the deal or don't close it. I don't care."

My son Pete was with us that day, and he walked out of the meeting with me. We went to the airport to catch the next flight back to Omaha and I suggested we stop at an airport bar for a beer. Pete was shocked. He knew I never drank when I flew for business. But I was feeling like the IPO might not be worth the misunderstanding and humiliation, and I felt done with it.

After we walked out, Bob and Joe were on their own. They

decided that if I had wanted to kill the deal, I would have killed it before I left. They signed the agreement on behalf of the company. We offered our initial public offering in March 1997, and our shares, trading under the symbol AMTD, were initially priced at fifteen dollars. They finished the day at $19.50. We raised more than $22 million. Later, when our stock price shot up much higher, the bankers acted surprised. "Joe," they said, "why didn't you tell us you were going to have this success?"

And I thought: *For crying out loud. I was trying to tell you all along. You didn't believe.*

We held no formal celebration of the IPO, but that Friday afternoon I went to talk to Jerry Gress at his office. He worked as part of the Aufhauser operation. I said, "Hey, everybody, I want you to know what a loyal friend did for me. I am presenting this check for $1,185,000. Jerry, what are you going to do now?"

"If you don't mind," he said, "I'd like to buy you a drink."

We went to a bar called the Green Onion. There was a phone at the bar, and Jerry called his wife. He held the phone in one hand and the check in the other. "Pat," he said, "you have to come down to the Green Onion and see this. You're not going to believe what I have in my hand."

Soon we held Ameritrade's first public shareholder meeting. It felt like old home week, with employees and clients in attendance from as far back as my days at Dean Witter. In a speech, I tried to acknowledge everyone who had taken risks and stayed loyal through the years. I thanked my attorney, Tim McReynolds, and my mentor, Mike Naughton, who had helped the company survive the SEC and NASD investigations of 1976. I thanked Marlene for holding the family together. My kids said later that I had been unusually emotional—they talked about how rare it was, my voice cracking and my eyes tearing up, and how, for a moment in front of all those people, I was speechless. I felt such joy to see so many who had believed in me get rewarded.

The disappointing response we had received to our road show had stoked a growing feeling within management that our multiple brands with different names and separate marketing campaigns were too confusing. The ever-changing retail subsidiaries on the Ameritrade organizational chart at this time included Accutrade, offering discount brokerage; Ceres, offering eight-dollar flat-fee trades; eBroker (which had been All-American), offering Internet-only trades with no toll-free customer service; and K. Aufhauser & Co., offering research and customer service.

Our strategy of diversifying our subsidiaries had proved excellent for testing different approaches, but confusing, and therefore expensive, to advertise. According to one analysis in the business press, the company's marketing costs were somewhere betwecn $235 and $305 per customer, while E*Trade, a single brand, had to spend only $166 to add a new customer. Our competitor's approach was also attracting the most valuable kinds of customers: while E*Trade had 182,000 "electronic" accounts, far below Schwab's 860,000, its customers traded far more often than Schwab's, averaging 2.3 trades each month.

I asked Professor Mark Mitchell, an economist who had taught all three of my sons at the University of Chicago, to prepare a report on meeting the challenge of our thriving competitor. He concluded that E*Trade was killing us because their advertising developed not just new accounts but a consistent reputation for their brand, while our multibrand strategy was diffusing the enthusiasm into multiple reputations. I couldn't prove that Professor Mitchell was correct, but I knew that we were losing and E*Trade was winning.

At the next meeting of our new board of directors, I said that the time had come to consolidate into a single brand. I laid out a plan to spend $200 million on advertising. The board seemed uncomfortable. The advertising budget I had in mind was bigger than the book value of the company, and board members debated alternative approaches that would move more slowly and take less risk. I told them, "Time isn't on my side. E*Trade is going to eat my lunch." Ameritrade was a public company now, but I was still the majority shareholder and I still made the decisions. I was ready to move forward.

In July, at a mandatory Saturday morning meeting for the company's fifty-six managers, I announced that we would consolidate all our services under one name and brand. Mike Anderson, president of Accutrade, argued that we should leave the touch-tone-service brand alone because it charged the highest commissions and was our cash cow, and I agreed to keep that separate. I also announced that the new brand would lower the price per trade to eight dollars.

My employees were shocked. Joe Konen and Bob Slezak, my closest deputies, both opposed the move. Bob complained later that I had pulled the number 8 out of thin air. Joe insisted privately that eight dollars was below our cost to make a trade. How could we make a profit at that price? It seemed to me, though, that if I spent $200 million on advertising and another $200 million on tech to support the eight-dollar trades, there would be huge benefits in market share and economies of scale. By this point, our competitors had Internet-trading websites that were similar to ours. Our chance to be disruptive was no longer through technology but through advertising.

Would the benefits be enough to make the new strategy pay? No one could know for sure, but I had the feeling, the intuition, and intuition had succeeded for me before. I took it on faith and told my managers to get to work.

With the decision made to launch the new campaign in the fall, Joe called all the senior managers into a conference room and wrote the number 59 on a whiteboard. That was the number of days I was giving them to reorganize the company, consolidate the brands, notify the regulators, and be ready to relaunch under the new name. A more typical timetable might have been a year. When they learned they had less than two months, Mike Anderson, the new president of the new brand, told me, "People were throwing up in the aisles."

Curt Conklin proposed that we name the effort Project Lazarus, but Lazarus had been dead four days before Jesus raised him, so that seemed a discouraging analogy. We settled instead on Project Phoenix. We would rise from the ashes.

Next, Joe Konen assigned managers to committees as though they were in high school choosing players for teams for a football game. People began to feel the excitement. Later, many of those involved would say that those fifty-nine days were the most exciting, satisfying time of their careers.

To pick our new company name, we brought in a consultant from California, the branding star who had named Saturn for General Motors. I remember he didn't wear a suit, just a brown sweater and a pair of loafers. He came up with all kinds of creative ideas, but finally, Mike Anderson said, "Joe, we already have the best name out there. It's Ameritrade."

"But it's taken," someone said.

"Well, but it's taken by our own company. Screw them. It's the best name; let's use it. It connotes everything you want to connote."

"You're right." I said. "We'll make up a new name for Ameritrade Clearing. Nobody cares what you call a wholesale business anyway."

While Joe oversaw the consolidation of multiple brands into one, with all the changes that entailed, I turned my focus to the advertising campaign that would launch the new brand. I wanted humor, a warm feeling, but most of the advertising consultants I talked to cautioned me against that approach. They tried to school me on how money was serious business. "You don't put humor into brokerage and bank commercials," they said. I called in nine different nationally recognized advertising companies and they all gave me boring responses. They seemed to believe it would sully their reputation to put humor into a campaign they created.

OgilvyOne Worldwide, however, was willing to work with my vision. They designed advertisements that featured ordinary people whose lives included taking pleasure in being successful online investors. A businesswoman in a suit says, "I bought Disney for eight bucks." A man says, "I shifted into Mercedes Benz for eight bucks." Another says, "I bought Coca-Cola for eight bucks." We meet a firefighter, the owner of a donut shop, folks on vacation, Japanese businessmen, and they've all bought a stock that speaks to their lives in some way, for a commission of only eight dollars.

For the first time, our ads were not simply making a direct marketing pitch. We were cultivating a brand image: a new generation of Americans of many backgrounds and professions, all so comfortable with investing for themselves that they could have fun with it. Previously, our ads had appeared on CNBC or in financial publications, but now we placed ads during popular television shows that the community of our potential customers enjoyed, like *Nightline*, *NYPD Blue*, and *Seinfeld*. I wanted Ameritrade to become a part of people's lives.

We pulled out all the stops to finance the most ambitious advertising effort the company could afford. In addition to the capital raised with the public offering, Ameritrade negotiated a line of credit of about $75 million. There was speculation in the business press that this could become a very expensive campaign. I told one reporter, "They can estimate whatever they want. As long as the advertising is successful, we're going to continue to push."

Ameritrade also looked for ways to promote its services on the Web. We negotiated an agreement that allowed Yahoo users to connect directly to their Ameritrade accounts for stock quotes and trades. The deal added to similar agreements already in place with Microsoft Investor Relations, America Online, and Intuit's Quicken.

To celebrate the launch, we organized an event at a local sports bar in Omaha called Scorecard to watch the ads debut on *Monday Night Football*. Two undefeated teams—the Dallas Cowboys and the New England Patriots—were playing that night, making for an exciting game with a big national audience. When the company's first spot appeared, we shouted and whistled. Confused regulars at the Scorecard turned to look toward the back room and saw Ameritrade employees standing on chairs and clapping as if we'd just won the Super Bowl.

In the short term, analysts had predicted that Ameritrade would lose money in the last quarter of 1997. As the advertising campaign continued, we opened as many as a thousand new accounts each day. One analyst asserted that each of these accounts cost the company approximately $300 to acquire but had a net present value of nearly $1,300. Over the next nine months, the company opened 181,000 accounts, doubling the firm's customer base. By the end of October, Forrester Research reported that more than 1.5 million investors had online trading accounts, growth that far exceeded their mid-1996 predictions.

Many in the business had doubted that we could survive charging only eight dollars per trade, but now I could see a day when customers might pay nothing per trade or get reimbursed part of the spread in some way, like gas station customers received green stamps. Companies like Ameritrade that had their own clearing operations could afford to offer trades at very low prices because they charged the customer for other banking-related services, like margin loans and stock lending.

Ameritrade more than doubled its share of the total online

brokerage market from 3 percent in September 1997 to 6.4 percent in June 1998. More investors meant more customers opening margin accounts on which we collected interest. By the fall of 1998, the company had more than $600 million on loan to investors, charging rates as high as 9.25 percent. Cash flows also provided opportunities to make money. At any given time, Ameritrade had nearly a billion dollars in cash deposits paying 3 percent. Put to work in the money markets, this cash earned Ameritrade a profit margin while still generating the interest needed to pay investors.

In the end, the response to the massive advertising campaign exceeded all expectations. The eight-dollar pricing strategy unlocked the economies of scale I had suspected were waiting for us. I could never have proved they were there, though, until we achieved them.

Once again, success nearly overwhelmed us. In the first quarter of 1998 alone, the volume of our business doubled. In the next three months, it doubled again. We had only around two hundred employees at the time the new brand launched, and suddenly we were desperate to hire. We set up tables in the lobby of our main office where job applicants could take tests and wait for interviews, while nearby new hires were fingerprinted and photographed. Every day our employees were stepping up to new responsibilities. We had a saying: "If you've worked here three months, you're training someone else."

We leased an old J.C. Penney store plus additional space in the dying Southroads Mall in nearby Bellevue, Nebraska, and turned it into a call center. All the technology we needed to run the business had to be installed, and Susan Hohman, our head of human resources, oversaw that work though she had never done anything like it before. Some staff was moved to an old dress shop with pink carpeting and mirrors on the walls. Every Monday morning at Southroads, we held an orientation for fifty new employees. Meanwhile, to handle all the new brokerage accounts, the company had to train people to take license exams so they could become registered representatives.

We realized we needed another location as a backup, in case a disaster such as a tornado struck our headquarters in Omaha. Susan flew to Texas to open a facility expected to accommodate as many as a thousand customer-service representatives. When she took me to view the site, it was nothing but a dusty stretch of land with a few cows somewhere between Dallas and Fort Worth. Our hope was to attract talent from both cities. A couple of years later, it was a thriving community.

Signing up new accounts and hiring new employees at this rate was astonishing to me, to all of us, I think, and utterly exhilarating. Two years after the launch of the new advertising campaign, the company had grown from two hundred employees to two thousand.

Back in Omaha, our growing computer system strained under the workload. In a locked room at headquarters, a hundred servers with flickering lights hummed twenty-four hours a day, monitored by a team of more than sixty technicians. A backup power system could keep the computers going for two to three hours when the power failed. A six-hundred-gallon diesel-powered generator provided a secondary emergency source of electricity.

Surges in volume threatened to overwhelm our systems at times, but this seemed to be true for all the discount brokerages. At the opening of the market in the morning, when many customers placed their first trades of the day, our computers sometimes crashed and stayed down for forty-five minutes. We also had trouble half an hour before the market closed. On September 10, 1998, a heavy trading day, both Ameritrade and Waterhouse Securities reported that their systems had been down from between twenty-five minutes to two hours. In one week in February 1999, Ameritrade's Internet and touch-tone trading systems both went down, and E*Trade's systems crashed four times for a total of more than four hours.

When our computers went down, frustrated customers called in with their orders or questions. Sometimes they had to wait a full hour to talk to a representative. When they got through, they were furious. Some threatened to sue, claiming they had lost money because their trades wouldn't go through. Mike Anderson kept a bottle of Rolaids on his desk and passed them out to employees like candy. Customer frustration threatened to undermine the massive investment we were making in the brand, especially when our system problems were reported in the press. Eliot Spitzer in the New York Attorney General's Office received widespread complaints about technology problems among all the deep discounters and opened an investigation.

The SEC responded in July 2000 by proposing a new rule that would require online brokers to issue monthly public reports detailing the efficiency of their trades. The SEC also wanted brokerages to tell customers how their orders had been routed so that if an order went wrong, the customer could see where the mistake had been made. The government increased the pressure in October when the SEC detailed 4,258 complaints against online brokers received during the twelve months ending September 2000. The largest number of these complaints related to failures to process orders, or delays in execution. Others reflected difficulties in using the account or contacting a broker. According to the government, the rate of all these complaints was increasing faster than the rate of increase of new accounts opened by online brokers.

At times, it was true; Ameritrade would fall behind in our order flow. We might receive an order at ten in the morning but not be able to execute it until five minutes later. If the price had gotten worse from the customer's point of view, they were entitled to the earlier price. In these years of tremendous and unpredictable growth, with systems sometimes badly overwhelmed, the regulators could have come at us very hard, but instead, they did their jobs in a way that was respectful and constructive. We worked to treat our customers appropriately, and when we made mistakes, we paid for them. I wish the country could get back to that understanding that a degree of regulation is necessary, but there is no need to treat the financial industry, or any industry overall, as criminals. There may be bad actors, like the penny brokers in the '90s, but that doesn't mean that entire industries need to be treated as guilty until proven innocent.

So-called discount brokers had been treated at times like the bastard children of the industry, but now we were being treated as legitimate. After twenty years building a discount brokerage, I felt great satisfaction at the change. Moreover, I felt free to go on trying things that had never been tried before. The regulators had finally recognized that I was doing something good for my customers and the market.

As advertising budgets swelled, regulators were also increasingly uneasy about what they took to be the implied message in the ads: that making money in the stock market was risk-free and took little thought or research. One ad by a Morgan Stanley Dean Witter subsidiary featured a tow-truck driver who had made enough money trading online to buy a tropical island. Officials at the SEC and leaders at the NASD were not happy.

Advertising was driving the hurtling pace of stock orders, so the regulators might have required us to slow down or even stop our advertising. But again, their attitude was changing. They showed patience with us because now the so-called discount brokers were the biggest force in the industry. I volunteered to be on some of the committees on the NASD to get to know some of the regulators and to have the chance to help them understand that we were allowing ordinary people to perform their own analysis of the data and come to their own judgment. It seemed that, for a change, a dialogue with the regulators was possible.

Even as we enjoyed an improved relationship with the regulators, our technology shortcomings grew severe. We were relying on the middleware we had originally designed for Accutrade for Windows to translate the orders that came in from customer PCs to our computer system, but when we added more new features to our trading site, the middleware couldn't handle the complexity. *Barron's Online* ranked the reliability of all the online brokers, and out of twenty-two companies, they judged Ameritrade's website to be second from the worst. We received poor ratings for customer service, availability, price per trade, and ease of use. I realized it would do me no good to have been right about the potential for online trading if I couldn't provide a reliable product.

I gave the IT department a deadline to replace the middleware, but they lacked the technical experience to do it. I began a search for a visionary technologist to guide us, but half the corporations in America were looking for someone who could overcome the challenges of bringing their business to the World Wide Web. Meanwhile, most of the people capable of tackling that job were looking for venture capital so they could start their own companies and get rich by taking their company public.

Finally, a headhunter in New York arranged a meeting with Thomas Lewis. A Philadelphia native from a working-class family, Tom had been head of technology development for Marriott and then for the Reagan White House. Unlike many technologists, though, he was easy to talk with and spoke in layman's terms that made sense to me.

Unfortunately, he wanted to start his own company and said he had no desire to move to Omaha. He offered instead to visit for a week to assess Ameritrade's technology crisis and make recommendations.

At the end of that week, he walked into my office, closed the door, and said, "It's worse than you think." After outlining what needed to be done, he said, "You're probably talking about two hundred million in technology, and it can't all be done here. You're going to need two hundred people with skills in such high demand that you couldn't pay them enough to move to Nebraska."

I was impressed by his analysis. He offered to advise me in finding the right leader for this project, but I told him, "Here's what I really want to know: What will it take to get you to come here and do this for us?"

"I'll come to Omaha," he said, "if I can have your job. I'll come as CEO."

We sat for a long while in silence. I thought about my life. I had always wanted to work. On the weekends, I waited for Monday morning. When the alarm clock went off, I couldn't wait to get into the office. What Tom Lewis was suggesting was almost unimaginable. Even so, there were parts of the business, especially concerning the technology, that were beyond my reach. Didn't my business deserve someone to do for it what I could not?

"Let me think it over," I said, finally.

If I was going to replace myself, I felt, I wanted to make sure I had vetted my choice. Lewis agreed to fly to Denver to be one of several candidates evaluated by an executive search firm. He did very well in the evaluation, but still, I wasn't sure. Several weeks later, I called him with a proposition.

"What would you think of this? You would begin as co-CEO for a year, and if you're successful working with me, hand in hand, after a year I'll make you CEO."

The board was skeptical. My children seemed unconvinced I could exit the business on any timetable. Lewis, though, agreed to give it a try. When he arrived for his first day, having driven his BMW all the way from his home and family in Maryland, he suggested, "Let's talk about how we're going to manage this co-CEO position."

"You'll run technology, Tom," I told him. "I'll oversee everything else."

"Joe," he snapped, "I told you from day one. I didn't come here to be your head of technology."

"I built this company!" I shot back. "I built it from scratch, and I'm not just going to hand it over!"

"Well, I'll tell you what," he said. "I'm getting in my car, and I'm going back to Maryland. Thanks anyway."

Neither of us moved. We sat in my office, fuming. In the quiet, I thought: *We have an enormous issue with unreliable service. It's a technical problem, and I'm running out of time to solve it. This guy seems like he could do the job. Am I really going to send him away and start over?*

Gingerly, we began the conversation over again. We agreed to the dramatic step of slowing the company's advertising and, with it, our rate of growth, then averaging 10 percent a month, to address the deeper problems.

The best thing Tom did for us was hire James Ditmore, a computer systems expert with experience in banking, to serve as chief information officer. We were lucky he took the job—he said later, "If I had understood how much they needed done, I would have said no." After evaluating Ameritrade's entire computer system, Ditmore found some good news: the technological architecture for our web-based business, which was anchored in Sun Microsystems' Unix server-based systems, was sound. Streamlining the computer code and adding selected components to make specific processes run the way they had been designed to run could increase productivity dramatically. Ditmore also addressed our need for redundancy to keep the business afloat in the event of a disaster or a significant system crash. He planned to increase capacity by adding new data centers in Kansas City, Missouri, and Annapolis, Maryland.

With the board's support, the company embarked on a $100 million effort to retool its systems, focusing mainly on the middleware that routed customer requests for information and transactions through the core computer servers. Lewis and Ditmore opened a technology development center outside Baltimore, Maryland, where they felt Ameritrade would more easily attract high-tech workers.

Within eighteen months, having fallen to the bottom of the *Barron's Online* rankings, Ameritrade now soared to the top. Along the way, the web interface was redesigned twice. New accounts processing was restructured so that it could handle eight times the volume with 90 percent fewer employees. With faster processors and software, the average transaction time dropped from more than thirty-five seconds to less than eight. No one had ever imagined that a customer could say "Buy that stock" and it would be done in eight seconds. By the year 2000, Ameritrade would tie with Fidelity for first place in *Money* magazine's rating of overall performance by online brokers.

While the company was making these changes, we ramped up our advertising again with a new series of television spots that launched in the spring of 1999. Ogilvy scripted a spot in which a young office assistant, attractive and irreverent, would teach his boss how easy it was to trade online. They hired Michael Maronna, a twenty-two-year old, red-haired former bike messenger and film student from the State University of New York at Purchase to play the character of Stuart.

On the shoot, Maronna didn't stick to the script. He ad-libbed the first take, and the director had to start over. Then he improvised again. However, the ad-libbed sections, spliced together, had an energy that was fresh, funny, and reassuring, and that became the core of the ad and the campaign that followed.

Stuart is first seen photocopying his face and getting caught by his boss, who calls him into his office. An older coworker shakes her head: *What is wrong with this guy?* But when the door is closed, instead of chewing Stuart out, the boss asks the young man for help making his first trade. "Let's light this candle," Maronna improvised, a slang term for "let's get started" that became a catchphrase in the industry. The message was that trading stocks with your computer could be simple and fun. "It's so easy," the ad explained, "even grown-ups can do it."

The Stuart ads were so successful that the character began to take on a life of his own. Fans demanded autographed photos of Maronna. He seemed cool and smart, a maverick for whom everything works out. "That's the way people who are online traders feel about themselves," my son Pete told one reporter asking about the Stuart mystique. Maronna even made a cameo appearance at President Clinton's annual White House Correspondents' dinner.

On the strength of the Stuart ads and our top-rated systems and service, Ameritrade surpassed not only analyst expectations but also the growth rate of most of its competitors. According to FleetBoston Financial, we were on pace to increase our total number of accounts by 92 percent—growth that was double that of the rest of the industry. *Institutional Investor* wrote, "Hundreds of millions of dollars of Stuart ads have turned Ameritrade into a brand more powerful than some of its larger rivals." At the top of a bull market, the little discount broker from way out in Omaha was at the top of its industry, a business and cultural phenomenon.

CHAPTER 11

By April 1999, during a feeding frenzy for Internet stocks, the company's share price had risen 840 percent. This Internet bubble made a number of our employees millionaires, but only in the retirement accounts that they were forbidden to touch according to the rules of my profit-sharing plan. They knew the sky-high stock price could fall again, but they had no way to make permanent the new wealth that, for many, represented their entire net worth unless they quit. Many felt pressure to resign while the stock was sky-high.

Some employees asked permission to sell a portion of their stock, but I was adamantly opposed. I had worked so hard to build the value of that stock and I could not see why they should want to sell when they had every reason to stay with the company for another twenty years. Could they not see that the world was our oyster? As long as we had good management, I felt sure the company would continue to thrive.

I had designed our profit-sharing plan to align my employees' interests with the long-term interests of my shareholders. Instead, I thought, the Internet bubble was turning them into short-term gamblers, looking to cash out their winnings when the market landed on a high-enough number. I also worried that if the press found out that Ameritrade employees were unloading their stock, it would spread doubt about the company.

The soaring stock price also damaged the motivation to work. Many employees were too distracted by watching the market move on their computer screens to concentrate on their responsibilities. I don't mean, however, to single out my employees for criticism. The Internet bubble was undermining motivation at companies all over the country. It became common to hear people in tech companies talk as if the sole purpose of starting a business was to make a public offering of stock, wait for the price to rise, and cash out. That casino mentality among founders of tech businesses has been with us ever since.

As the Dow continued to soar at the end of 1999, the feeling seemed widespread that the rules of economics had changed. History was irrelevant. Congress repealed significant portions of the Glass-Steagall Act, tearing down many of the walls that had separated commercial banking from the securities industry. Legislation known as the Gramm-Leach-Bliley Act also repealed portions of the Bank Holding Company Act of 1956, which had separated commercial banking from the insurance industry. For the first time in sixty-six years, a single holding company could offer a broad range of banking, securities, and insurance services and products to their customers. These changes expanded the size of the market, though it also removed the barriers to improper actions.

In the changed regulatory environment, banks and brokerages now raced to find partners. Rumors circulated on Wall Street in early March 2000 that Ameritrade was up for sale, but although

I understood that the company might be attractive to a large bank looking to diversify into investing, I continued to feel that our fundamentals and our future were sound. I had no more interest in selling now than I had before.

As the stock market bubble pushed my employees to leave, the pressure was further magnified for some by personal considerations. Many of our top executives had been with the company for years, working long hours, sacrificing both time with family and the chance to pursue private interests. They had spent most of their waking hours as part of the Ameritrade family culture, but now Tom Lewis, my co-CEO, was changing that culture, bringing the kind of professionalism and bureaucratic oversight expected in a public company. Some of the old guard found it hard to adapt. Now they had neither our family feeling nor their financial self-interest to hold them close. The old guard began to leave.

Bob Slezak, our chief financial officer, retired in November, announcing that he planned to sell 550,000 shares of Ameritrade stock worth nearly $10 million. Joe Konen, our president, resigned. Mary Fay, who ran Ceres, and Susan Hohman, head of human resources, left me as well. Other executives departed to spend more time with family or to pursue other interests and ambitions.

I was losing the people who had built my business with me. It was gut wrenching, but it did not change my feeling that they should have held their stock and stayed loyal to the company. The hard truth, which the business journalists never acknowledge, is that there are different stages in the life of a business and the employees and even the management suited to one stage are often not what the company needs for its next stage. When the needs of the company change, people generally can't change with it. I didn't enjoy all the decisions Tom made as CEO, but he was successful. The company needed him, and the unavoidable result was that the old guard departed.

Around this time, my youngest son, Todd, got engaged. He was working at Knight Securities with Ken Pasternak and Walter Raquet, based in Jersey City, New Jersey, and happy with his job. But his fiancée, Sylvie, who was on track to become a partner at the consulting firm Accenture, was based in Toronto and working with a client in Washington, DC. The young couple only saw each other on weekends. I suggested to Todd that they both come work at Ameritrade. It seemed an excellent opportunity to bring new family members into the business.

When they arrived, however, the timing could not have been worse. Tom Lewis had brought in his own people to handle positions and responsibilities that might have suited Todd or Sylvie. They arrived without specific job titles, expecting that where they saw a need they could step in and fill it, but instead Todd told me, "Everything I try to do is someone else's job." Sylvie had a similar experience. Maybe I was naïve, or maybe I didn't want to look too deeply at how the organization and the spirit of the company had changed. When I had invited them to come to Omaha, I hadn't understood that they were not going to be welcomed. Within a year of joining my flourishing, now-public company, they quit and left for Chicago. I was coming to feel that while many fathers dream of having their children come into the family business to work together and make everyone happy, once a company goes public, it's an almost impossible dream.

Around the same time, it also became clear to me that my middle son, Tom, resembled me in his gifts—not an especially motivated student but a natural entrepreneur. Back when he was in college, I had helped him get a job on the Chicago Board Options Exchange. After graduation, he became a trader there. Later he had the idea to sell investment-grade bonds, usually sold to institutions, directly to individual retail investors. The concept had some similarity to the way

Ameritrade had broken with investing tradition and begun to sell stocks directly to individual investors. Tom made a great success of it, first with his colleagues at the Dutch bank ABN AMRO, and then founding his own firm, Incapital. That gave us a lot to talk about, but it also showed me that he was never going to be content to help run someone else's company. He was never going to come work with me at Ameritrade.

My daughter, Laura, was not going to join the management of Ameritrade either, for reasons I did not at first understand. In her early thirties, she told Marlene and me that she was a lesbian. I suppose there had been signs. I can remember her as a little girl, preferring to dress up in trousers and a work shirt, carrying one of my briefcases. But growing up in Omaha, in a Catholic, Republican family, she fought the knowledge within her for years. At her high school, she's told me, the kids who were gay didn't speak about it. Gays were treated as people to feel sorry for. When my brother Bob came out to the family, we discussed it only as part of the story of his death.

For years, Laura had felt the truth but kept it to herself. When she finally came out to us, I wept. I looked over at Marlene and saw that she was not crying, not surprised. She had understood the signs. She told Laura, "I wanted you to come to us in your own time. You're the same person to me. I'm just concerned about what you might face."

Laura explained to me that she had been born this way, and to me, that made all the difference. She was God's creation just like anyone. Through my tears, I told her, "God loves you as much as he loves anybody. Never hang your head. Never take second place. Conduct yourself as an equal and hold your head high and be proud of who you are because I am proud of you. And if anyone gives you any trouble about it, you tell me."

"Oh yeah, Dad?" she answered. "Are you going to beat them up?"

Laura went to law school, and ever since she has made it her mission that gay people should be treated as equal to those who are not. She has gone against social conventions and religious convention. I can see that it has taken a tremendous amount of courage. Marlene has said, "Laura is the only one of the children that you did not intimidate." I think Laura is the bravest person in the family and that makes me very proud. But she was never going to come work with me at Ameritrade.

In May 2000, Tom Lewis took over as sole CEO of Ameritrade, handling day-to-day operations while I continued as president. Almost immediately, however, personal concerns arose that interfered with Tom's work. It became known that he was having an inappropriate relationship with an employee he had hired. Tom and I were comfortable with each other by then, and we decided to take a motorcycle trip to get some perspective. We rode from Helena, Montana, through the Canadian province of Alberta and down to Jackson Hole, Wyoming. I knew that some people's attitude about inappropriate relationships was that boys would be boys, but I felt he had made a choice that was immoral. If he was immoral in this way, I worried he could be immoral in ways that could hurt the company. I felt it was impossible for him to continue with us, and by August he had resigned.

Now, once again, I was the sole CEO of Ameritrade. I knew that people doubted I would ever let someone else run my company and that they might see Tom's departure as evidence that I could not let go. It was indeed true that it was tough for me to give up some control. Very, very tough. Ever since the company had gotten in trouble with the regulators back in 1976, I had taken responsibility for it on myself. I had bought out my original partners back then, and I never pursued new partners seriously, never wanted them, even when they might have brought an infusion of much-needed capital. I was not comfortable giving up my responsibility for the company.

At the same time, I did not relish the idea of remaining CEO. I had done nothing but work my whole life, sixty to eighty hours a week, and now I had a lot of money and wanted to take advantage of it. To be honest, though, enjoying the money I made was never enough motivation for me to give up my responsibilities. I wanted to pull back in part because the quality of my work and the satisfaction I drew from it were changing for the worse.

For all these years, I had managed to align three goals: to run the company to deliver an annual return on investment of 30 percent or more, to create a family business to pass on to my children and grandchildren, and to use the skills for innovation and marketing that I most enjoyed. Now I found I could no longer do all three.

Instead of focusing on innovation and marketing, my company needed me to capture imaginations—of the shareholders, the stock analysts, the general public. I didn't want to do that. I hated taking questions at shareholder meetings. At times, I almost choked on my answers.

I also found it awkward to work with the board of directors, which was tasked with making sure that my choices reflected my fiduciary responsibility to my stockholders. Of course, I had always felt responsibility to my stockholders—my closest friends and family—ever since I had taken control of the company in the '70s, but now I had to chair meetings of a board that questioned my strategic judgment.

Unlike some heads of companies, I had not stacked the board with cronies who would agree with me. Instead, I had sought the guidance of a headhunting firm to help me identify candidates with expertise in different areas I needed, from accounting to regulations to strategic planning and technology. Some of the board members had participated in an advisory group I had put together in the years before we went public, and I was grateful for their expertise. To me, though, advice seemed to be the natural limit of what they should do for me. This was before the Enron scandal had led to changes in laws regarding the independence of boards of directors. Important decisions, I believed, were still mine.

At the first board meeting, we discussed executive compensation.

"We'll need to form a committee to look at that," someone said.

"You can discuss it," I said, "but what you say is not going to impact what I do."

The board also challenged my strategic judgment when I placed big bets, such as the massive investment in advertising right after the IPO. That was uncomfortable for me, but because I was still the majority stockholder, it did not hold me back.

Even when the board provided advice that was helpful to my thinking, the relationship felt uncomfortable to me. I didn't like to make decisions in the middle of a meeting. I preferred to take a walk by myself and let any given question percolate in my mind. Then I would come to a conclusion and tell the other people what they had to do.

With the changes I've described in the laws that had once separated commercial banks, investment banks, and insurers, I saw a new opportunity for Ameritrade. We had succeeded as a low-priced provider of stock trading nationwide. Why couldn't we do the same for insurance? I presented my vision to the board, but they just rolled their eyes.

Wait, I thought. *That's me. That's what I do. I have a vision and I try new things. They don't all work, but insurance feels to me like it could be huge. Why couldn't a trusted discount broker be able to sell insurance to our brokerage customers?*

Some board members were open to doing a market study to test the viability of selling insurance, but I knew that wasn't going to tell us anything. I wanted to bring a product to market and find out what it could do. That did not sit well with the board, and the idea died. It was an unhappy time for me.

In addition to dealing with the board, I also had to deal with stock analysts who seemed to second-guess every decision made by a tech CEO, which is what they now considered me. The big brokerage firms that produced the stock analysis reports were intimidated by the new technology, so they turned the writing over to young writers more familiar with the digital world. These writers were smart people from good schools, but they were very young and lacked real-world experience of running a company. They were quick to say that I was making mistakes, but of course, it was not their money at risk, it was mine. Their stories would be picked up by the press, and then investors would believe the information came from knowledgeable sources, but it did not. The result was twenty-one-year-old kids dictating what major tech companies should be doing. Once these wrong ideas were in circulation, it was up to me as CEO to try to intervene with the media to correct the inevitable inaccuracies and misrepresentations. These were crazy times.

Nevertheless, once Tom Lewis left in 2000, the company needed a CEO, especially at this moment when the industry and the entire country finally had to admit that the Internet bubble was ending. The rules of economics had not, in fact, changed. A professor at Yale named Robert Shiller published a book in April 2000 arguing that share prices in the stock market were unjustifiably high. Stocks then were worth $17 trillion, 1.7 times the value of the nation's gross domestic product. From 1994 to the end of 1999, Shiller pointed out, the Dow Jones had risen from around 3,600 to nearly 11,700, more than tripling its value in just six years, yet during this period, US personal income and GDP rose less than 30 percent, and nearly half of that increase was due to inflation. Corporate profits were up less than 60 percent from lows during the recession of the early '90s. "Viewed in the light of these figures," Shiller warned, "the stock price increase appears unwarranted and, certainly by historical standards, unlikely to persist."

Sure enough, investors soon began to retreat. On April 14, 2000, the Dow dropped 616 points, capping a week of declining values that saw the Nasdaq lose nearly 25 percent of its market capitalization—almost a trillion dollars in wealth vanished in five sessions. The biggest losers in this massive sell-off were the dot-com companies. Employees were laid off by the thousands. Unlike past drops in the stock market, which affected only a relatively small percentage of Americans, this decline hurt one out of two households in the nation.

As the downturn continued and trading volumes declined, Ameritrade was forced to cut overhead. Fortunately, our recent investments in technology produced dramatic savings. With the systems newly upgraded, we could now handle more than two out of every three incoming phone calls with no human involvement. Online orders went from the keyboard of the customer all the way to us and back without anyone intervening. The percentage of transactions handled by a registered representative fell from 14 percent to almost zero. That meant that when our call volume shrank, we didn't need so many layoffs. As a result of automating so many of our calls and transactions, our average cost of processing a trade declined by nearly 25 percent. These were vast improvements. We now spent less money executing and processing a trade than anyone in the business. Meanwhile, our revenue per trade, including earnings on margin loans and payments for order flow from market makers, rose to twenty dollars per trade.

All that cost cutting put us in a strong position to weather a downturn, so even as market conditions altered, we could maintain our traditional approach. Schwab and E*Trade, however, changed course. If the market was turning, they seemed to reason, many self-directed investors would feel less confident in their ability to pick stocks and start looking to buy investment advice. In June 2000, E*Trade announced a joint venture with Ernst & Young to provide financial planning services to its brokerage customers. Schwab did something similar.

Those two companies also took advantage of the recent changes in the investment laws to move into banking. E*Trade spent $1.8 billion to buy Telebanc Financial Corporation, an Internet bank, and acquired Card Capture Services, a company that operated 8,500 ATMs around the country. It also bought Private-Accounts.com, a business that offered personalized asset management services to high-net-worth clients. Schwab, similarly, purchased U.S. Trust Corp., a private bank, for $2.7 billion.

Stock analysts seemed to like these moves, but Ameritrade did not change course. As the market retrenched in the middle of 2000 and many discount brokers began to struggle in the new environment, I believed a massive consolidation in the industry was on the horizon. The stronger would acquire the weaker. I directed my management to hire enough new employees to open a million new accounts.

In June 2000, the company acquired Ten Bagger Inc. In February 2001, we bought TradeCast for $40 million in stock and rebranded it as Ameritrade Pro, a new service for professional and active stock traders. As the bear market continued, we bought National Discount Brokers from Deutsche Bank in a stock deal worth $154 million. They had previously paid $823 million. At roughly $500 per account, the National Discount Brokers deal added 316,000 accounts representing more than $6 billion in customer assets to Ameritrade's business.

Some analysts criticized our "dogmatic focus" on online brokerage and US (not international) markets, especially as we, like most other brokerages, lost money—twelve to fourteen cents a share in the last quarter of 2000. The losses were two and a half to three times what analysts had been expecting. In January 2001, we announced that we would lay off 230 full-time employees and eliminate our entire temporary workforce in response to the slowdown in online trading. It was a worrisome time. Some pundits predicted the end for "any online broker that insists on slogging it out as a transaction-oriented business." Deep-pocketed traditional brokers were set to buy or bury any online broker who refused to give in. Richard Strauss of Goldman Sachs went so far as to tell *Fortune*, "I think the majority of these [discount brokers] are toast."

Internet stock trading volumes continued to slide. In the first six months of 2001, among all online brokers, they fell 50 percent. By early April 2001, Ameritrade's once-skyrocketing stock price had fallen to $5.28. E*Trade slashed its spending on advertising by 50 percent. Schwab cut 3,400 workers. Once again, rumors circulated on Wall Street that Ameritrade was about to be bought. *American Banker* reported in May 2001 that Canadian Imperial Bank of Commerce was negotiating to buy Ameritrade for $1.8 billion or approximately $9 to $10 a share.

"We do not want to be bought," I told the *Wall Street Journal.* Reflecting on the state of the market, I acknowledged, "At these prices, everyone in the world would love to buy us, but we are not for sale, and I think everyone knows it." Because my family and I still owned about 63 percent of Ameritrade's stock, a deal without my approval was impossible.

Through all the ups and downs of those hard years, what mattered was our consistency. My son Pete likes to say that the most important lesson he learned from me—not by hearing me talk but by watching me work—was "mission first." Our mission as ever was to make the company grow by reinvesting our earnings and remaining a low-cost provider. When the market was up and trading volume went up along with it, we spent on acquiring more of the tools we needed and on spreading our good name—in other words, we bought technology and advertising. When the market fell, we kept our costs as low as we could and went bargain hunting among our competitors. Our success in the new millennium was consistent with the mission I had established in the 1970s, and it was not so different in philosophy from my father and grandfather's approach to the Ricketts home-construction business—hard work, the latest tools (like that long-ago buzz saw), and reliable quality to give meaning to the phrase "Ricketts built." Their approach in the 1940s and 1950s, in turn, was not much different from that of my forebears in the nineteenth century. Ameritrade survived and thrived after the bursting of the Internet bubble because we remained old-fashioned pioneers.

With Tom Lewis gone and my own satisfaction with the job of CEO fading, my choice for a new CEO was my son Pete. Although I might have underestimated him early in his career, I had come to believe he was capable of handling anything. He understood my vision, yet he felt comfortable challenging me when he thought I was wrong. He asked the hard questions and was highly professional in his management style, focusing on process and discipline. He had worked in almost every part of the business and had a personal touch and a down-to-earth style that made people comfortable. He even played in the company's paintball league.

But because we were a public company, it was unlikely Pete could become CEO at that point. He was still young, and the board had concerns about how it would look if I picked my son to succeed me, especially given that we had several older candidates within the company who also deserved consideration. The market analysts expressed skepticism. "The market would not look favorably on it," one analyst told a reporter. "It's nothing against Pete, but they need to bring in a world-class manager like Tom [Lewis]." The market's reaction to the choice of a new CEO was especially critical for us given the economic pressure on Ameritrade and all online brokers at the end of 2000.

I asked the board to create a selection committee to consider all our senior executives for the job. The committee members interviewed them but came away with a strong feeling that the company needed someone with greater experience running a public company. The board concluded that they would be better off hiring a candidate with a proven track record who could mentor Pete and position him to be a successor in five years or so. It was another disappointment of being a public company.

In March 2001, Ameritrade recruited Joe Moglia from the investment products and strategies section of Merrill Lynch's private client division. A former football coach at Dartmouth, he had grown up in an Italian neighborhood in Columbia Heights, Brooklyn. Hard-driving and energetic, he was also charismatic and inspirational. Moreover, unlike Tom Lewis, he planned to move his family to Omaha, which to midwesterners was an essential sign of commitment. Wall Street applauded the appointment: when news leaked that he had been tapped, Ameritrade's stock rose 8.4 percent.

Moglia took over in an especially tough year. On September 11, 2001, terrorists using commercial jetliners as missiles attacked the World Trade Center and the Pentagon. In the wake of the attacks, the New York Stock Exchange closed for four days. That fall, the weak market turned worse, and Ameritrade struggled to balance cost cutting to maintain profitability with investing for the future. After the 9/11 attacks, the company closed the books on its fiscal year and reported a $14 million loss. Joe Moglia called the final quarter "one of the most difficult in the last twenty years."

The immediate circumstances that contributed to Ameritrade's financial woes in the fall of 2001 were bad enough, but long-term factors were even more disturbing. Many of our customers and self-directed investors in general had stopped trading. Many others abandoned the idea that they could manage their financial futures and returned to traditional brokerage firms, hoping that greater expertise would protect the assets they still owned. The numbers were bleak. As recently as early 2000, 45 percent of all trades on the New York Stock Exchange and the Nasdaq had come from online brokers. Two years later, online brokers handled only 22 percent of this volume. Many companies in the brokerage industry were in trouble. By mid-October, the index for the S&P 500 had fallen to 776, half its value at the top of the dot-com bubble. The Nasdaq had fallen near 1,100, which was 78 percent below its peak during the bubble. Of some 825 companies that had gone public in 1999 and 2000, 715 were below their offer price and more than a third were trading for less than a dollar a share or had been delisted.

Once again, there seemed to be a widespread feeling that recent events had changed everything—this time, for worse and not for better. Yet I could not forget how the stock market had collapsed in the 1970s after I first entered the brokerage industry. It had seemed then that no one wanted to invest in stocks anymore, but the customer is always going to come back. I believed that a downturn, however severe, was only going to be temporary, and so it represented a chance to grow. I never lost my faith in the old laws of economics.

Late in 2001, a remarkable opportunity materialized. Datek Online Holdings Corporation put itself on the auction block. The brokerage had flouted the rules in the 1990s, and after being charged with securities fraud by the SEC, the company had paid a $6.3 million fine. It seemed the regulators would put Datek out of business, but the investment firm Bain Capital, an investor in Datek, negotiated for its survival with the Justice Department and the SEC. The regulators agreed that the company could survive if it could find a white knight to buy it. Following Bain's plan, the company put itself on the auction block.

Datek's accounts were very valuable. We estimated that a merger could achieve a $100 million in annualized savings. We won the bidding war with an offer of $1.29 billion in stock, and shareholders for both companies approved the deal in September 2002.

That was how, in this extremely bleak time for tech stocks, the Datek acquisition made Ameritrade the number-one online broker as measured by trading volume. We became number one despite holding customer assets equal to just 5 percent of the assets held by Schwab. Meanwhile, Schwab had now effectively abandoned the discount market and, by adding a growing array of services and facilities, focused on asset aggregation, moving to compete with full-service brokers like Merrill Lynch. In contrast, with the acquisition of Datek, Ameritrade's position with savvy, self-directed investors, including day traders, seemed more secure than ever.

As we integrated Datek's accounts with our own, the advantages of Ameritrade's strategy became increasingly apparent to the market. By the end of 2003, Internet stocks were once again in favor on Wall Street. Consumers had never truly abandoned the online trading world, despite the predictions of analysts at the full-service brokers. That made sense to me: Once you give someone freedom, they won't want to go back. While analysts noted that with the resurgence of Internet stocks, Ameritrade and E*Trade were both back in favor again, "of the two, Ameritrade should have more upside in a stronger market," *Fortune* wrote, "especially since, unlike E*Trade, it doesn't have banking and mortgage operations that could weigh on the share price if interest rates continue to tick higher." *Fortune* also noted that the company had a "pristine balance sheet and strong management that keeps a lid on costs." As the economy began to recover in 2004, Ameritrade found that its decision to stay focused had paid off. Charles Schwab struggled to control costs related to less profitable diversified lines of business, and E*Trade faced similar issues, while Ameritrade returned to solid profitability.

It was a tremendous feeling to achieve the goal that no one had believed I would ever meet, becoming the biggest broker in the world as measured by number of trades, and especially to reach it at a time of unrest and decline for the industry. To reach that goal, however, had required me to make changes to the company and my role that could never be undone. The acquisition agreement required that we form a new board of directors that reflected the combined interests of both Ameritrade and Datek shareholders. My share of the total equity fell from 55 percent to 28 percent. For the first time, I had no majority interest in my company. Giving up that kind of authority scared the crap out of me, but forced to choose, I chose the company's success over my authority.

Although I remained the largest single stockholder and, as chairman, exercised a great deal of influence over the company's future, I felt increasingly out of place. I remember the first time I made a proposal at a board meeting and a member responded, "We're going to need to get buy-in on that."

I thought: *Are you kidding me? "Buy-in" at Ameritrade?*

I had always believed that the leader of a company has to do what he or she thinks best. You can't listen to market research or anyone else. I had succeeded as an entrepreneur in a private company *because* I didn't listen to others. In a public company, though, you have to listen. You have to bring people around to your point of view.

One day, angered by people in the company who were not doing as I said, I complained to Pete: "They're insubordinate!"

"Dad," he said, "that's only in the army. People here work for us because they want to work here. If they don't like it, they'll quit. You've got to bring them along, help them buy into the mission and vision." Pete was great at that. He had a gift for management and politics. I did not.

As uncomfortable as these changes in the company were for me, I was happy that the successful integration of Datek had put Ameritrade in an even stronger position to acquire other companies. In April 2003, we purchased Mydiscountbroker.com's 16,500 online retail accounts and integrated them into Ameritrade's client base. In September, Ameritrade's total number of accounts surpassed the three million mark. Acquisitions of BrokerageAmerica and Bidwell & Company added approximately one hundred thousand accounts and nearly $5 billion in client assets. The company then acquired the online retail accounts of JB Oxford Holdings for roughly $26 million. We were able to integrate all of these types of operations smoothly into our own.

Feeling the pressure from Ameritrade and E*Trade, Schwab announced in May 2004 that it would cut prices for some online stock trades to remain competitive. Schwab told analysts that the move would reduce overall revenue by 2 to 3 percent. Relative to the price/earnings ratios of Ameritrade and E*Trade, Schwab stock was still expensive, indicating that the market put a premium on Schwab's brand. However, the markets worried that Schwab's price cut reflected continuing uncertainty about how to position the company and its services in the market, and the share price fell 3 percent on the news. Schwab's difficulties became all the more apparent in January 2005, when the *Wall Street Journal* reported that while Ameritrade's earnings had risen 29 percent in the last quarter of 2004, Schwab's profits had dropped by 64 percent. They had finally tried to compete with us on price, but they had started too late. We were now too big and too successful to be driven out of business with that tactic.

Precisely because Ameritrade showed itself to be so healthy financially, we became a target for another merger. In 2004, TD Waterhouse and Ameritrade discussed a possible combination, but the conversation faltered after TD Waterhouse insisted on more management control than Ameritrade was inclined to give. TD Waterhouse also talked to E*Trade, but no deal was reached because, again, corporate governance issues could not be resolved. Then in spring 2005, E*Trade made a bid to acquire Ameritrade while at the same time Ameritrade resumed conversations with TD Waterhouse. These were high-stakes negotiations for all three companies. The future of the brokerage industry was being determined.

At this point the board included me, my sons Pete and Tom, Professor Mark Mitchell, who had advised us on meeting the challenge of E*Trade, and a number of representatives of Datek and its investors, Bain Capital and Silver Lake Partners. Overall, the board was leaning toward accepting the offer from TD Waterhouse. Pete, though, felt strongly that he didn't want us to be owned by a stodgy bank. He thought that E*Trade was a company more like ours and that they would work with us better.

The board held a weekend conference call. I remember that Pete and I took the call in the library of my home. It became clear that nearly everybody wanted to accept the offer from TD Waterhouse, but Pete asked for the chance to call Mitch Caplan, CEO of E*Trade, to ask if his company would make a better offer. The board agreed to let him take that shot. We got off the phone and Pete and I hugged.

Pete called Mitch at home, and soon E*Trade made a counteroffer. Then TD Waterhouse, to stay competitive, offered about $400 million more, an all-stock deal worth $2.9 billion. We were in the office of the investment bank. Pete told the board, "I didn't want to do the TD deal, but I don't know how we can vote against an offer that good."

"Pete!" I said after the call ended. "Do you know what you just did? Do you realize you just made us an extra four hundred million dollars?"

Then Pete called Mitch Caplan at E*Trade and said, "I'm so sorry."

The deal was an amazing triumph for our company. It made me and Marlene and our children wealthy beyond what we had ever imagined. The deal also marked the end of the work that made up my adult life and of the last hope I had that Ameritrade would be run by Ricketts family members. When management went out to dinner that night to celebrate, Pete begged off and went back to his hotel. Now that we were merging with Toronto-Dominion, he knew he would never fit in to the banking culture. He would never succeed me as CEO. From the night we closed the deal, Pete was already making plans to resign.

The new board of TD Ameritrade let me know very quickly that I was not in any way running the company, and gradually I stepped down as chairman and became a board member. Now, what I said did not go. Not at all.

Did I feel proud of what we accomplished that day? I felt certain, intellectually, that I had made the right choice. I also understood that the company had now outgrown all of its old guard, including me. Did I attend that dinner celebration after we closed the Toronto-Dominion deal? I don't remember the rest of that night. My career was over. Emotionally, I had blacked out.

EPILOGUE

The TD Ameritrade deal proved to be one of the best and worst events of my life. The good part I saw coming—wealth beyond anything I had imagined. The deal was valued at about a billion dollars in stock for my family and me, but I was in no rush to sell our shares. I took the same advice I'd always given my employees and held the stock because I believed in the company. A few years later, it was worth $6 billion.

Wealth gave me the freedom to do as I pleased. I bought a ranch in Wyoming near Yellowstone National Park on beautiful land that was, in many ways, unchanged from frontier days. Marlene and I began to travel the world. In England, we enjoyed the chance to meet former prime minister Margaret Thatcher and her husband, Sir Denis Thatcher. We also met former chancellor Helmut Kohl, who gallantly kissed Marlene's hand and became her smoking buddy. We discovered we had the opportunity to meet almost anybody if we put the introduction the right way. We also found, though, that the thrill wears off fast. At some point, you want to go home and get back to the rest of your life. The rest of my life, though, had been my work, and now my work was gone.

That next period for me became a kind of limbo. "When Joe stepped down from being CEO," Marlene would explain to friends and family members, "I think it broke his heart. He got so quiet. Someone else could have walked away and spent the rest of his life having fun, but Joe wasn't born that way. He needs to be needed by a business. He has his family, and that's fun, but that's on weekends. During the week he needs something to do." I had always found fulfillment in setting goals and working hard to achieve them. The flip side, I learned, was that having no goals and no use for your talents produces emptiness.

For most of my adult life, I had focused on three goals: to employ the skills I loved to use, to work to make my company prosper, and to create an enduring business my children and grandchildren could run when I was gone. Now I felt as though I'd retired when I was still only one for three. I worried especially about the future of my family. Without Ameritrade as its center, the sun for our solar system, what would hold us together? Each of my children had gone off in their own direction professionally: Pete into politics, Tom into business, Laura advocating for equal rights for gay people, and Todd working for conservative causes—"saving Western civilization," as he likes to tell me. Each was blessed to marry well, and their wives—Susanne, Cecilia, Brooke, and Sylvie—were truly daughters to me. My children were all finding personal satisfaction in their lives, but what was going to hold the generations together?

I had seen other families drift apart when they became wealthy and I didn't know what would make us any different. Back when the children were little and they would argue, Marlene had always told them, "Fight all you want when you're in the house, but when you go out of doors, go as a group." Once Marlene and I were gone, I wondered, what would be left to remind them that family comes first? When economies and governments go bad, and you have to find a way to survive, family cohesiveness is what helps you get through. A lot of people are alive today because their cousin told them or their parents or grandparents to get out of Germany in the 1930s. Family, to me, is our crowning achievement, our greatest good. But after the TD Ameritrade deal, I could not see a happy future ahead for either my family or me.

One day, my middle son, Tom, approached me with a proposition. Back when he had applied to business school, he had written an essay describing his dream job: owning and managing the Chicago Cubs. At that time, he and Pete lived in an apartment above a bar across from Wrigley Field. When I telephoned them and the El train went by, we had to pause because the noise drowned out our voices, but Tom loved living so close to the ballpark. Now he suggested that our family make an offer to buy the Cubs. Over the years, I had put Ameritrade stock into trusts for all my children, and with the TD Ameritrade deal, those trusts had become extremely valuable. The kids had the means to make an offer on their own, but he still wanted my blessing.

Tom pitched me his proposal, and I said, "That's the stupidest idea I've ever heard." Tom, however, was a natural entrepreneur with an entrepreneur's optimism. He told me later that he felt my response, harsh though it might have been, was a step forward. *Yes!* Tom thought to himself. *Dad didn't say no!*

I had never had any interest in baseball, but he had described his plan as a business venture, which I understood very well. I was also compelled by the idea that my four children would go in on this venture together. I could see that it would be a complex and ongoing project, something that would require them to stay in frequent contact and manage their differences. Could this become the keystone that the family lacked? We differed on politics, differed in our religious beliefs, but this could be something the entire family had in common. What finally convinced me was seeing all my grandkids at a Cubs game, seated together in one row. I told Tom that if his siblings supported the idea of buying the franchise, I would support it, too.

In a way, it was a perfect business for my kids to take on, because I didn't know anything about running a sports franchise so I couldn't interfere. People told me we were going to lose money if we got into the sports business, so I warned my four children, "You can't come back to the honey pot. Take the money to make the purchase, but after that, you have to run it successfully or sell it to someone who can."

As it turned out, I was wrong. Buying the Cubs was not a stupid idea at all. From the start, my children ran the franchise successfully. With new management, the team won their first World Series in more than a century, and the value of the franchise multiplied. The four siblings have weekly phone calls in which they navigate around the challenges of owning the organization together. I could not be happier to see them close and connected, and also to know that I was able to model for them how a family can unite around the work they must do together, focused on being creators and not just consumers. In this way, although Ameritrade did not become the family business, Ameritrade money and Ameritrade values helped my children establish the family business that will last beyond my lifetime.

There was still the question of what I would do with my days and my skills. Some of my time I just enjoyed myself with traveling and vacations. Two high school friends and our wives would get together once a year and go to the Black Hills of South Dakota to ski. Now, that was the stated purpose of these trips, but we never actually skied because in the morning we would start drinking Bloody Marys and light a fire in the fireplace and sit around telling jokes and enjoying one another's company. One time, driving across South Dakota, the weather was temperate, and my friend asked if we would like to see a bison ranch. It was managed by his wife's cousin, and he liked to hunt deer there in the fall. The farm was only seven miles from the interstate.

The rancher took us out on a tractor to look at the animals. And because we were going to be with him over lunchtime, he invited us to stay for the meal, as any good rancher or farmer would. His wife, who made the meal, served creamed corn, several salads, mashed potatoes, and gravy—it was like Easter Sunday. Then she brought out of the warming oven a pile of bison T-bone steaks, huge and thick. Having just seen examples of the bison that produce this steak, I knew it was a big, hardy animal, a tough animal, and I worried the steak would be tough. I saw that my hosts had only provided me with a butter knife, and I pictured myself trying to cut that thick steak and flipping it into my wife's lap.

To my surprise, though, the meat was juicy, delicious, and tender. I could cut it with a fork. I thought, *Man, if I could sell this meat to the public, I could make a fortune*. It had the potential to be one of those ventures where everybody wins—the customer gets a great piece of meat, the company's employees make a good living, and I make a profit. Another Ameritrade waiting for someone to believe in it. But I didn't know anything about raising bison. I said to my host, "Tell me about this meat."

When the "skiing" trip was over, I wanted to learn more, so I went to the National Western Stock Show in Denver to see prize animals and learn how they were treated. I read there that a fellow was offering white bison for sale. I had never heard of white bison. I called the number on the note, and the guy explained that he had a farm where he raised wild game from different parts of the world. For a fee, he would release the game onto forest service land so a hunter could shoot it. How did he get white bison? I asked him. He mated ordinary bison with Charolais cows to get the Charolais' white genes. Not all the calves came out white, so he had some brown ones for sale, too. I bought two of the brown bison to live on my ranch in Wyoming so I could see what that was about.

Gradually, I developed a brand around bison meat for sale to grocery stores. Once again, after so many years, I was starting a business. I was in charge, and I could hire talented people and risk my own money and not have to answer to anyone, just as I had loved doing for Ameritrade.

That first venture led to other for-profit adventures and philanthropic pursuits: restaurants, educational institutions, conservation, a film company, some local news services, and an Ignatian Catholic silent meditation retreat. The most recent is a pie company. I sometimes say that I start new businesses for my grandkids to run, but that's not entirely true. I hope some of my grandchildren will manage my companies and that some will be the entrepreneurs who take the existing companies in new directions, but it's just as true that I start new businesses because it's exciting and it lets me use my skills.

Entrepreneurship is an art, a kind of painting you do in your mind of what could succeed in a future that doesn't yet exist. Entrepreneurship is an applied science, like surviving in the wilderness. When you bring that art and science together and you risk your capital in the marketplace with the chance of real failure and practical reward, you get one of the most magnificent and fruitful activities that human beings can attempt. We started Ameritrade from nothing, just a glimmer of an idea that we hardly understood ourselves, and we were giddy with joy when we were able to do a handful of trades. Forty-five years later, the company sometimes handles more than a million trades a day. It employs ten thousand people, all of who can build lives for themselves and their families. Successes like that made this country, and they are what will keep it strong in the future. The principle I learned as a young man still holds: the way to relieve misery and bring happiness is through free enterprise. I prefer that term to *capitalism*, which sounds as if you need a lot of capital to participate. But we started Ameritrade, as many entrepreneurs do, with almost no money.

Many Americans, I'm afraid, no longer respect free enterprise. The term has come to seem the property of conservatives, while liberals appear drawn instead to socialism. Many Americans, especially young people, apparently do not understand what economists have clearly shown, that for this country to provide jobs for our graduates and our immigrants, we need to increase gross national product by at least 3 percent per year. Free enterprise is what creates jobs and makes the economy expand. I don't see how we can be America without it. And while I'm not going to get on my soapbox here, I do have to point out that in a socialist country there would have been no Ameritrade.

Among conservatives, meanwhile, there is lately an extreme focus not on creating the best conditions for free enterprise but on eliminating regulation. The truth, though, is that for the country to do well, we will always need some regulation. The question is how not to overdo it. In my industry, for example, someone must look out for the customer. Someone must weed out the bad actors, such as the unscrupulous penny brokers of the 1990s. Even on the frontier, back when beaver trappers—the ultimate entrepreneurs—moved into unmapped lands, sometimes a newcomer would be unethical. He would find an established trapper working a good stream and kill that man to take his stream. If he killed a good man, someone else in the area might kill him for revenge. If he killed a bad man, they might slap him on the back and say well done. The only justice they had was what they made themselves. So, we needed the covered wagons to come, bringing sheriffs and courts—imperfect justice, still, but better.

Free enterprise can't function without an ethical government that enforces necessary regulations judiciously. When free enterprise does work properly, I believe, it is our best chance of practical salvation in the world. Its accomplishments are more significant than those of any system of government or religion. America learned it on the frontier, and those lessons from the frontier still hold today. They could be the key to my next success, or yours.

Moreover, as I know from my own experience, free enterprise does far more than create wealth. When I go to work, it's not because I need more money. I'm working at my businesses because that kind of work brings not just prosperity but joy. To see people make good wages, do well, and send their kids to college—that's what gives me joy today. That's what brings me pleasure. When I get up in the morning, and Marlene says goodbye, she says, "Have fun!"

Acknowledgments

There are several people I want to acknowledge and thank for their contributions to this book project. First and foremost, I want to thank my wife, Marlene, who has been my partner in life, both working with me at Ameritrade and raising four amazing kids. I also want to thank my children, Peter, Tom, Laura, and Todd, who lived through many of the adventures in this book and have each grown up to be smart, independent adults with ethical values. I could not be more proud of you.

My thanks to G. F. Lichtenberg, my cowriter, for helping me to bring out not just the facts but also the spirit of this story. Thanks to Alfred Levitt and Bob Barnett for their encouragement to write this book in the first place. And, finally, I want to thank Priscilla Painton, my editor, and the entire team at Simon & Schuster, who helped to guide this book to completion.

Notes

Chapter 2

38 *For the first time since the stock market crash of 1929*: John Brooks, *The Go-Go Years: The Drama and Crashing Finale of Wall Street's Bullish 60s* (New York: Allworth Press, 1998), 101.

38 *As trading volumes rose to record levels*: Lee Berton, "Reluctant Bosses: Brokerage Firms Find Prospering Salesman Shun Managerial Jobs," *Wall Street Journal*, January 29, 1968. For median income in 1965, see "Consumer Income," US Bureau of the Census, *Current Population Reports*, Series P-60, no. 49 (August 10, 1966).

Chapter 3

49 *the number of Americans who owned stock*: "The Death of Equities," *Businessweek*, August 13, 1979, cited in Roger Lowenstein, *Origins of the Crash: The Great Bubble and Its Undoing* (New York: Penguin, 2004), 2.

49 *American manufacturing had slowed*: Stuart Bruchey, *The Wealth of the Nation: An Economic History of the United States* (New York: Harper & Row, 1988), 211–14.

49 "*'story peddlers'*": Steven Fraser, *Every Man a Speculator: A History of Wall Street in American Life* (New York: Harper Perennial, 2005), 536.

51 "*Ideas rule the world*": George C. Roche III, "Why Not a Campaign

for National Leadership?" *imprimis*, August 1983, 2. https://imprimis.hillsdale.edu/wp-content/uploads/2016/11/Imprimis-Why-Not-A-Campaign-For-National-Leadership-Aug-1983.pdf.

54 *The Dow would lose three-quarters of its total value*: Ibid.

Chapter 4

87 *At the same time, there was evidence that some full-service brokers were colluding*: Timothy D. Schellhardt and Richard E. Rustin, "U.S. Probe of Brokerage-Rate Practices Isn't Expected to Produce Indictments," *Wall Street Journal*, April 11, 1978.

Chapter 5

92 *"willfully aided and abetted"*: "First Omaha Securities, 4 Aides to Be Subject of SEC Proceedings," *Wall Street Journal*, March 31, 1977.

96 *"We would like to fight these very old charges"*: "First Omaha Securities Gets 5-Day Suspension, Settling SEC Complaint," *Wall Street Journal*, August 4, 1977.

109 *equal to the firm's entire net worth*: Terence P. Pare, "How Schwab Wins Investors," *Fortune*, June 1, 1992, 54.

119 *The Gallup organization conducted a study*: Art Kleiner, "How to Build a Stronger Economy," *strategy+business*, September 4, 2018, https://www.strategy-business.com/article/How-to-Build-a-Stronger-Economy.

Chapter 6

132 *Volcker pushed for an increase in the federal funds rate*: Richard A. Posner, *The Crisis of Capitalist Democracy* (Cambridge, MA: Harvard University Press, 2010), 23–24. See also Charles R. Geisst, *Wall Street: A History: From Its Beginnings to the Fall of Enron* (New York: Oxford University Press, 2004), 325.

132 *Volcker did succeed in slowing the pace of inflation*: Posner, *The Crisis of Capitalist Democracy*, 24.

132 *increasing deregulation of global banking systems brought a flood*: Robert Brenner, *The Boom and the Bubble: The US in the World Economy* (London: Verso, 2002).

132 *hostile takeovers and leveraged buyouts*: Steve Fraser, *Every Man a Speculator: A History of Wall Street in American Life* (New York: Harper Perennial, 2005), 543.

144 *William Porter and Bernard Newcomb founded a company*: E*Trade Group, Inc., "Prospectus," August 16, 1996, 23, 54.

152 *"raging bull market"*: Maggie Mahar, *Bull!: A History of the Boom and Bust, 1982–2004* (New York: Harper Business, 2004), 50.

152 *20 percent of stock trading*: J. Ernest Beazley, "Financial Planning (A Special Report): Investing—Narrowing the Gap: Changing Costs, Services Blur the Distinction Between Discount Brokers and Full-Service Firms," *Wall Street Journal*, December 2, 1985.

Chapter 7

153 *Commission revenues dropped 20 percent*: Joe Ricketts, "Reports to Stockholders," November 27, 1984, 3, Ricketts Archives.

156 *the Douglas Building, a former Masonic temple*: Jim McKee, "Freemasons Build a Home in Lincoln," *Journal Star*, January 16, 2016, https://journalstar.com/lifestyles/jim-mckee-freemasons-build-a-home-in-omaha/article_e5c9faa4-d4cf-5c4f-a746-66d2ae42235a.html.

162 *software, and services would cost between $150 and $200 million*: "AT&T and Quotron Set Pact to Develop Business-Data System," *Wall Street Journal*, June 21, 1985.

163 *Both the NYSE and the American Stock Exchange had developed*: Scott McMurray, "Three Brokerage Firms Moving Toward Automated Over-the-Counter Trading," *Wall Street Journal*, January 11, 1985.

176 *signs of weakness*: Maggie Mahar, *Bull!: A History of the Boom and Bust, 1982–2004* (New York: Harper Business, 2004), 62.

177 *share prices stalled*: Charles R. Geisst, *Wall Street: A History: From Its Beginnings to the Fall of Enron* (New York: Oxford University Press, 2004), 348–49.

180 *The markets overall were experiencing volatility*: Mark L. Mitchell and Jeffry M. Netter, "Triggering the 1987 Stock Market Crash," *Journal of Financial Economics* 24, no. 1: 37–68. See also Mahar, *Bull!*, 64.

Chapter 8

204 *With the launch of Accutrade, we grew tremendously*: Richard E. Croker to J. Joe Ricketts, July 10, 1991, in "Reports to Stockholders" binder, Ricketts Archives.

205 *an exponential change*: Joe Ruff, "Ameritrade Moves from Upstart to Mainstay," *Denver Post*, March 29, 2004.

205 *Ameritrade outpaced most of its peers*: Securities Industry Association, *1995 Securities Industry Fact Book* (New York: Securities Industry Association, 1995), 39–40.

208 *The case first came to light*: "Columbiana County Calls in FBI Over Missing $6 Million," *Dayton Daily News*, September 22, 1993.

208 *the son had opened a brokerage account*: *SEC v. Stephen T. Strabala*, U.S.D.C. N.D. Ohio, Civil Action No. 4:95 CV 02060, filed September 25, 1995, http://www.sec.gov/litigation/litreleases/lr14667.txt. See also Securities and Exchange Commission, *1995 Annual Report* (Washington, DC: Securities and Exchange Commission, 1996), 43–44.

208 *three hundred thousand dollars in public funds*: Stephanie Ujhelyi, "City's Treasury Investment Board Agrees to Maintain Current Investment Course," *Alliance Review*, October 8, 2008.

208 *pleaded guilty*: "Criminal Actions: Stephen T. Strabala," *Ohio Securities Bulletin* 94, no. 4 (1994): 18.

208 *Sentenced to nine years*: "Criminal Actions: Stephen T. Strabala," *Ohio Securities Bulletin* 95, no. 1 (1995): 6.

Chapter 9

212 *I always kept one eye on the possible threats from our competition*: Anthony Bianco, "Charles Schwab vs. Lee Quick," *Businessweek*, May 12, 1986, 80.

212 *Schwab was referred to as a discount broker*: Ibid.

220 *repeal of the regulatory barriers*: Charles R. Geisst, *Wall Street: A History: From Its Beginnings to the Fall of Enron* (New York: Oxford University Press, 2004), 366.

220 *"people talked about stocks in their homes and offices"*: Roger Lowenstein, *Origins of the Crash: The Great Bubble and Its Undoing* (New York: Penguin, 2004), 23.

222 *In response to this new low commission*: Michael Trimarchi, "The Duel of the Discount Brokerages," *Washington Post*, July 10, 1994.

228 *"The Cheap Get Cheaper"*: Francis Flaherty, "Discount Brokers: The Cheap Get Cheaper," *New York Times*, June 18, 1994.

231 *the organization that would collect the $20 million*: Rebecca Buckman, "On-Line Firms Poised to Reap Hefty Rewards in Stock Deal," *Wall Street Journal*, June 29, 1998.

233 *increase more than 2,000 percent*: Rebecca Buckman, "Online Trader

Knight/Trimark, amid a Boom, Faces Threats," *Wall Street Journal*, January 19, 1999.

237 *the first discount brokerage to trade stock over the Internet*: Steven T. Goldberg, "Goodbye Wall Street, Hello Omaha," *Kiplinger's Personal Finance Magazine*, October 1998.

Chapter 10

243 *"The Internet is still the Wild, Wild West"*: "Brokerages Become First to Let Investors Buy, Sell Stocks through Internet Innovation," *Los Angeles Times*, March 12, 1995.

245 *"The Internet Tidal Wave"*: John Heilemann, *Pride Before the Fall: The Trials of Bill Gates and the End of the Microsoft Era* (New York: HarperCollins, 2001), 64.

246 *In the mid-1980s, the company employed over two thousand people*: "Lettuce Entertain You Enterprises Inc," *Encyclopedia of Chicago*, Chicago Historical Society, http://www.encyclopedia.chicagohistory.org/pages/2749.html.

249 *The* Motley Fool *had become the most popular personal-finance site*: "The Motley Fool, Inc. History," FundingUniverse, http://www.fundinguniverse.com/company-histories/The-Motley-Fool-Inc-Company-History.html.

251 *software went into production in mid-February 1996*: Joe Konen, "Fabulous February!" *TransTerra Times* 2, no. 1 (February 1996): 1.

251 *We sent a mailer to more than a million people*: Mary Fay, "Ceres Securities," *TransTerra Times* 2, no. 1 (February 1996): 2.

252 *early days for online trading*: Vanessa O'Connell and E. S. Browning, "Stock Orders on Internet Poised to Soar," *Wall Street Journal*, June 25, 1996.

252 *"the Internet is taking Wall Street by storm"*: "Cyberspace and Your Nest Egg," *Los Angeles Times*, June 4, 1996.

252 *These were still very early days for online trading*: James F. Peltz, "The Cutting Edge: Markets and Modems, the Internet Is Making Online Trading Faster, Cheaper and Easier Than Ever," *Los Angeles Times*, August 5, 1996.

253 *Competition intensified*: Ibid.

253 *online trades for twelve dollars*: O'Connell and Browning, "Stock Orders on Internet Poised to Soar."

253 *E*Trade closed 1995 with total revenues of $23.3 million*: E*Trade Group, Inc., "Prospectus," August 16, 1996, 4.

253 *The surging volume of trades strained everyone's systems*: Vanessa O'Connell, "On-line Trades Surge, Causing Some Glitches," *Wall Street Journal*, July 18, 1996.

255 *E*Trade filed papers to make an initial public offering*: O'Connell and Browning, "Stock Orders on Internet Poised to Soar."

259 *According to one analysis in the business press*: Kimberly Weisul, "Study of On-Line Brokerage Casts New Light on Leaders," *Investment Dealers' Digest*, August 25, 1997, 14.

262 *"They can estimate whatever they want"*: Kimberly Weisul, *Investment Dealers' Digest*, December 1, 1997, 4.

263 *the company opened 181,000 accounts, doubling the firm's customer base*: Jim Rasmussen, "Online Trading: Omaha's Ameritrade Seeks Recognition," *Omaha World-Herald*, November 2, 1997.

263 *1.5 million investors had online trading accounts*: Rajiv Chandrasekaran, "Online Trading Delayed," *Washington Post*, October 28, 1997.

263 *Ameritrade more than doubled its share of the total online brokerage market*: Steven T. Goldberg, "Goodbye Wall Street, Hello Omaha," *Kiplinger's Personal Finance Magazine*, October 1998, 85.

266 *The SEC responded in July 2000 by proposing a new rule*: Pallavi Gogoi, "Rage Against Online Brokers," *Businessweek*, November 20, 2000, 98–102.

267 *regulators were also increasingly uneasy*: Ianthe Jeanne Dugan, "Brokerage Ads Veer from Mainstream," *Washington Post*, April 23, 1999.

268 Barron's Online *ranked the reliability*: Mathew Schwartz, "Test Case," *Computerworld*, August 14, 2000, 62.

271 *Ameritrade would tie with Fidelity for first place in* Money *magazine's rating*: Hal Lux, "Omaha Stakes," *Institutional Investor*, September 2000.

271 *Ogilvy scripted a spot*: Andy Serwer, "Ad Nauseam: Rating E-Broker TV Spots," *Fortune*, March 6, 2000, 451–52.

272 *The character began to take on a life of his own*: Rebecca Buckman, "Rock On! Stuart Rules as Web Trader," *Wall Street Journal*, December 7, 1999.

272 *President Clinton's annual White House Correspondents' dinner*: Mercedes M. Cardona, "Ameritrade: Anne Nelson," *Advertising Age*, June 26, 2000, S12.

272 *"a brand more powerful than some of its larger rivals"*: Lux, "Omaha Stakes."

Chapter 11

282 *"the stock price increase appears unwarranted"*: Robert J. Shiller, *Irrational Exuberance* (Princeton, NJ: Princeton University Press, 2000), 4. See also Joseph Stiglitz, *The Roaring Nineties: A New History of the World's Most Prosperous Decade* (New York: W. W. Norton, 2003), 138.

282 *investors soon began to retreat*: Mark Ingebretsen, *NASDAQ: A History of the Market That Changed the World* (Roseville, CA: Forum, 2002), xiv.

282 *The biggest losers in this massive sell-off were the dot-com companies*: Stiglitz, *The Roaring Nineties*, 138.

282 *investments in technology produced dramatic savings*: Hal Lux, "Omaha Stakes," *Institutional Investor*, September 2000.

283 *Schwab and E*Trade, however, changed course*: Megan Barnett, "Ameritrade Stays Its Rocky Course," *Industry Standard*, June 12, 2000, 77.

283 *two companies also took advantage of the recent changes*: Lux, "Omaha Stakes."

283 *In June 2000, the company acquired Ten Bagger Inc*: "Ameritrade Meeting Founders Asset Management," November 12, 2002, Executive Historical Files.

283 *In February 2001, we bought TradeCast*: "Online Brokers Continue Consolidation," *Mergers and Acquisitions*, September 2001, 19.

283 *Some analysts criticized our "dogmatic focus"*: Emily Thornton, "Why E-Brokers Are Broker and Broker," *Bloomberg*, January 22, 2001, 94.

284 *"the majority of these [discount brokers] are toast"*: Nelson D. Schwartz, "Can't Keep a Good Day Trader Down," *Fortune*, February 19, 2001, 146–50.

284 *Internet stock trading volumes continued to slide*: Pallavi Gogoi, "Ameritrade Might Just Claw Its Way Back," *Businessweek*, August 13, 2001, 71.

284 *stock price had fallen to $5.28*: Stacy Forster, "Ameritrade Plans Layoffs, McDonnell Quit," *Wall Street Journal*, April 2, 2001.

284 *E*Trade slashed its spending on advertising*: Susanne Craig, "Ameritrade Sets Another Round of Staff Cuts Amid Market Drop," *Wall Street Journal*, April 13, 2001.

284 *Schwab cut 3,400 workers*: "Ameritrade Lays Off an Additional 7% in Customer Service," *Computerworld*, April 2, 2001.

284 *Once again, rumors circulated on Wall Street*: Matthias Rieker, "Ameritrade Stock Up 8% on Report of CIBC Talks," *American Banker*, May 14, 2001, 24.

284 *"We do not want to be bought"*: Susanne Craig, "Ameritrade Scoffs at Sale

Talk, But Hopes for Deal Spur Shares," *Wall Street Journal*, May 21, 2001.

285 *"The market would not look favorably on it"*: Lux, "Omaha Stakes."

286 *he planned to move his family to Omaha*: Joe Moglia, "My First Day on the Job," *Fortune*, November 18, 2002, 126.

286 *Wall Street applauded the appointment*: Charles Gasparino, "Merrill Lynch Veteran to Take Top Post at Ameritrade, a Move Investors Applaud," *Wall Street Journal*, March 5, 2001.

286 *"one of the most difficult in the last twenty years"*: "Ameritrade Holding Corp.; Online Brokerage Firm Reports Loss of $14 Million," *Wall Street Journal*, October 24, 2001.

287 *long-term factors were even more disturbing*: Timothy J. Mullaney, "Hunkering Down May Not Save Ameritrade's Skin," *Businessweek*, April 22, 2002, 88.

287 *Many companies in the brokerage industry were in trouble*: Roger Lowenstein, *Origins of the Crash: The Great Bubble and Its Undoing* (New York: Penguin, 2004), 211–12.

287 *Datek Online Holdings Corporation put itself on the auction block*: Virgil Larson, "Ameritrade CEO: No Plan to Move Ameritrade Stock Price per Share Companies' Timelines," *Omaha World-Herald*, B1.

288 *We won the bidding war*: Ryan Naraine, "Ameritrade Shells Out $1.29B for Datek," Ecommerce-Guide.com, April 8, 2002.

288 *the Datek acquisition made Ameritrade the number-one online broker*: Michael Santoli, "Beyond the Wall," *Barron's*, April 15, 2002, 15.

288 *"pristine balance sheet and strong management that keeps a lid on costs"*: Yuval Rosenberg, "E-stocks Rise Again After a Stomach-Churning Descent," *Fortune*, September 1, 2003, 163–66.

290 *In April 2003, we purchased*: "Asiff Hirji of Ameritrade Holding Corp.: Ready to Merge—Again?" *Institutional Investor*, June 1, 2003, 1.

290 *acquired the online retail accounts of JB Oxford Holdings*: "Ameritrade to Buy Online Retail Accounts of JB Oxford," *New York Times*, June 8, 2004.

290 *Schwab announced*: Susanne Craig and Gregory Zuckerman, "Schwab Misses Market's Gains," *Wall Street Journal*, June 2, 2004.

290 *Schwab's difficulties became all the more apparent*: Gaston F. Ceron, "Brokers Ameritrade, Schwab Post Mixed Results," *Wall Street Journal*, January 19, 2005.

Index

About the Author

JOE RICKETTS is the founder, former CEO, and retired chairman of online brokerage TD Ameritrade.